BLACK MIDDLE-CLASS BRITANNIA

RACISM, RESISTANCE AND SOCIAL CHANGE

FORTHCOMING BOOKS IN THIS SERIES

Race talk: Languages of racism and resistance in Neapolitan street markets:
Antonia Dawes

The Red and the Black: The Russian Revolution and the Black Atlantic:
David Featherstone and Christian Høgsbjerg (eds)

Revolutionary lives of the Red and Black Atlantic:
David Featherstone, Christian Høgsbjerg and Alan Rice (eds)

Urban unrest: Black resistance to policing in contemporary England:
Adam Elliott-Cooper

African and Mexican American men and collective violence, 1915–65:
Margarita Aragon

East London Jewish radicals: Ben Gidley

PREVIOUSLY PUBLISHED IN THIS SERIES
In the shadow of Enoch Powell: Shirin Hirsch

Race and riots in Thatcher's Britain: Simon Peplow

Black middle-class Britannia

Identities, repertoires, cultural consumption

Ali Meghji

Manchester University Press

Copyright © Ali Meghji 2019

The right of Ali Meghji to be identified as the author of this work has been asserted by him in accordance with the Copyright, Designs and Patents Act 1988.

Published by Manchester University Press
Altrincham Street, Manchester M1 7JA
www.manchesteruniversitypress.co.uk

British Library Cataloguing-in-Publication Data
A catalogue record for this book is available from the British Library

ISBN 978 1 5261 4307 5 hardback
ISBN 978 1 5261 5608 2 paperback

First published 2019

The publisher has no responsibility for the persistence or accuracy of URLs for any external or third-party internet websites referred to in this book, and does not guarantee that any content on such websites is, or will remain, accurate or appropriate.

Typeset by Deanta Global Publishing Services

Contents

	List of tables	vi
	Series editors' foreword	vii
	Acknowledgements	viii
1	Introduction – Taking off the colour-blind goggles: crafting a study on Britain's Black middle class	1
2	Towards a triangle of Black middle-class identity	23
3	White spaces: consuming traditional middle-class culture	53
4	Constructing and using Black cultural capital	77
5	Revisiting race and nation: double consciousness, Black Britishness, and cultural consumption	99
6	Race, class, and culture in the British racialised social system	120
	Appendix: Building a reflexive case study of the Black middle class	142
	References	158
	Index	177

Tables

2.1　Introducing the triangle of identity　30

2.2　Identity modes and their corresponding cultural repertoires　31

Series editors' foreword

John Solomos, Satnam Virdee, Aaron Winter

THE STUDY of race, racism and ethnicity has expanded greatly since the end of the twentieth century. This expansion has coincided with a growing awareness of the continuing role that these issues play in contemporary societies all over the globe. *Racism, Resistance and Social Change* is a new series of books that seeks to make a substantial contribution to this flourishing field of scholarship and research. We are committed to providing a forum for the publication of the highest quality scholarship on race, racism, anti-racism and ethnic relations. As editors of this series we would like to publish both theoretically driven books and texts with an empirical frame that seek to further develop our understanding of the origins, development and contemporary forms of racisms, racial inequalities and racial and ethnic relations. We welcome work from a range of theoretical and political perspectives, and as the series develops we ideally want to encourage a conversation that goes beyond specific national or geopolitical environments. While we are aware that there are important differences between national and regional research traditions, we hope that scholars from a variety of disciplines and multidisciplinary frames will take the opportunity to include their research work in the series.

As the title of the series highlights, we also welcome texts that can address issues about resistance and antiracism as well as the role of political and policy interventions in this rapidly evolving discipline. The changing forms of racist mobilisation and expression that have come to the fore in recent years have highlighted the need for more reflection and research on the role of political and civil society mobilisations in this field.

We are committed to building on theoretical advances by providing an arena for new and challenging theoretical and empirical studies on the changing morphology of race and racism in contemporary societies.

Acknowledgements

My first acknowledgement goes to the participants of this study. None of this research would have been possible without these wonderful participants volunteering their time, and their narratives and experiences are the foundation of this book.

I have also received a great deal of academic support in writing this book. At Cambridge, Dr Mónica Moreno Figueroa – a wonderful colleague and mentor whom I will always look up to – supported my research with the Black middle class from day one. Mónica gave me invaluable support on my research methods, writing, and overall thinking – she taught me what sociological imagination is all about, and accompanied me all the way down to the depths of critical race studies. Dr Filipe Carreira da Silva has supported my sociological studies and writing since I became interested in the topic, and his ongoing advice has been influential in my thinking around social theory and cultural sociology. I have had the pleasure of having my work – both in its infancy and in its more developed stages – commented on by Dr Manali Desai, Professor Patrick Baert, Professor John Thompson, Dr Brendan Burchell, and Professor Sarah Franklin. Conversations with my friends Valentina Ausserladscheider, Tanisha Spratt, Me-Linh Riemann, and many of the undergraduate and graduate students that I have had the pleasure of teaching have helped form the arguments in these pages. Professor Sarah Franklin kindly gave me research time, offered by Sidney Sussex College, to complete the writing of this book.

Outside my institution there is a whole network of people who have strongly influenced and supported the writing of this book. A friend and collaborator, Rima Saini, helped me form ideas around whiteness and middle-class identity, and her own work on race and class is going to shake up sociology. Professors Les Back and Satnam Virdee both provided deep critiques of my work which have significantly developed many of the ideas and themes and much of the writing in this book. Both Les and Satnam (in Les's words) taught me about remembering the 'morality of criticism' – I hope we all take that forward with us in sociology and academia more generally. Satnam also edits the series *Racism, Resistance and Social Change* (RRSC), within which this book is published, along with Dr Aaron Winter and Professor John Solomos. When I attended the symposium for John Solomos, everyone mentioned that there is not a single person in Britain working on racism, race, and ethnicity that doesn't owe at least something to John. In my case, John has offered me great support and advice, on this work and much more broadly. Again, I hope the academic community keeps building this kindness. Aaron was the first person I talked to about publishing this book in the RRSC series, and he has given invaluable support throughout the process. And of course, Tom Dark, the editor at Manchester University Press, has been fantastic, moving this project from a book proposal to a completed monograph.

Conversations and exchanges with a host of other scholars also gave me indispensable help with this book's arguments. Dr Derron Wallace has given me enthusiastic support and advice with my work on the Black middle class; his own work on the Black middle class is pushing the field forward, and I am grateful for his kindness and mentorship. Professor Claire Alexander kindly invited me to present my research at Manchester's Centre on Dynamics of Ethnicity, where I received invaluable feedback on my preliminary research interpretations. We often tell our students that research and writing is a messy process, but struggle to say exactly how. For me, a lot of the 'messiness' was cleared up in an email exchange with my now sponsor at the Weatherhead Centre at Harvard, Professor Michèle Lamont, who suggested I look beyond the more predictable focus on solely 'cultural capital'. The framework in this book is indebted to Michèle's developments in cultural sociology, boundaries, and cultural repertoires. (Again thanks to John) I had the pleasure of attending the *Ethnic and Racial Studies* journal's fortieth anniversary conference, where I was able to discuss some of my research with eminent thinkers in the field, including Professor Karyn Lacy, whose work on Black middle-class identity is very formative to my thinking. On the theme of journals, I thank all the reviewers and editors who have worked with me on my papers that have been foundational for this manuscript, as well as the reviewers of this manuscript itself.

Lastly, there is my partner, Emily Chan. Emily continually gives me love, care, affection, and encouragement. She celebrates each of my accomplishments, no matter how small or large, and she is also the first person to pick me up when things aren't going well. Having Emily by my side has helped me deal with all the trials and tribulations of academia.

Thank you, everybody.

1

Introduction – Taking off the colour-blind goggles: crafting a study on Britain's Black middle class

IN THE summer of 2017, I was involved in a back-and-forth email conversation with someone whom I had been trying to interview for seven months. I received an email late at night, inviting me to an event run by the Powerlist Foundation, a foundation composed of the most 'powerful' Black Britons. It read

> Hi Ali,
>
> I have been really poor with communication and I am so sorry.
>
> We begin our Annual Summer Leadership Programme, in partnership with BT, tomorrow and I would like to extend the invitation for you to join us if you think it would be useful for your work.

I was slightly annoyed that I had not been given ample time to prepare myself for such a social event, not to add that I had no clean shirt to wear. The following day I arrived at the BT headquarters in London, dressed in a suit despite the baking heat. As I left St Paul's underground station, I was surrounded by white suit-wearing professionals on their lunch breaks. However, as I entered the BT headquarters, where the Powerlist Foundation were beginning their annual mentoring programme, not a white face was in sight. The room was filled with established members of the Black middle class, as well as young, aspiring Black professionals.

Throughout the course of this Powerlist event, it became clear to me that there was a paradox at the heart of being a member of the so-called Black middle class. On the one hand, this event featured some of the wealthiest Black Britons as keynote speakers. On the other hand, in all their keynotes, these speakers emphasised the narrative that Black people have to work at least twice as hard as their white counterparts for the same recognition of worth. Similarly, the young, aspiring professionals at the event were mostly recent university graduates, about to join large corporations in the City. Yet, as many told me, to gain entry into this corporate world, they had struggled through at least three years of isolation at an elite higher education institute, where there were often few other Black folk on their degree courses. These feelings of non-recognition and isolation were also acknowledged by the Black professionals who were at the Powerlist event to act as mentors. Folk working as managers of international firms, through to those who had started their own internationally successful businesses, all emphasised the narrative that they were exceptions to the rule; they had been let through the 'coloured' glass ceiling, recognising that Black people are still marginalised in British society. Indeed, many of these mentors claimed they were at the event so that they could help young Black people move into professional occupations, knowing that this 'social capital' is often exclusive to the white middle class. Put simply, my takeback from this event was that economic wealth does not shield Black folk from racism.

This book delves into the ways that racism shapes the lives of the Black middle class.[1] At the foundation of this book is a desire to unearth how, and why, being in a privileged class location does not make one immune to racism. However, my study engages with how the racism that affects the Black middle class is *more than individual acts of bigotry and violence*, but something structural and systemic. Thus, the people at the Powerlist event talked about racism not in terms of racist name-calling, but in terms of the differences in how white and Black people are recognised as having worthiness, how higher-paying occupations still rely on white middle-class social networks, and how middle-class spaces such as elite educational institutions are dominated by whites. These are all *structural* processes which stretch far beyond the acts of individuals, signalling a 'racism without racists'.[2] This book aims towards unearthing Britain's systemic 'racism without racists', and locating where the Black middle class are positioned in this structurally organised racial hierarchy. Given my focus on a structural approach to racism, I use this book to develop a *critical race theory* account of British society. Through a critical race approach, I work with the idea of racism as involving the construction of racial groups into a racial hierarchy, with societal resources being distributed unequally according to this hierarchy.

Within this paradigm of structural racism, the Black middle class become an interesting case study. In terms of societal resources, by virtue of their class status, the Black middle class possess relatively privileged amounts of economic capital. Indeed, as one white colleague recently commented to me on finding out that I research how racism affects the Black middle class, 'It doesn't matter what colour you are if you're earning £200,000 a year and driving a BMW!' This comment, although seemingly inane, represents the wider commitment that many Britons have towards post-racial ideology. Namely, the *existence* of a Black middle class is taken to be representative of the *non-existence* of structural racism.

Against this post-racial argument, my work turns towards the cultural sphere, and looks at the unequal distribution of *cultural resources* across Britain's racial hierarchy. In this book, I am particularly interested in addressing the question 'Do racism and anti-racism affect Black middle-class cultural consumption?' This book, therefore, seeks to draw fundamental links between the macro, material British racial hierarchy and the micro phenomenon of Black middle-class cultural consumption. I address questions such as 'How does the unequal distribution of dominant cultural capital affect the Black middle class, and what do they do about this?'; 'Do Black middle-class people exclude themselves from arenas of dominant cultural capital, and if so, what logic underlies this self-exclusion?'; 'Do the Black middle class use the middle-class cultural sphere to challenge ideological representations of Blackness?'; and 'Do Black middle-class cultural spaces challenge the material dimensions of the racial hierarchy?' As with most sociology, these questions only achieve meaning within the current state of the field.

The rabbit hole of colour-blindness

Presently, we have a limited understanding of how racism shapes middle-class identity and culture. Social classes, including the middle class, exist twice: first as statistical clusters, measured by the distribution of material (and mostly economic) resources, and second as *practical groups that must be made* through symbolic struggles, cultural practices, and group identification.[3] In other words, social classes do not just exist a priori and 'out there' with purely objective contours. Rather, social classes have both social boundaries (measured as material differences) and symbolic boundaries ('conceptual distinctions made by social actors to categorize ... [which] separate people into groups and generate feelings of similarity and group membership').[4] Indeed, these symbolic boundaries – conceptual distinctions made and reproduced between different social-class groups – often become the necessary basis on which social (material) boundaries can then develop. I thus propose that social classes (including the middle class) are *economic locations with rules for cultural membership*. While we now know a fair amount about how the Black middle class occupy a different economic location to the white middle class, in terms of ethnoracial wage gaps and mobility trajectories,[5] there is a lack of research addressing how racism affects the non-economic dimensions (including the cultural consumption) of the British middle class.

This gap in research is exacerbated by the fact that the British middle class are often treated as a colour-blind category.[6] This means that sociologists of Britain's middle class often avoid any 'race talk' in their analysis, making it seem as though middle-class identity and culture exist in a realm 'beyond race'. For example, many studies claim to be about the middle class but have almost exclusively white samples.[7] In this case, the studies reproduce what Bonilla-Silva and Zuberi refer to as a 'White logic, White methods',[8] what Bhambra terms 'methodological whiteness',[9] or what Bhatt simply terms 'White sociology'.[10] These colour-blind studies follow a logic that the white middle class are a *non-racial category* – their whiteness is merely an incidental skin colour and not connected to, or influenced by, processes of racial hierarchisation. Such studies can thus claim to be about the entire middle class, because if the white middle class are a *non-racial* category, then having exclusively white samples ceases to be a methodological problem. Through this logic, we thus see how 'the whiteness of the white middle classes remains universal, silent and unmarked',[11] while our understanding of how whiteness structures middle-class identity and culture is patently truncated.

This invisibility of whiteness in middle-class studies becomes even more apparent in those studies that *do* have racially diverse samples. In this case, such studies often reproduce a (post-)racial grammar that claims that the whiteness of the white middle class is incidental, whereas race is essential to the identities and cultural practices of other racialised middle-class groups (such as the Black or Asian middle classes). For instance, studies such as the Cultural Capital and Social Exclusion Survey,[12] as well as research into the British middle class and education,[13] will often refer to their 'Asian middle-class' and 'Black middle-class' participants, but when talking about their white middle-class participants they simply label them as 'middle class'. Even studies that have racially representative samples, therefore, often reproduce the notion that when it comes to the middle class, 'Whiteness constitutes normality and acceptance without stipulating that to be White is to be normal and right'.[14]

Putting colour-blindness into the rear-view mirror

While colour-blindness is the norm in middle-class studies, there are a handful of studies that encourage us to see the racialised dynamics underlying British middle-class identity and culture. These studies can be split into two streams: that which focuses on the whiteness of the white middle class, and that which focuses on the Black middle class.

What's 'white' about the white middle class?

Within the sociology of education, there are studies that show how the white middle class seek social closure.[15] This closure is often seen in white middle-class parents only wanting their children to be schooled among other white middle-class children, and white middle-class parents only wanting their children to maintain close social networks with other white middle-class families.[16] Importantly, these white middle-class parents who look for social closure rationalise their choices through a logic of 'anything but racism' which exonerates them from reproducing racism. For instance, in Raveaud and Zanten's[17] study of a secondary school in Hackney (London), the white middle-class parents rationalised their decision for choosing socially homogeneous schools by arguing either that their children will experience 'social mix' later in their educational lives (at university), or that they had no other choices because the local state schools were not of sufficient 'quality'.

Furthermore, there is a body of literature that shows how many white middle-class folk who do *not* seek social closure in education still use their white middle classness to distinguish themselves from raced and classed others, therefore reproducing their material privilege(s). In particular, the work of Diane Reay and her colleagues draws on interviews with 125 white middle-class families in London and two anonymised cities, who deliberately chose inner-city, *socially mixed*, comprehensive schools for their children.[18] Three points are pertinent in this discussion. First, the white middle-class students in these comprehensive schools are allowed to maintain their hegemonic whiteness through the differential treatment they get compared to their lower-class, and Black and minority ethnic peers.[19] For instance, they receive much more attention from teachers, are free from negative stereotypes, and get streamlined into the 'top sets' in the classrooms and 'gifted student' extra-curricular programmes.[20] Second, despite being in 'socially mixed' schools, the white middle-class children are encouraged by their parents to *deliberately form* homogeneous social capital networks with other white middle-class children.[21] Finally, the white middle-class parents draw on stereotypes of classed and racialised others as being less intelligent, thus arguing that sending their children to these schools is good for their confidence because they will be at the top of their classes, whereas they would be mediocre in exclusively white middle-class schools.[22]

Thus, research both on the white middle class who seek social closure in schooling and on those who seek social mix shows how the 'whiteness' of the white middle class is much more than an incidental skin colour. The deliberate formation of closed, white middle-class social capital networks is a patent way the white middle-class construct and protect their hegemonic whiteness (compared both to racialised and classed others). In contrast to the colour-blind approaches to the middle classes, therefore, there is a significant literature which justifies the view that middle-class identity, culture, and practice often overlap heavily with whiteness.

Given the infeasible approach to colour-blindness in middle-class studies, in this book I question whether the large surveys and colour-blind studies of (white) middle-class cultural lifestyles remain accurate when we analyse the *Black* middle class. If we know that many studies of the middle class focus mostly on the *white* middle class, and if we know that the whiteness of the white middle class is more than just a skin tone, then it is logical to infer that many practices of the white middle class may be down to their intersecting whiteness and class position. We can thus scrutinise the universality of the findings of many middle-class studies. For instance, research finds that (white) middle-class folk consume cultural forms – including 'highbrow' arts, literary novels, classical music, opera, and theatre – *while also being perceived (by themselves or by the lower-classes) as the most legitimate consumers of these cultural forms*.[23] This book engages with these findings by asking questions such as 'Does this supposedly middle-class reality of cultural consumption and distinction work when we focus on the Black middle class?' and 'Do the Black middle class consume these listed cultural forms, and perceive themselves to be legitimate consumers of the said cultural forms?' Alternatively, do Black middle-class people think that the legitimacy of their consumption of these cultural forms is doubted? Moreover, do they even consume these cultural forms at all? These are all questions which study middle classness in a way that is attentive to the dynamics of racialisation and racism.

Nevertheless, my research is not only positioned against the former 'colour-blind' studies of middle-class identity and culture. I additionally engage with a recent stream of literature which focuses on the Black middle class.

Black middle-class identity and cultural consumption: developments and limitations

The view that the middle class is a racialised category becomes even more convincing when we turn attention to the literature on those who are occupationally middle class, but are not racialised as white. If we look at *Black* middle-class identity and cultural consumption, we can unearth how the middle class is often construed as a space of rarefied, hegemonic whiteness (hegemonic whiteness being the form of whiteness that is both materially dominant and culturally normative).[24]

One of the most systematic studies of Britain's Black middle class was conducted as an Economic and Social Research Council (ESRC)-funded project entitled 'The Educational Strategies of the Black Middle Classes'.[25] This ESRC project drew on interviews with sixty-two Black people in professional occupations, finding that most Black middle-class folk switch identities when they are around white middle-class people.[26] As I elaborate on later, this is justified under a mode of identity labelled 'strategic assimilation', where the Black middle-class person engages in a routine of code- or 'script-switching', taken on different performative personas in different interactional settings as they deem appropriate.[27] For example, when around the white middle class, many Black middle-class people will deliberately put on a particular accent (displaying middle-class 'linguistic capital'), and wear particular clothes (displaying middle-class embodied cultural capital), to assimilate with white middle-class norms.[28] Given this regular identity switching, such Black middle-class folk are often 'ambivalent' about their class status, recognising its tentative nature.[29] This finding is further corroborated by Wallace's research on Black middle-class children in an inner-city school in London, where they will often switch performances between what they construe as an urban, 'Black identity' when among Black working-class peers, and a 'refined' middle-class identity when among white middle-class peers.[30] Both the ESRC project[31] and Wallace's[32] research thus highlight how racism influences Black middle-class identity formation. Namely, these individuals 'switch' identities to appear respectable to white middle-class others; they centre their identities according to white middle-class norms. The experiences of these Black middle-class folk thus show how, within Britain, *hegemonic whiteness is essential in gaining legitimate middle-class cultural membership.*

Beyond cultural membership, Wallace's research highlights how Black middle-class folk have different cultural lives to their white middle-class counterparts.[33] Drawing on interviews with Black middle-class school children and their parents, Wallace shows how Black middle-class parents will equip their children with knowledge of diasporic authors (such as Chinua Achebe) to signal to their teachers that they are 'cultured' middle-class children, but in a way that maintains a connection to Black diasporic identity and culture.[34] Wallace thus highlights how Black middle-class families will encourage their children to consume 'forms of dominant cultural capital racialised as Black' to resist teachers stereotyping them as unintelligent.[35] This strategy allows for such Black middle-class families to show their children that they can be Black *and* partake in middle-class culture at the same time. Wallace's research thereby further develops our understanding of the relation between 'race' and middle classness.[36] Namely, Wallace's research points to the fact that many Black people – on becoming middle class – will still make an especial effort to support *Black* cultural producers; their racialised membership thus influences their middle-class identity, just as I have shown that the racialised membership of whites also influences their middle classness.

Picking up where others left off: considering a triangle of identity

While the current scholarship on the Black middle class has made significant steps forward in understanding the intersection of race with middle classness, it has some limitations that I overcome in this book. These limitations stem from the overreliance on strategic assimilation for explaining Black middle-class identity, and the focus on 'strategic anti-racist' cultural consumption.

Present understandings of Black British middle-class identity have an overreliance on 'strategic assimilation'.[37] While it is true that many Black middle-class folk do code-switch when around the white middle class, my research also points to many Black middle-class people who are *against* this code-switching. Moreover, while strategic assimilation may constitute an identity mode for some, there is yet to be a comprehensive understanding of how this identity mode has implications for such individuals' cultural lives more generally. For instance, in the area of cultural consumption, if it is the case that Black middle-class people tend to be 'class ambivalent', does this mean that they display no particular affinity towards middle-class cultural forms? Alternatively, does the strategic assimilation with white middle-class identities also result in a strategic consumption of white middle-class cultural forms?

It is in this area of cultural consumption that we see another limitation in present understandings of the Black British middle class. Namely, Wallace suggests that Black middle-class people show a preference for middle-class cultural forms mediated in a way that maintains an ethnoracial affinity.[38] However, within my research I show that some Black middle-class folk have no predilection towards 'Black' cultural forms at all, while others prioritise consuming the same culture as the white middle class to establish a cultural equity with them. Furthermore, Wallace's work remains within the locale of the education system.[39] Alternatively, I examine Black middle-class cultural lives more generally, exploring what Black middle-class people consume (culturally) outside their strategising in educational markets, and *why* they consume what they do.

The main way I overcome these described limitations is through constructing a dynamic triangle of Black middle-class identity. This triangle of identity enables me to appreciate the diversity in Black middle-class identities, cultural consumption, and cultural repertoires.

Towards a triangle of identity

In this book, I argue there are three Black middle-class identity modes: strategic assimilation, ethnoracial autonomous, and class-minded. A key argument developed in this book is that people towards each identity mode draw on different cultural repertoires to guide their consumption of cultural capital. The division between cultural capital and cultural repertoires is thus essential to the argument in this book.

The notion of cultural capital can be traced back to Du Bois,[40] or indeed Veblen,[41] although it was later popularised by Bourdieu.[42] Du Bois stressed that a project of 'racial uplift' must involve creating not just an economic equality with whites, but also a *cultural equality*.[43] Du Bois argued that, because of enslavement, ghettoisation, and exclusion from cultural and educational institutions,[44]

> most Negroes in the United States today occupy a low cultural status; both low in itself and low as compared with the national average in the land. There are cultured individuals and groups among them. All Negroes do not fall culturally below all Whites. But if one selects any one of the obviously low culture groups in the United States, the proportion of Negroes who belong to it will be larger than the Negro proportion in the total population.

In response to this downpression, Du Bois's thesis was that Black folk ought to become skilled in 'high status' cultural forms – the arts, music, and intellectual production – to achieve a cultural equity with their white counterparts.[45] In present-day language, Du Bois's argument is that Black folk should strive to have equal economic capital and equal *cultural capital* with white folk. This Du Boisian cultural approach was incorporated into a more systematic notion of cultural capital by Bourdieu,[46] although the presence of a 'Jim Crow sociology', which segregated Black sociologists from white canons, meant that Bourdieu displayed no cognisance of such work.[47]

From the Bourdieusian tradition, we get the view that cultural capital can exist in three states: embodied, objectified, or institutionalised.[48] Embodied cultural capital includes not only appearance and bodily 'hexis' (the way one presents oneself), but also the knowledge one possesses of given academic subjects. Objectified cultural capital exists within objects – for example, paintings, books, and artworks that are ascribed value within grander models of cultural hierarchisation. Institutionalised cultural capital refers to capital bestowed on an individual or group by a recognised institution, for instance educational qualifications. Using Bourdieu's work as a springboard, I argue that cultural capital serves two particular functions: to (re)produce material inequalities, and to curate and sustain symbolic boundaries between different social groups.

Within British society, research shows how cultural capital produces and reproduces economic forms of inequality. First, there is the research which focuses on the economic returns of institutionalised cultural capital – particularly educational credentials.[49] The point developed here is that certain British universities are 'ranked', and that a degree from higher-ranked institutions (institutionalised cultural capital) is rewarded with higher economic returns than lower-ranked institutions. For instance, graduates from the University of Cambridge, on average, annually earn £20,000 more than graduates from their lower-ranked neighbouring university, Anglia Ruskin.[50] Similarly, Wakeling and Savage found that of all the British universities, the highly ranked universities of Oxford and Cambridge were sending the highest proportion of graduates into elite occupations.[51] Furthermore, in terms of objectified and embodied cultural capital, drawing on UK Household Longitudinal data from 2009–11, Reeves and de Vries found that there is a positive correlation between one's volume of cultural capital and one's earnings.[52] Reeves and de Vries's research thus highlights that participating in cultural activities (including both 'highbrow' and popular cultural forms) garners economic returns.[53]

While cultural capital is therefore important for (re)producing material inequality, it is equally important for curating and sustaining symbolic boundaries. By this I mean that cultural capital is often used to draw boundaries between 'insiders' and 'outsiders' of certain social groups, to exclude the said outsiders, and to legitimise this exclusion. The point being developed here is that there is a general homology between social groups and cultural practices, whereby 'effective membership of the group or network depends, in part, on the individual's ability to share cultural interests and experiences'.[54] This helps explain, for instance, the finding that those in professional occupations are much more likely to visit art galleries and attend classical music concerts than those in working-class occupations; these cultural practices have become necessary (although not sufficient) components for professionals to establish legitimate middle-class cultural membership, while working-class people often see themselves as 'unnatural' consumers of these cultural practices.[55] It is in this line of thought, therefore, that Lamont and Lareau highlight the function of cultural capital to justify exclusion of people from particular social groups[56] – cultural capital has a symbolic value just as much as it has a material value.

While cultural capital is thus a societal resource, *cultural repertoires* refer to something entirely different. Indeed, whereas the notion of cultural capital stems from the sociology 'of' culture, cultural repertoires stem from 'cultural sociology'.[57] A cultural repertoire can be understood as a '"tool kit" of habits, skills, and styles from which people construct "strategies of action"'.[58] Cultural repertoires thus refer to the 'set of tools available to individuals to make sense of the reality they experience'.[59] A cultural repertoire thus refers to the concepts, frames, and arguments people use to make sense of their experiences, to comprehend their worlds, and to guide their action; cultural repertoires are conceptual schemes just as much as they are strategies for action.

We can show empirical examples of cultural repertoires. For instance, Lamont and Fleming,[60] researching the African American elite, found that some of their respondents would draw on a cultural repertoire of 'essentialist universalism'. This repertoire holds that all humans are created equal in the eyes of God, and all humans are of equal moral worth. Such members of the African American elite used this repertoire to justify their involvement in anti-racism. Their belief, or cultural repertoire, that all humans are equal thus guides these African American elites to make sure that certain folk – other African Americans, in this case – are not unfairly discriminated against. To use a different example, Khan's ethnography of St Paul's School in Concord, New Hampshire, shows that many members of the elite will draw on a repertoire of meritocracy to justify their societal standings.[61] Such individuals thus construe the world, or 'the reality they experience',[62] through the cultural repertoire of meritocracy to exonerate themselves from reproducing inequality (i.e. 'we are ahead because we worked hard, not because of structural privilege').

Indeed, although there is little acknowledgment of this similarity, many critical race theorists, or 'race critical' theorists, implicitly use the notion of cultural repertoires through their own alternatively defined concepts. Critical race theorists use the notion of 'racial ideologies' (and counter-ideologies) to refer to 'the racially based frameworks used by actors to explain and justify (dominant race) or challenge (subordinate race or races) the racial status quo'.[63] These racial ideologies encompass the frames, styles, and stories that actors use to justify, obfuscate, or contest their position in the racial hierarchy. In other words, they are the cultural repertoires used by actors to justify or challenge their position in the racial hierarchy. For example, post-racial ideology can be understood as a cultural repertoire because it involves frames and understandings (such as that we live in a meritocracy, or that Black people are workshy) which reproduce the racial hierarchy.[64] Contrastingly, we can understand the 'Black is beautiful' counter-ideology as a cultural repertoire; it involves meanings and frames (such as that Black women ought to be proud of their features) that contest reproductive ideologies such as the dominant, Eurocentric notions of beauty.[65] Recognising that racial ideologies (and counter racial ideologies) are essentially 'types' of cultural repertoires is especially important within this book, as it allows us to see how Black middle-class people construct, and are guided by, repertoires that work to contest (counter racial ideologies) or reproduce the racial hierarchy (racial ideologies).

The dynamics of racism, anti-racism, cultural repertoires, and cultural capital are tied together in this book's theory of a triangle of Black middle-class identity. The argument presented in this book is that people towards each Black middle-class identity mode (strategic assimilation, ethnoracial autonomous, and class-minded) incorporate their consumption of cultural capital into different cultural repertoires, each therefore showing a different relationship between racism, anti-racism, and cultural consumption. This argument is summarised in the following section.

Strategic assimilation

Individuals towards the strategic assimilation identity mode adopt repertoires of code-switching and cultural equity. Through the repertoire of code-switching, those towards strategic assimilation often switch identities when around white middle-class people to establish legitimate middle-class cultural membership. This commitment to code-switching interrelates with the repertoire of cultural equity, the desire to be equal to the white middle class in levels of economic *and* cultural capital. Through their repertoire of cultural equity, individuals towards strategic assimilation make sure to consume traditional middle-class cultural forms – even though they decode such cultural capital as 'white' – to avoid exclusion from the white middle-class milieu.[66] Nevertheless, through their commitment to code-switching, individuals towards the strategic assimilation identity mode do retain an ethnoracial affinity, and thus make sure to also consume culture they decode as 'Black'.

Ethnoracial autonomous

Individuals towards the ethnoracial autonomous identity mode adopt cultural repertoires of browning and Afro-centrism. Through the repertoire of 'browning', those towards the ethnoracial autonomous identity mode resist white norms of middle-class identity, and stress that people ought to be 'proud' of being Black.[67] Unlike individuals towards the strategic assimilation identity mode, therefore, individuals towards the ethnoracial autonomous identity mode do not 'switch' identities when around the white middle class. Indeed, such individuals argue that this code-switching leads to inauthenticity and simply reproduces the racial structure within which whites are deemed more acceptable and respectable than Black folk. Browning is connected to the repertoire of Afro-centrism. Individuals towards the ethnoracial autonomous identity mode adopt a repertoire of Afro-centrism to stress that they have a duty to positively uphold Black diasporic histories, experiences, knowledges, and identities. Through this repertoire of Afro-centrism, those towards the ethnoracial autonomous identity mode often consume cultural forms which give 'authentic' representations of Blackness. Furthermore, such individuals remove themselves from traditional middle-class cultural spaces, such as mainstream art galleries, opera houses, theatre halls, and classical music concert halls, arguing that these cultural spaces are 'Eurocentric' and 'white'.

Class-minded

Lastly, individuals towards the class-minded identity mode adopt repertoires of de-racialisation and post-racialism. Through the repertoire of post-racialism, such individuals believe that racism is no longer a significant issue in British society. Through the repertoire of de-racialisation, these individuals see their Blackness as merely an incidental skin colour, and not as an identity they display any affinity towards. They therefore construe themselves as 'middle class', rather than 'Black', and often construe these two group memberships as incongruous. Such individuals thus often de-racialise themselves, but *re-racialise others*; they compare their middle-class cultural consumption with the cultural myopia of other 'less cultured' Black people. Such class-minded individuals thus reproduce negative ideologies of other Black people as being uncultured, culturally myopic, or constantly 'playing the race card'.

Benefits of a tripartite approach

Through theorising a triangle of Black middle-class identity, three particular benefits can be realised. The benefits of this tripartite approach thus not only enable us to develop the literature on Black *British* middle-class culture and identity, but also allow us to engage with more international research on the Black middle class.

First, my tripartite approach has a conceptual advantage in that I focus on cultural capital *and* cultural repertoires. The statement that cultural capital is often incorporated into cultural repertoires may seem a relatively uncontroversial comment; yet within sociology, the 'cultural capital' and 'cultural repertoires' approaches have sometimes been seen to belong to distinct subfields (the sociology 'of' culture verses 'cultural sociology').[68] However, through admitting that the consumption of cultural capital is often incorporated into cultural repertoires, we gain the ability to focus not only on *what* cultural capital people are consuming, but *why* they are consuming such culture.

Through focusing on the 'why' of cultural consumption, we can then explain instances where people may have the same *attitudes* towards cultural forms, but differing patterns of cultural consumption.[69] We can also explain instances where people engage in the same cultural consumption, but have different attitudes towards this culture and thus radically different reasons for their cultural consumption. For instance, through my triangle of identity I show that individuals towards the class-minded and strategic assimilation identity modes *both* consume traditional middle-class cultural capital. However, while those towards the class-minded identity mode justify this consumption through a repertoire of de-racialisation, wanting to separate themselves from 'common', culturally myopic Black people, those towards the strategic assimilation identity mode justify consumption of this cultural capital through a repertoire of cultural equity – the idea that Black folk ought to be equal to the white middle class in terms of cultural capital. While both groups of people thus consume the same cultural capital, they do so for radically different reasons, justified through different cultural repertoires. To use another example, those towards both the ethnoracial autonomous and strategic assimilation identity modes decode traditional middle-class cultural pursuits as 'white' – their *attitudes* thus remain the same. However, as mentioned, those towards strategic assimilation, on the one hand, still consume such cultural capital justified through their repertoire of cultural equity. On the other hand, those towards the ethnoracial autonomous identity mode draw on the repertoire of Afro-centrism to remove themselves from these 'white' cultural pursuits because they are decoded as Eurocentric and 'not for them'. In this case, the two groups share similar attitudes, but engage in different forms of action.[70]

Through focusing on the 'why' of cultural consumption, paying attention to cultural repertoires, we thus gain deeper insights into how cultural consumption can be connected to wider processes of reproducing or contesting the racial hierarchy. Research on Black middle-class cultural consumption in the United States has approached this question, albeit from a very particular angle. Namely, both Banks[71] and Grams,[72] in New York and Georgia, and Chicago, respectively, found that Black middle-class people make an especial effort to support Black artists and Black cultural institutions (particularly Black-owned or Black-led art galleries). This support, both authors argue, *contests* the racial hierarchy in two main ways. First, by supporting Black artists and Black cultural institutions, these Black middle-class folk can establish a 'Black presence' in the racially exclusive space of middle-class cultural production and consumption.[73] Second, through their support of Black artists and Black cultural institutions, such Black middle-class folk can foster associations between 'Blackness' and high culture, in a racial hierarchy whereby Blackness is often associated with urban and lower-class culture.[74] Though a tripartite approach to Black middle-class identity in my research, I demonstrate some more significant ways that Black middle-class cultural consumption is connected to racial reproduction and contestation.

Those of the strategic assimilation identity mode clearly contest the racial hierarchy through their cultural consumption. If we understand racism as *structural* and partly to do with the unequal distribution of *material resources*[75] (including cultural resources), then the strategic assimilation repertoire of cultural equity is necessarily anti-racist. Towards the strategic assimilation identity mode, individuals see it as a necessity to consume dominant, middle-class cultural capital *being cognisant that such dominant cultural capital circulates within racially exclusive (white) spaces*. Such consumption is necessary for building an equal standing with the white middle class, not only in terms of economic capital but in terms of cultural capital. Through the repertoire of cultural equity, therefore, those towards strategic assimilation are contesting the unequal distribution of dominant cultural capital across the racial hierarchy.

Those of the ethnoracial autonomous identity mode also contest the racial hierarchy through their cultural consumption, albeit in a more ideological manner. While racism is material, it partially relies on the ideological level for its reproduction;[76] it is predominantly this ideological level that those towards the ethnoracial autonomous identity mode contest. Through their connected repertoires of Afro-centrism and browning, those towards the ethnoracial autonomous identity mode first and foremost *reject* and *resist* the negative 'controlling images' of Blackness as being urban, dangerous, pathological, and aggressive.[77] Those towards the ethnoracial autonomous identity mode thus consume cultural forms that uplift Black diasporic histories, cultures, identities, and knowledges. Similarly to those Black middle-class folk found in Banks's and Grams's studies,[78] therefore, those towards the ethnoracial autonomous identity mode contest the racial hierarchy by using the cultural sphere as a means to promote positive imagery of Blackness and Black people. At a more *material* level, those towards the ethnoracial autonomous identity mode reject the *cultural arbitrary* – that is, the hierarchy which discriminates between 'dominant' and high, and subdominant and lower culture.[79] While ethnoracial autonomous individuals are comfortably middle class, they remove themselves from arenas of 'dominant' cultural capital, arguing that such cultural forms are Eurocentric, 'white', or not for them. To this extent, such individuals refuse to 'play by the rules of the game'; they reject the hierarchy of cultural capital that ranks Eurocentric cultural forms dominant above all others, *and attempt to create their own systems of cultural hierarchisation and valuation that give proper representation and recognition to Blackness and Black people.*

Last are those towards the class-minded identity mode. These individuals actually *reproduce* the racial hierarchy through their cultural consumption. Namely, through their repertoires of post-racialism and de-racialisation, such individuals come to reproduce negative ideologies of other Black people as being culturally myopic, having uncultivated taste, and continually 'playing the race card'. A similar group of people was found in Moore's research on the Black middle class in Philadelphia, where such 'middle-class-minded' Black people would work to symbolically separate themselves from other Black people.[80] However, my research shows how this symbolic boundary that these class-minded Black people deploy against other Black people is partly fostered through cultural consumption. Namely, such class-minded folk compare their consumption of middle-class cultural capital with other Black people, who they deem to be culturally myopic, or uncultivated. Furthermore, through their repertoire of post-racialism, class-minded folk come to see middle-class cultural spaces as being 'beyond race' and not connected to processes of racism. While such individuals are patently aware that middle-class cultural spaces – from art galleries through to classical music concert halls – are dominated by white audiences, this is interpreted not as racism but as the result of Black cultural myopia. Such class-minded folks' cultural consumption thus reproduces the racial hierarchy in two main ways: first, by reproducing negative ideologies of Black people as being uncultivated and culturally myopic, and second, by dismissing claims from other people that middle-class cultural arenas are spaces of racial domination.

This triangle of identity thus provides the backbone to much of the argument throughout this book, and I spend much of the rest of this book outlining the empirical and conceptual dynamics of this triangle of identity. However, before proceeding to discuss these dynamics, I wish to make a brief note on the methodology I used to organise my research presented in the following pages.

Methodology

The data for this book comes from a project on Black British middle-class cultural lives, drawing on interviews with thirty-two middle-class Black Britons, and ethnographic work across middle-class cultural spaces in London.[81] Within this research, I adopted a broad and porous definition of 'middle class' according to the points 1.1, 1.2, and 2 in the National Statistics Socio-Economic Classification Scheme (NS-SEC), thus incorporating those in managerial, directorial, and professional occupations.

Underlying my qualitative approach was a case-study logic. Following the likes of Small[82] and other advocates of the case-study approach,[83] I used a case-study logic to form *logical* inferences in my research. Unlike quantitative 'statistical inferences', which seek to provide descriptive, representative information on a total group, logical inference aims at a 'looser generalisation' that builds tentative explanations about the social world, *and invites other scholars to critique and develop one's explanations*.[84] To this extent, I stress that the explanations and analyses presented in this book are not intended to be the 'final word' on Black middle-class cultural lives. Rather, I see all research – including my own – to be part of a grander mosaic, whereby 'each piece added to a mosaic adds a little to our understanding of the total picture'.[85] I intend the empirical analyses and conceptual points made in the following chapters to enter into a wider dialogue with other scholars to move towards a more complete picture of the Black middle class, racism, anti-racism, and the cultural sphere.

Outline of the book

This book follows a straightforward outline. Chapter 1 contextualises the growth of Britain's Black middle class and highlights how the growth of this category non-coincidentally coincides with the solidification of post-racial ideology.

Chapter 2 introduces the triangle of Black middle-class identity. As mentioned in this chapter, I argue that there are three Black middle-class identity modes: strategic assimilation, class-minded, and ethnoracial autonomous. I discuss how each of these identity modes draws on different cultural repertoires in their identity formation. Strategic assimilation involves repertoires of code-switching and cultural equity; ethnoracial autonomous involves repertoires of browning and Afro-centrism; and class-minded involves repertoires of de-racialisation and post-racialism. I show how this tripartite model develops both UK and US approaches to Black middle-class identity. I then use the next three chapters to put this triangle of identity to practice in the analysis of Black middle-class cultural consumption. Each of these chapters focuses on one dimension of Black middle-class cultural consumption.

Chapter 3 examines how the Black middle class consume (or do not consume) traditional middle-class culture. I argue that those towards the ethnoracial autonomous identity mode, through their repertoire of Afro-centrism, remove themselves from traditional middle-class culture because it is decoded as 'Eurocentric' and 'white'. Those towards the class-minded and strategic assimilation identity modes *do* consume such cultural forms, albeit for different reasons. Those towards strategic assimilation consume such culture because they want to establish a cultural equity with the white middle class, whereas those towards the class-minded identity mode use their consumption of traditional middle-class culture to separate themselves from those whom they deem to be 'common', uncultured Black folk.

Chapter 4 turns attention to how the Black middle class consume (or do not consume) middle-class cultural forms that are decoded as 'Black'. I argue that through their repertoire of de-racialisation, those towards the class-minded identity mode have no affinity towards 'Black' cultural forms. On the other hand, those towards the strategic assimilation and ethnoracial autonomous identity modes make an especial effort to consume middle-class cultural forms (such as theatre plays, literary novels, and 'highbrow' arts) which have some authentic focus on 'Blackness'. I discuss this through engaging with the recent literature on 'Black cultural capital'. I then highlight how those towards strategic assimilation, through their repertoire of code-switching, make sure not to get overly comfortable in 'Black spaces'. Contrastingly, those towards the ethnoracial autonomous identity mode use Black cultural spaces to create and sustain *Black* middle-class spheres sheltered from the reach of the racial hierarchy.

Chapter 5 involves a discussion of how Britishness and Blackness are still seen as incompatible, and how this affects Black middle-class cultural consumption. Within this chapter I look at the specific 'double consciousness' of Black Britishness, and how this double consciousness varies among those towards the ethnoracial autonomous and strategic assimilation identity modes. I argue that those towards the ethnoracial autonomous identity mode use the 'second sight' of double consciousness, using their cultural consumption to challenge British post-racialism, and to highlight the contributions that Black folk have made towards Britain. Such individuals therefore try to raise the profiles of Black British cultural producers by seeking out cultural forms (such as artworks or novels) which centre the Black British experience. Contrastingly, those towards strategic assimilation display a double consciousness as an identity mode. Blackness and Britishness are said to be two identity components, and those towards strategic assimilation consume cultural forms that bring these two aspects of their identities together. Those towards strategic assimilation, therefore, try to find cultural forms which synthesise elements of 'Black diasporic' and 'British' culture – such as Shakespeare performed through rap music. This cultural consumption helps those towards strategic assimilation appreciate that both Blackness and Britishness inform their identities and that these two facets of their identities can be combined into a holistic articulation.

The book concludes in Chapter 6 by looking at the broader lessons that can be learned from Black middle-class cultural consumption. First, I summarise how each of the three Black middle-class identity modes shows a different relationship between racism, anti-racism, and cultural consumption. Second, I consider how traditional middle-class cultural capital is being used to sustain *white* middle-class supremacy. I also review my contributions in cultural sociology and critical race theory, before defending my argument that we must *resist* colour-blindness in social-class studies.

Notes

1 By Black, I am referring to those from the African and Caribbean diasporas. I capitalise the 'B' for similar reasons identified by Du Bois (1967 [1899]: 1) in his study of Philadelphia: 'I shall, moreover, capitalize the word, because I believe that eight million Americans are entitled to a capital letter.'

2   Bonilla-Silva, 2017a.
3   Bourdieu, 2013; Lamont and Molnár, 2002; Wacquant, 1992.
4   Lamont and Molnár, 2002: 168.
5   See Clark and Drinkwater, 2007; EHRC, 2016; Lessard-Phillips et al., 2018; Li, 2015; Meghji, forthcoming; TUC, 2017.
6   Perhaps this reality stems from the fact that many studies on British middle-class identity and culture import a Bourdieusian cultural capital approach, where dominant cultural capital was studied as a classed resource, but not so much connected to gender and race domination. This is not to say that Bourdieu 'ignores' race in his oeuvre – revisionist scholars have shown us that this is not the case (for example, Wacquant and Akçaoğlu, 2017; Wallace, 2015) – but that Bourdieu's particular work around cultural capital was inattentive to the dynamics of racism (Meghji, forthcoming; Puwar, 2004).
7   For example, Bacqué et al., 2015; Ball, Bowe and Gewirtz, 1996; Butler and Robson, 2003a, b; Benson and Jackson, 2013; Friedman, Savage et al., 2015; Oría et al., 2007; Prieur and Savage, 2013; Savage, 2015a; Savage, Bagnall and Longhurst, 2001; Savage et al., 2013.
8   Bonilla-Silva and Zuberi, 2008.
9   Bhambra, 2017.
10 Bhatt, 2016.
11 Lawler, 2012: 419.
12 See Bennett et al., 2010.
13 Power et al., 2003.
14 Bonilla-Silva, Goar and Embrick, 2006: 231.
15 Ball, 2003; Raveaud and Zanten, 2007; Reay, 1998; Vincent and Ball, 2007.
16 Ball, 2003; Raveaud and Zanten, 2007; Reay, 1998; Vincent and Ball, 2007.
17 Raveaud and Zanten, 2007.
18 Crozier et al., 2008; Reay, 2007; 2008; Reay, Crozier and James, 2011; Reay et al., 2007; 2008.
19 Crozier et al., 2008; Reay et al., 2008.
20 Crozier et al., 2008.
21 Reay et al., 2007.
22 Crozier et al., 2008; Reay et al., 2007; 2008.
23 Atkinson, 2017; Bennett et al., 2010; Bull, 2016; Silva, 2006; 2008; Warde and Bennett, 2008; Warde and Gayo-Cal, 2009; Warde, Wright and Gayo-Cal, 2008.
24 Hughey, 2010; Lewis, 2004.
25 This project resulted in the publication of journal articles (Ball et al., 2013; Gillborn, 2015a; Gillborn et al., 2012; Rollock et al., 2011; 2013; Vincent et al., 2012a, b; Vincent, Ball et al., 2013; Vincent, Rollock et al., 2013), a report (Vincent et al., 2011), and a book (Rollock et al., 2015). Throughout this book, I use the term 'the ESRC project' to refer to these texts as a whole.
26 Rollock et al., 2011; 2015.
27 Lacy, 2007: 91.
28 Rollock et al., 2011; 2013; 2015.

29 Rollock et al., 2011; 2013; 2015.
30 Wallace, 2015; 2017.
31 Rollock et al., 2011.
32 Wallace, 2015; 2017.
33 Wallace, 2017; 2018.
34 Wallace, 2017; 2018.
35 Wallace, 2018: 477.
36 Wallace, 2017; 2018.
37 Rollock et al., 2011; 2013; 2015; Wallace, 2015; 2017.
38 Wallace, 2017; 2018.
39 Wallace, 2017; 2018.
40 See Du Bois, 1922a, b; 1926; 1990 [1944]; 2007 [1903]; 2007 [1940].
41 Veblen, 2005 [1899].
42 See Bourdieu, 1979; 1986; 2010.
43 Du Bois, 1926; 2007 [1903]. See also Banks, 2012; Hyra, 2017.
44 Du Bois, 2007 [1940]: 9.
45 Du Bois, 1926; 2007 [1903]; 2007 [1940].
46 Bourdieu, 1979; 1986; 2010.
47 See Bhambra, 2014; 2015; Wright II and Calhoun, 2006.
48 Bourdieu, 1979; 1986.
49 Hey, Grimaldi-Christensen and Savage, 2017; Savage, 2015a, b; Wakeling and Savage, 2015.
50 Savage, 2015a.
51 Wakeling and Savage, 2015.
52 Reeves and de Vries, 2018.
53 Reeves and de Vries, 2018.
54 Chan and Goldthorpe, 2007: 382.
55 See Atkinson, 2017.
56 Lamont and Lareau, 1988.
57 Alexander, 2003; Lamont, 1992. On the particularities of cultural sociology and cultural repertoires, see Hannerz 2004 [1969]; Lamont, 1992; 2000a, b, c; Lamont and Fleming, 2005; Lamont et al., 2016; 2017; Swidler, 1986.
58 Swidler, 1986: 273.
59 Lamont et al., 2016: 21.
60 Lamont and Fleming, 2005.
61 Khan, 2010.
62 Lamont et al., 2016: 21.
63 Bonilla-Silva, 2010: 9.
64 See Bonilla-Silva, 2012; 2017a; Meghji and Saini, 2018; Mueller, 2017.
65 Tate, 2013.
66 'Traditional' or 'dominant' middle-class culture refers to those cultural forms – including the arts, classical music, and opera – that (often colour-blind) large social-class surveys have shown to be disproportionately consumed by the middle classes (for example,

Atkinson, 2017; Bennett et al., 2010; Savage, 2015a). While recognising that multiple classes consume these traditional middle-class cultural forms, I follow Atkinson's (2017) research that highlights how there is still a doxic belief that such cultural capital is more 'normal' to middle-class cultural lifestyles.

67 As highlighted in the following chapter, the concept of 'browning' is taken from the work of Shirley Tate (2013).
68 For instance, Alexander, 2003; Lamont, 1992; McLennan, 2005.
69 For an analysis of actions versus attitudes, see Jerolmack and Khan, 2014.
70 In this discussion between the ethnoracial autonomous and strategic assimilation identity modes, I thus tap into the argument made by Anderson (2011; 2015) in his work on the Black middle class in Philadelphia. Namely, while Anderson (2011; 2015) argues that many Black middle-class people will remove themselves from cultural pursuits they decode as 'white', I pay attention to the cultural repertoires that justify this self-exclusion, as well as the repertoires that justify the consumption of these putative 'white' pursuits.
71 Banks, 2010a, b; 2012.
72 Grams, 2010.
73 Banks, 2010a, b; 2012; Grams, 2010.
74 Banks, 2010a, b; 2012; Grams, 2010.
75 See Bonilla-Silva, 1997; 2015; 2017a.
76 See Bonilla-Silva, 2003; Collins, 2004; Doane, 2017; hooks, 2014.
77 For analysis of these controlling images, see Collins, 2004; hooks, 2014.
78 Banks, 2010a, b; 2012; Grams, 2010.
79 Bourdieu, 1993.
80 Moore, 2008: 505.
81 See Appendix 1 for a more systematic discussion of my methodology.
82 Small, 2009.
83 For example, Becker, 1992; Flyvbjerg; 2006; Ragin, 1992a, b; Thomas, 2010; 2011.
84 Thomas, 2010: 577.
85 Becker, 2002: 80.

2

Towards a triangle of Black middle-class identity

SOCIOLOGISTS ARE often committed to the view that identity is 'restless, fickle and irresolute'.[1] Contrastingly, the very reason that 'race' (and particularly 'Blackness') was brought into existence was to *deny human difference to certain people*.[2] As critical social scientists, therefore, we must walk a tightrope between appreciating that individuals are individuals while also appreciating that systems of domination often aim to homogenise people into restrictive categories. One way that sociologists originally walked this tightrope was by paying attention to the heterogeneities – including class differences – within groups racialised as Black.[3] In this line of thought, simply studying the Black middle class – thus appreciating the class differences in a racialised group – provides some fightback to the homogenising lure of racialisation. However, my research goes a step further by analysing the heterogeneities *within* the Black middle class.

While my research is not the first to posit that there are differences within the Black middle class,[4] it is the first study to show how different Black middle-class identity modes lead to different modes of cultural consumption, justified through different cultural repertoires. The way I pay attention to these nuances within the Black middle class is through constructing a triangle of identity – composed of the strategic assimilation, ethnoracial autonomous, and class-minded identity modes. This triangle of identity is an important intervention, given that *strategic assimilation* is the predominant way that Black middle-class identity is presently understood in three nations where Black middle-class literature is flourishing[5]: the United States,[6] South Africa,[7] and the United Kingdom.[8]

Theorising strategic assimilation

The notion of strategic assimilation was most cogently theorised by Lacy in her research on the Black middle class in Washington, DC.[9] Drawing on interviews with thirty Black middle-class respondents, Lacy demonstrated how these participants would use 'inclusionary boundary work' to emphasise similarities with the white middle class, while also displaying an affinity towards their ethnoracial roots.[10] Such boundary work forms the basis for strategic assimilation, as Lacy argued that her respondents were involved in a form of 'segmented assimilation' whereby they privileged the 'Black world' as a 'site of socializing' while assimilating with white standards in public spheres of action.[11] This understanding of Black middle-class identity has been reiterated in British research, where Black middle-class people are said to emphasise cultural similarities (for example, through manners of speaking) with the white middle class to establish legitimate middle-class cultural membership.[12]

It is important to realise *why* scholars have predominantly studied Black middle-class identity through the lens of strategic assimilation. The reason is because much research has highlighted the 'emotional labour' that Black middle-class people perform to 'gain some level of legitimacy and acceptance within white society'.[13] Key to this emotional labour is that members of the Black middle class learn how middle-classed spaces – including the professional workplace – are inherently racialised as white, and that to successfully attain legitimate middle-class cultural membership in these spaces requires carefully thought out, consistent performances to counter the *negative ideologies* of Blackness.

Strategic assimilation has therefore been theorised as a way to explain *how* and *why* Black middle-class people use their public identities to counter negative racial ideologies (stereotypes) of Blackness. In my own research, for example, many participants talked about confronting the negative ideology of Black people all being urban and 'lower class' – what Wallace refers to as 'class-imaging'.[14] Many participants also talked about confronting the negative ideology of Black people as being hyper-aggressive. Rather than recount all of these instances, I will focus on the case of Martin to show the link between strategic assimilation, emotional labour, and racial ideologies.

Martin is a barrister in his forties, who also holds a governmental position. We met in a café near London Bridge. As I did with many of my interviewees, before we began the interview I asked Martin what he thought of the project brief that I had sent him in an email. Martin commented that he saw great value in shedding light on Black middle-class experiences; using his own example of being a barrister for two decades, he made the point that representation in middle-class occupations does not seem to be changing that much, which makes professional life as a Black person very isolating. Within the interview, we therefore discussed how racism and racial prejudice cut across class divides, affecting both poorer and richer Black people. Martin's first point was that negative ideologies of Blackness 'kind of mutate into more nuanced variations than the cruder versions you face if you're not in a professional environment'. He elaborated on this comment by discussing various board meetings he had attended as a barrister:

> You just have to be aware that people will *receive information* from you probably slightly differently depending on who you are. I think for the Black professional it is quite a point to be aware of. So, one illustration of that is that I noticed that if I said something which, sort of put some *passion* into what I was saying, it was sort of overpowering. It was like throwing a whole ton of seasoning into the soup. It was, it just overpowered people. I could turn down my 'passion level' to *two*, or three, and it would be more than enough, right? Whereas my white counterpart could turn up [their] passion level to a six or a seven, that would be, you know, could easily be understood – they were making a forceful point. But if I went past four or five, somehow it's just too overpowering, it didn't get received, the shutters came down.

The first point to note in Martin's narrative is that he is confronting the negative ideology of Blackness as being hyper-aggressive. Indeed, this ideology of Blackness is *centuries* old.[15] The second point to note in Martin's narrative is that he understands that he has to *act strategically* to navigate the racial ideologies he faces. This is seen in how he turns down his 'passion level' to two, knowing that four or five will be 'too overpowering'. Martin thus engages in emotional, performative labour to appear more palatable to the white middle class, and to minimise the chances that he will be stereotyped according to a negative racial ideology.

The case of Martin thus shows the link between emotional labour and negative racial ideologies, which characterises strategic assimilation. Martin realises that being 'rich' does not shelter you from the negative racial ideologies of Blackness. He thus points to the construction of a racialised (white) border at the frontier of legitimate middle-class cultural membership. However, he engages in performative, emotional labour to counter negative racial ideologies. Scholars have thus approached Black middle-class identity through the lens of strategic assimilation to highlight how Black middle-class people are constantly involved in such interactional games, or 'emotional gymnastics',[16] where they must appease the white middle class to gain legitimate middle-class cultural membership.

However, my research seeks to go beyond just a focus on cultural membership, turning towards the link between Black middle-class identity modes with Black middle-class cultural consumption. To theorise this link, I pay attention to the *cultural repertoires* espoused towards each Black middle-class identity mode. In the case of strategic assimilation, this identity mode is characterised by two repertoires: code-switching and cultural equity.

Code-switching and the burden of strategic assimilation

Code-switching refers to how in the public sphere, on the one hand, members of the Black middle class will adhere to a specific code which enables them to assimilate with the norms of white middle classness, such as dressing in particular manners, speaking in a refined tone, and regulating one's emotions, as previously analysed. In the private sphere, on the other hand, such people will adhere to a different code, whether that is manifested by wearing 'natural' hair (as opposed to a weave at work), or speaking in Patois or 'Black English' to Black others.[17] Indeed, Martin's aforementioned example of deliberately turning down his passion level to 'two' is an example of code-switching; by turning down his passion level, he switches to a performance he thinks is more palatable to the white middle class.

Underlying the repertoire of code-switching is thus a view that there are specific interactional rules in (white) middle-class spaces, whether that means the professional workplace, art institutions, classical music concert halls, or even 'trendy' cafés. Dawn, who is currently a PhD candidate and has previous experience working in the arts, demonstrates this view that code-switching is about 'learning' the interactional rules of white spaces. We were talking about how since she was a child, Dawn has expressed an interest in pursuits such as European arts which are often understood as being very white and middle class. Being a Black child, this always made Dawn feel uncomfortable. However, she comments,

> And that's why, I don't know, I felt like, I've always felt like those things can be learned. But it's a matter of do you learn them because it's an uncomfortable place to be in? But at the same time, yes it's uncomfortable, but I really like the music, I really like the art, so why shouldn't I be there? So

I learn the codes, and I learn the practices, and it's ok, people are always shocked when they see me – but I know how to behave.

In Dawn's narrative, the code-switching is articulated in her comment that 'I learn the codes, and I learn the practices, and it's ok, people are always shocked when they see me – but I know how to behave.' Shortly after making this comment, Dawn claimed that because of her interest in these pursuits which are decoded as 'white', many Black members of her church would make fun of her when she was a child. She comments,

And I'd go to church and they'd be like 'You're white on the inside' or 'You're a coconut' and I'd be like 'No! Actually, I know more about Black history than you!'

Taken as a whole, Dawn's narrative succinctly summarises the cultural repertoire of code-switching. To those individuals towards the strategic assimilation identity mode, code-switching is a strategy of action that focuses on learning the interactional rules that govern white middle-class spaces and settings, such that one can confidently move within such racially tainted areas of (social) space. However, while engaging in this code-switching such individuals still retain an affinity towards their Blackness, as Dawn commented to those who criticised her: 'I know more about Black history than you!'

The very fact that such individuals towards the strategic assimilation identity mode adopt a repertoire of code-switching shows us how racism lurks behind their everyday experiences. Namely, while engaging in code-switching, Black middle-class folk are aligning their performative identities to the gaze of hegemonic whiteness. This shows how Black middle-class people often carry a 'deficit of credibility'[18] – the default assumption is that they are lower class, and the onus falls on them to convince people otherwise.[19] Code-switching thus burdens the Black middle class psychologically and emotionally, as their public identity becomes structured vis-à-vis the ubiquity of hegemonic whiteness. This burden is well exemplified by Danna, an education consultant in her late twenties, when we were discussing the pressures of being Black and middle class under a white gaze:

Not only does it make our day-to-day living absolutely horrendous, because I think, it's just, implicitly, explicitly, in many ways Black people are meant to feel like 'others', outside of this homogeneous white

> middle-class mass. I think what happens also is that consciously, or unconsciously, middle-class Black people feel [pause] *pressure* to assimilate in their thoughts, erm to be this more acceptable, not to be 'so other'.

Danna's comment on the pressure to be 'more acceptable' cuts to the core of strategic assimilation. Strategic assimilation is based around making one's Blackness palatable to the white middle-class custodians of middle-class cultural membership. However, just as in Skeggs's ethnography of white working-class women, respectability and acceptability are key concerns for the Black middle class because such cultural capital is 'usually the concern of those who are not seen to have it'.[20] It is this issue of a 'cultural capital deficit' that relates to the second cultural repertoire that typifies strategic assimilation: cultural equity.

Cultural equity: overcoming the capital deficit

The cultural repertoire of code-switching is necessarily connected to the repertoire of *cultural equity*. Cultural equity is the principle that Black folk must establish equal levels of not just economic but *cultural* capital with the white middle class. Jacob, who is a retired consultant with an interest in pre-twentieth-century Black British history, exemplifies this repertoire of cultural equity. We were beginning the interview, seated in the National Gallery café. In our previous email exchange, Jacob had commented to me that my research is important because we need to 'recognise the Black middle-class presence'. Therefore, I began the interview conversation by asking him what he meant by this, to which he answered,

> I think Black people are *obsessed* with economical capital. That is what they are looking for – to be an engineer, a doctor, wanting to be making money. And I always, and I, I argue that [pause] the English middle class has known this for centuries: it's not what you know, it's who you know … And I feel that Black people don't realise the importance of that network. There's a trope, six degrees of separation, now, I believe that you always are six degrees away from anybody. I know someone, who knows somebody, who knows somebody. And to make that chain work, you've got to push it, push the piece of information which will bring value to the next person along the chain. So that's how you find your place in society, that's why I talk with, erm, Black people need to get up move up, not just economic, but social capital, and cultural capital.

The repertoire of cultural equity is well stressed at the end of Jacob's quote: 'Black people need to get up move up, not just economic, but social capital, and cultural capital'. Jacob stresses that it is one thing to be economically wealthy, and economically equal to the 'English [read: white] middle class', but it is another thing to be rich and equal to the white middle class in terms of social and cultural capital. This repertoire of cultural equity is essential to theorising the strategic assimilation identity mode. Just as with code-switching, the repertoire of cultural equity is formed around the anti-racist agenda to achieve some equal footing with the white middle class. Indeed, in my following chapter, I thus pay attention to how those towards the strategic assimilation identity mode engage in the strategic consumption of traditional middle-class culture to establish an equal standing with the white middle class in levels of cultural capital.

Strategic assimilation and beyond

Nevertheless, my own research goes beyond just a focus on strategic assimilation as a Black middle-class identity mode. While I acknowledge that code-switching and 'segmented assimilation' typify the identities of many of my Black middle-class participants, I believe there are two further identity modes which are in need of further theorisation: the class-minded, and the ethnoracial autonomous. Appreciating this 'triangle of identity' is essential for understanding the full dynamics of how racism and anti-racism affect Black middle-class cultural consumption. Focusing solely on strategic assimilation overlooks the differences in how Black middle-class people incorporate their cultural consumption into differing cultural repertoires; not everyone adopts repertoires of code-switching and cultural equity. Furthermore, strategic assimilation overlooks both those who deny that Blackness has any bearing on their identities (those towards the class-minded identity mode), and those who dedicate their performative identities and cultural lives to challenging the hegemonic whiteness of middle-class identity (those towards the ethnoracial autonomous identity mode). In the remainder of this chapter, I further elaborate on these dynamics underlying Black middle-class identity, racism, anti-racism, and cultural lives.

Introducing the triangle of identity

Strategic assimilation, ethnoracial autonomous, and class-minded are the three identity modes that together form the triangle of identity. The identity modes are presented next, with some of their corresponding general characteristics and the cultural repertoires they draw on (Tables 2.1 and 2.2). Before reading these tables, it is worth clarifying two points about the triangle of identity, which I will elaborate on throughout this chapter. First, the triangle constitutes a *dynamic space of positions*. Thus, the aim is not to fix an identity statically to each individual

TABLE 2.1 Introducing the triangle of identity

Strategic assimilation:

- Class ambivalent.
- Adopt repertoires of code-switching and cultural equity.
- Differ from the class-minded identity mode in that they believe society is still structurally racist.
- Differ from the ethnoracial autonomous identity mode in that they consume traditional middle-class culture (which they see as 'white') as well as 'Black' cultural forms.

The triangle of Black middle-class identity

Ethnoracial autonomous:

- Class confident.
- Adopt repertoires of Afro-centrism and 'browning'.
- Have a preference for cultural forms they decode as 'Black'.
- Differ from the class-minded identity mode in that they believe society is still structurally racist.
- Differ from the strategic assimilation identity mode in that they reject the repertoire of code-switching.
- Differ from the strategic assimilation identity mode in that they remove themselves from traditional middle-class cultural spaces (which they decode as 'white').

Class-minded:

- Class confident.
- Adopt repertoires of de-racialisation and post-racialism.
- Have an ambivalence towards (and sometimes a distaste for) 'Black' cultural forms, and socialising with other Black people.
- Differ from the ethnoracial autonomous and strategic assimilation identity modes in that they believe society is no longer structurally racist.

TABLE 2.2 Identity modes and their corresponding cultural repertoires

Identity modes	Cultural repertoires	Example quotes
Strategic assimilation	Code-switching	'Being Black and middle class demands that Black individuals can be bi-cultural at the very least. Being able to operate in the white world, and that of other terrains' (Dominic).
	Cultural equity	'Black people need to get up, move up, not just economic, but social capital, and cultural capital' (Jacob).
Ethnoracial autonomous	'Browning'	'Having natural hair is about challenging white supremacist ideas' (Sarah).
	Afro-centrism	'We share roots. Yes geographically, but also culturally. Our cultural goods. We need to make sure we remember our cultural goods, pass this through the generations' (Mady).
Class-minded	De-racialisation	'Race is not a big part of my identity. It may matter to some people, but they are far and few between nowadays ... so, no, it isn't really a part of who I am' (William).
	Post-racialism	'If you're a middle-class Black girl, living in a middle-class suburb, you're not really gonna get it [racism] – you get insulated, so therefore the world is your oyster' (Thomas).

in the study; neither is it to assert there is a full consistency in people's identity modes and cultural repertoires. Rather, it is a theoretical model that allows us to appreciate the nuances in how racism and anti-racism configure into Black middle-class cultural lives. Indeed, this is one reason why I often write 'individuals towards the X identity mode' throughout this book, rather than saying 'people *of* the X identity mode'. Second, the repertoires common to each identity mode can be espoused to stronger or weaker degrees. Further, these repertoires only make full sense within the grander context of people's narratives, which I endeavour to show throughout the book in the way I introduce participants. However, for the sake of simplicity, in Table 2.2 I have attached a quote divorced from overall narratives to help clarify the meanings of the given cultural repertoires:

At a foundational level, the triangle of identity highlights the multiple ways that race (Blackness) and class (middle class) can be co-articulated. First, this heterogeneity can be seen in how individuals towards the three identity modes have differing attitudes towards their class status.

Towards the class-minded pole, individuals are class confident – they are assured of their middle-class status. A question I often asked my interviewees was 'Do you think class or race is more important to your identity?' The confidence of the class-minded identity mode can be captured in the response of William, an investment consultant, who straightforwardly stated,

> Definitely class. Because my job, if you look at the lifestyle I can afford because of that, definitely class.

In contrast to this position, those towards the ethnoracial autonomous identity mode are assured of their middle-class status but *additionally* claim the importance of their ethnoracial identity. Thus, in response to the same question 'Do you think class or race is more important to your identity?', Mady, a consultant in the third sector, also straightforwardly claimed,

> You can't really separate them. Obviously I can't deny being middle class, but I am always Black too.

Those oscillating towards the strategic assimilation identity mode, however, have more of an ambivalence towards being middle class, recognising that their Blackness often 'trumps' their class status. Importantly, this class ambivalence at the strategic assimilation identity mode is a *racialised* process. Researchers have highlighted how working-class (white) people upwardly mobile into the middle class tend to embody an ambivalence towards their new class status.[21] However, at the strategic assimilation pole, this ambivalence does not stem from a class trajectory inasmuch as a realisation that middle-class status is foundationally linked to an expression of hegemonic whiteness, and consequently that a Black person's middle-class status will always be tentative. Indeed, it is this realisation of the link between middle classness and hegemonic whiteness that encourages those towards strategic assimilation to engage in a repertoire of code-switching, as previously analysed. Such individuals thus define as 'professionals' rather than middle class, to stress their *occupational similarity* with, but *racialised difference* from the white middle class. For instance, when I began to interview Catherine, a doctor who lives and works in Oxford, she immediately talked about how more work needs to be done on 'Black professionals'. I asked whether she deliberately uses 'professionals' rather than 'middle class' as a label. She replied,

> I think middle class in my mind has, erm, particular connotations which certain individuals may or may not want to be associated with. So, I

dunno, I think of middle class as, when you think of middle class I think of middle-class England. And the thing that pops up, or pops into my mind is that well-spoken, southern, *white* individual, who normally have a nuclear family and shop at Waitrose. That, to me, is what middle class *says*. And I don't fit into that idea that quite a lot of people have of middle class, which is why I use the term professional, as opposed to middle class.

Therefore, clear differences exist between how those towards the class-minded, ethnoracial autonomous, and strategic assimilation identity modes articulate race and class in their identities. However, a large part of my research focuses on the different *cultural repertoires* which characterise the different identity modes. Indeed, it is through analysing these different cultural repertoires that I am able to show the different ways that racism and anti-racism configure into Black middle-class cultural consumption. While I have already discussed the strategic assimilation repertoires of code-switching and cultural equity, I will now turn towards a more comparative analysis of the different repertoires within the triangle of identity.

Post-racialism in the triangle of identity

One of the central cultural repertoires which characterises the class-minded identity mode is *post-racialism*. Post-racialism can be understood broadly as the system of beliefs that argue society has 'transcend[ed] the disabling racial divisions of the past'.[22] Post-racialism thus 'denies the significance of race in ways that diminish, cover up, or naturalise ... a highly racialised structure of power'.[23] A common way that those towards the class-minded identity mode supported post-racialism was through an act of historical displacement. Thomas, a CEO in the third sector, was born towards the end of the 1950s with parents who had arrived from the Caribbean in the Windrush generation. Thomas used his own life story to demonstrate this 'historical displacement' of racism, talking about a shift within his own life-span from being racially discriminated against as a child (in the 1960s), then growing up in an era less determined by race and more by class, and now living as middle class with his own daughter, arriving at the view that

> If you're a middle-class Black girl, living in a middle-class suburb, you're not really gonna get it [racism] – you get insulated, so therefore the world is your oyster. You don't see anything holding you back.

This comment from Thomas displays a pertinent theme for analysing post-racialism as a cultural repertoire. Cultural repertoires influence how you comprehend the world; they act as conceptual schemes. We can see post-racialism, as a repertoire, affecting Thomas's own perception as he comments that 'You don't *see* anything holding you back' (emphasis added). Nevertheless, this leads to a situation where individuals towards the class-minded identity mode often support post-racialism even in the face of what others may interpret as counter-evidence. This can clearly be seen in the case of Keith, an international business chairman. Even when I presented Keith with statistical evidence that Black Africans are among the highest educational achievers in Britain, but one of the worst-performing ethnoracial groups in terms of underemployment,[24] Keith stated that this was not evidence of the continuing existence of racism in Britain. Rather, Keith stated that if Britain was still shaped by racism,

> Well, if that were the case no Black people would get on out doing anything at all [pause] but they do!

Similarly to Thomas, Keith then moved from his own personal story – discussing his own position as a chairman towards making a general assertion about the non-existence of systemic racism:

> So what does that tell everybody? You can be [occupational position] while being Black. *Therefore*, being Black was not a factor. So there must be some other reason why all those other people do not get through.

A consequence of this class-minded support of post-racialism is that such individuals come to adopt a 'more volitional and cultural ... interpretation' of racial disadvantage.[25] In other words, such individuals tend to recast 'racial inequality as a product of non-white communities and "cultures" themselves, and *not* the result of racism'.[26] One way that racial inequality is blamed on people of colour is through the argument that people of colour cling to a culture of victimhood, and thus 'play the race card' instead of looking for other reasons why they are not getting ahead. For instance, Keith's position was that 'race' is just an adjective used to describe people, similar to how people are described as 'tall'. Keith argued that if you are tall, apply for a job, and fail to get this job, it would be absurd to claim that you did not succeed because you are tall. The same logic, he argues, applies to one's 'Blackness'. He later commented,

> being Black is an interesting adjective, to which people then attribute failure, et cetera, et cetera, instead of looking at the other ninety-seven other factors that might have led to them not being able to make something else happen ... So to say it is only that reason is to miss self-reflection, analysis, and a real opportunity to change.

Individuals towards the class-minded identity mode, like Keith, therefore, often claim that people complaining about racism are 'playing the race card'. Such individuals towards the class-minded identity mode thus avoid 'diagnosing' racism, to the extent that they often blame racial inequality on people of colour who partake in a culture of victimhood and 'miss self-reflection, analysis, and a real opportunity to change'.

In contrast to this class-minded stance, the majority of my participants – those siding towards the strategic assimilation and ethnoracial autonomous identity modes – were unequivocal in their beliefs that structural racism continues. They discussed this structural racism not only through personal experiences of being stereotyped and discriminated against at an individual level, but also in terms of macro circumstances such as overrepresentation of Black and minority ethnic people in poverty, in underemployment, in unemployment, and in the criminal justice system. Thus, the cultural repertoire of post-racialism is particular to the *class-minded* identity mode. In fact, participants towards the ethnoracial autonomous and strategic assimilation identity modes would draw boundaries against such post-racial class-minded folk. For instance, Lawrence, an academic in his fifties, referred to such class-minded folk to demonstrate how money could go to some people's heads, making them oblivious to continuing racism:

> as far as they're concerned they've made it, their money insulates them from certain things that other 'Blacks' will experience. However, put them in a different context and they will realise that they have *no* class. And it happened with a good friend of mine ... he said it dawned on him when he went to a meeting – remember, he's a Black professional, highly educated blah blah blah – and he went to this meeting and he realised that all the white people in this room were looking at him like he was a monkey! And when he got up to speak, they were ridiculing him!

Another participant, Daniel, also drew a boundary against himself and those class-minded folk who tend to look down on the Black lower class. Daniel is very busy working for a global financial company but commented on how he volunteers in his free time to help lower-class Black people become upwardly mobile. Daniel contrasted his own 'climb and lift' strategy with the post-racial class-minded folk who are disdainful towards the Black lower class:

> I call them the Black bourgeoisie [laughs]. Erm, who are all pretty, all doing pretty well for themselves, and yeah all doing pretty well for themselves and it's good to see ... but I wouldn't necessarily say that I am [one of them] because I still like to think I'm able to help others erm because I don't feel it's right that just because you've got to a certain level you should just forget people and just look down at people who aren't on your level. I wouldn't say that for everybody, but there are some people – I have run into some highly successful individuals who don't believe in this whole 'Black thing', empowering Black people and this whole race thing, and in terms of that aspect of things there are people who do believe it's the case and *will* look down upon you with that.

For anyone who is familiar with sociological studies of the Black middle class, Daniel's narrative immediately makes one think of Frazier's *Black Bourgeoisie*.[27] However, my analysis of the class-minded, and Daniel's critique of this social group, bears a substantial difference to those folk studied by Frazier. Namely, Frazier argued that the 'Black bourgeoisie' in the United States had an inferiority complex which led the group to strive 'to make itself over in the image of a white man'.[28] This inferiority complex stemmed from the reality that members of this Black bourgeoisie were educationally and occupationally superior to most white Americans, but were still the subject of overt racism. In my research, the individuals siding towards the class-minded identity mode are different to this 'Black bourgeoisie', most saliently in that they *do not believe that racism still exists*.

It may appear that this issue of how Black middle-class people differ over their belief in 'structural racism' or post-racialism is divorced from my book's overall focus on cultural lives. Nevertheless, this is an issue central to my analysis of cultural consumption in the following three chapters. As an overview, if certain Black middle-class people do not believe that racism is a phenomenon which affects them (those towards the class-minded identity mode), then why would they engage in anti-racist cultural pursuits? Indeed, in my next two chapters I show that due to their support of post-racialism, individuals towards the class-minded identity mode show little affinity towards 'Black' cultural forms, and neither do they work hard to support Black cultural producers and Black-led cultural institutions, because they do not believe that the middle-class cultural realm is racially exclusive to begin with. Similarly, such individuals, through their cultural repertoire of post-racialism, argue that traditional middle-class cultural spaces are 'white' not because of racism (which 'does not exist'), but because of the cultural myopia of other Black people.

On the flipside, if individuals *do* construe British society as systemically racist, this similarly influences people's cultural lives. For instance, in the next three chapters I show that those towards the strategic assimilation and ethnoracial autonomous identity modes support Black cultural producers and Black-led cultural institutions to *increase* the legitimacy of a 'Black presence' in otherwise 'white' middle-class spaces. Indeed, in the next chapter I show that those towards the strategic assimilation identity mode draw on the anti-racist repertoire of cultural equity, and thus consume traditional middle-class culture to establish equal cultural footing with the white middle class. The extent to which Black middle-class folk do, or do not, adopt a cultural repertoire of post-racialism is thus central to understanding the dynamics of their cultural lives. Nevertheless, it is not the *only* important repertoire, and I will now proceed to discuss de-racialisation and 'browning'.

Racial salience: from de-racialisation to 'browning'

De-racialisation is a key cultural repertoire at the class-minded identity mode, and it can be directly contrasted to the cultural repertoire of 'browning' which characterises the ethnoracial autonomous identity mode. Throughout this book, I regularly claim that the triangle of identity is a *dynamic* space, and I am not aiming to 'fix' participants to static positions. To show this principle in practice, I will illustrate the differences between de-racialisation and browning through one participant, Sarah, and her overall identity development.

Sarah is a journalist in her late twenties. She graduated from the University of Cambridge, where she was one of the only Black women in her entire college (of over 500 other students), and previously attended an almost exclusively white, private secondary school in Kent. Given that Sarah also was brought up in a predominantly white area, she highlighted to me that she had lacked any social situation where she could have meaningful discussions about racism with other people. To exacerbate this issue, Sarah's parents avoided having a 'race talk' with her, as some of my other participants recalled having with their own parents. In her own words, she lacked both 'the vocabulary' and 'the social group' to engage in such discussions. When Sarah was describing her upbringing and early university years, therefore, it appeared that she was largely sided towards the class-minded identity mode. Talking about this period of her life, Sarah commented to me that

> I didn't really ever think of it [race and racism] as an issue. Like, it was obvious that I was different, I didn't *look* like all of my friends. But at that time, did I think I was being treated different? Was, erm, did I think it was disadvantaging? No.

For many of her years, therefore, we see Sarah committed to the cultural repertoire of post-racialism. Racism was never an issue she thought about, and she never had a suspicion that her visible difference was translating into a social difference (and indeed, that social difference makes 'visible difference' a legitimate term to use in the first place). However, skipping forward to the present, Sarah is deeply committed to anti-racist activism, taking an active interest in ameliorating British racial inequality. I am not going to focus too much on the individual experiences that led Sarah to this shift, but I will note that it shows a dynamic move from the class-minded space of the triangle of identity, towards the ethno-racial autonomous pole. This move, I argue, can be further demonstrated in how Sarah goes from adopting a cultural repertoire of *de-racialisation* towards adopting a repertoire of *browning*.

We can understand one dimension of de-racialisation and browning through the lens of racial salience. Racial salience refers to being *visibly* different to the norms of hegemonic whiteness,[29] thus highlighting how race is often 'fixed' and given reality through the visual field.[30] In this context, de-racialisation first involves a situation whereby those towards the class-minded identity mode only see their Blackness as a visual marker – it has no political or cultural meaning to their own identities; to use Rollock et al.'s language, they construe their Blackness as 'incidental'.[31] However, even these folk who see their Blackness as 'incidental' have to engage with the reality that when moving in white middle-class spaces, they are often construed as 'visibly different' to the rest of the audience. De-racialisation in this context is thus a repertoire used by those towards the class-minded identity mode to *downplay* their racial salience; using the words of Samuel, a politician in South London, de-racialisation thus refers to the efforts of such individuals to 'become neutralised' in those white spaces.

In her earlier years at school and university, Sarah demonstrates this repertoire of de-racialisation, of trying to 'become neutralised' in what was a white space. Importantly, Sarah commented to me that she only realised she was involved in such a cultural repertoire *retrospectively*, speaking from her present moment. Her adoption of de-racialisation as a cultural repertoire was thus subconscious. The key aspect of Sarah's earlier de-racialisation, and one of the most succinct phrases to describe this cultural repertoire, was (in her own words) concerned with 'Not just being white, but being *inconspicuous* in a white environment'. Sarah and I thus talked about how she attempted to achieve this de-racialisation, which involved her wearing makeup to make her skin appear lighter and wearing a weave to achieve the Eurocentric standard of straight hair. She then proceeded to discuss the moment where she was applying for corporate jobs in the City, saying

> I had a thing of wearing weaves … I realised part of it was that I was a bit embarrassed about how my hair looked, and so I think there was definitely a thing about challenging it. And also this worry I had, I was applying for jobs at the time and reading about, you know, where if you're in a corporate or any working environment certain hairstyles are looked upon unfavourably or deemed to be inappropriate – so there was definitely a thing of acceptance … and having natural hair is about challenging white supremacist ideas.

Sarah thus recounts how she started with the cultural repertoire of de-racialisation, she was wearing weaves, and was seeking 'a thing of acceptance'. However, as time went on, Sarah decided to wear 'natural hair', and as she said, this was framed around her desire to challenge 'white supremacist ideas'.

It is this desire to challenge such norms of whiteness which characterises the repertoire of 'browning', a key repertoire of the ethnoracial autonomous identity mode. Following Tate, browning is understood 'as a practice rather than a phenotype [that] gives us an aesthetic parsing of Black beauty as part of a "distinctive counter culture"'.[32] Drawing on Tate's concept, in my research I define browning as a repertoire of resistance to the norms of hegemonic whiteness, formed around concepts of Black beauty and Black pride. To this extent, racial salience, and appearing 'different' to the norms of hegemonic whiteness, becomes something to be celebrated at the ethnoracial autonomous identity mode through the repertoire of browning, rather than towards the class-minded identity mode where it is something that needs to be cast off altogether through the repertoire of de-racialisation.

It is through the repertoire of browning that we see how the intersection of 'gender' often combines with race and class towards the ethnoracial autonomous identity mode. Thus, similar to Sarah's narrative of how she can use her hairstyle to resist white norms, Mady was discussing with me how private and 'elite' British schools will force young Black students, particularly Black women, to either keep their hair shaved, or to straighten it to match Eurocentric standards of beauty. She commented on this, 'we are told not to be Black, and so soon you are not proud to be Black'. Continuing the conversation, she pointed to her own braided hair to make the point:

> This is why I have it [her hair] like this, because then people will know I don't care about what they think.

Indeed, an almost identical interchange happened between me and Rosetta, who works in organisation management in the third sector. Rosetta used the example of her hair, braided with shells, to make the point that she is 'proud' of her diasporic, African heritage. While discussing negative representations of Africa in Britain, she commented to me,

> Like to me, when I think of Africa, I think of art. That's one of the things — art and music, rather than war, famine, poverty [laughs]. I think of colour and art and I just love it. Hence with my hair [she holds her hair, braided with shells] — because that's a work of art to me, you know?

Through resistance to white norms and celebrating Black pride through the repertoire of browning, we thus see a central difference not only between the ethnoracial autonomous and class-minded identity modes, but also between the ethnoracial autonomous and *strategic assimilation* identity modes. As I argued earlier in this chapter, those towards the strategic assimilation identity mode adopt a repertoire of code-switching to become 'palatable' to the white middle class. However, those towards the ethnoracial autonomous identity mode, given their commitment to browning, argue that such 'segmented assimilation' is undesirable and a sacrifice to Black pride. In this respect, my approach differs to previous intra-racial studies of Black middle-class identity, as offered by Anderson, for example.[33] Anderson argues that Black middle-class people often switch between a cosmopolitan 'cosmo' code and an ethnocentric 'ethnos' code, and that even a Black middle-class person who defines as 'ethnos' will 'try to pass themselves off as cosmo' in particular (often majority white) settings.[34] However, as captured in my research, those towards the ethnoracial autonomous identity mode reject segmented, or strategic assimilation – Anderson's 'cosmo' code – instead adopting the repertoire of browning. This negative view towards strategic assimilation is well explained by Toby, a solicitor in his thirties, when I probed him on whether Black people are expected to publicly behave and appear in particular ways. Although he said he can understand why particular individuals do switch identities, he commented that

> As soon as you start presenting yourself as others kinda want to see you, then in my opinion – and it's just my opinion – then you're not really yourself. And I won't, couldn't be that kinda person and be proud of that.

Browning, as a cultural repertoire, is thus deeply connected to issues of Black pride, and unapologetic commitments to 'being Black', even in white spaces. Towards the ethnoracial autonomous identity mode, the cultural repertoire of browning thus directly interrelates with the repertoire of Afro-centrism. This commitment to Afro-centrism can also be contrasted with another aspect of de-racialisation, as I now explore.

Afro-centrism and de-racialisation

Afro-centrism has been understood as a Black nationalist movement which brings attention to the contributions Africa has made to the world's development, while rejecting the view that 'the Enlightenment' and 'modernity' were essentially Western projects.[35] As Gilroy thus argues, such Afro-centrism can be seen as problematic in the way that it reproduces the constructed divide between 'Africa' and 'the West'.[36]

While Gilroy's criticism is pertinent, I deliberately use Afro-centrism to describe the repertoire espoused by those towards the ethnoracial autonomous identity mode. This is because at the heart of Afro-centrism is a *rejection* of 'white' myths about Blackness, and a re-articulation of 'Blackness' as a positive diasporic group identity with moral worth.[37] This foundational understanding of Afro-centrism is akin to the repertoire adopted towards the ethnoracial autonomous identity mode. Indeed, the repertoire of browning necessarily interconnects with the repertoire of Afro-centrism. As Sarah articulated in the story recounted earlier in the chapter, browning is formed around a resistance to 'white supremacist ideas'; Blackness is re-articulated as something to be celebrated, and even code-switching is rejected on the basis of this Black pride.

Individuals towards the ethnoracial autonomous identity mode often use the repertoire of Afro-centrism to claim that they have a 'duty' as Black people to preserve and positively uphold dimensions of Black diasporic history, thought, 'culture', and contributions to the world. This dimension of Afro-centrism was often articulated by those interviewees either beginning to family-plan, or those who had young nephews and nieces, who stressed the importance of introducing this generation to the positive dimensions of 'Blackness' in a society where it is often devalued. Summarising this position, Mady herself thus talked of the need for her generation who are starting to family-plan to 'make sure we remember our cultural goods, pass this through the generations'. This notion to 'pass' cultural goods 'through the generations' was also clearly articulated by Abebi, a programme manager, who is currently family-planning with her husband. Abebi understood these cultural goods largely through the concepts of values, material culture (food), and general mannerisms such as the way you greet your elders, stating,

> it's the cultural things like what food I eat, you know, how you greet elders, when I got married – what clothes you wear. That drives my identity because that's what I've known since birth. It's to do with interacting with family. So, like making sure I ask my parents a lot of questions, so I can get loads of stories I can then pass on to my children. When I was younger, it was mostly my mum cooking, so now I listen to her, I ask her how do I make this, how do I make that, so I can do it irrespective of her, so again when I have kids I can pass that down.

Underlying Abebi's narrative is thus a desire to pass down a diasporic connection to her future children, to associate them with their grandparents' narratives, experiences, and trajectories, and to provide them with a sense of heritage that Abebi herself received while growing up.

Dominic, a consultant in his early sixties who had previously worked in the arts, also espoused this Afro-centrism which focuses around 'passing down' experiences and histories of the diaspora across the generations, an issue that became salient to him as he had recently become a grandfather. However, unlike Abebi, Dominic's adoption of Afro-centrism is a lot more visceral, and explicitly connected to his view that Blackness is devalued in British society. Later in this book, I explore how Dominic collects Black British art to support awareness of Black British stories, but for now I will highlight one section of his narrative that he said in the context of why he collects Black British art:

My worry is that as the white structure negates our presence and stories, we too also do that by default. What I mean by that – because I can see your question mark frown – what I mean by that is erm, our schools will bombard us with white stuff, white writers of stories, white writers of history, white perspectives of history, the lot. If you do Black history, so called, it starts with slavery – who wants to know about that story? And, erm, any other stories are about empire. So, so you end up with having no sense that there is another side, another dimension, another shared history to explore. You spend your time doing, therefore, your A-levels on the same narrow band of knowledge, because it has been passed on. You go to university, and you *might* stumble upon a book or, some characters, but that is somewhat late in the day – but that's the only time you may have. And *even then* you might find, as my daughter did, that lecturers aren't keen to explore race-related topics, even if it's in psychology, because it's uncomfortable. So where is the knowledge base going to come from? We need to feed our people, that they have stories, and they have a presence, and there is a dynamism that is beyond racial tension.

Dominic's view is therefore that if 'they' (members of the Black diaspora) do not uphold and value their stories, experiences, and histories, then no one will. The duty for this recognition falls on their shoulders, otherwise 'the white structure negates our presence and stories'. This cultural repertoire of Afro-centrism can be directly contrasted to the repertoire of de-racialisation practised and upheld towards the class-minded identity mode.

Revisiting de-racialisation

When I was comparing de-racialisation to browning earlier in this chapter, I highlighted how de-racialisation was about making oneself inconspicuous in white spaces, trying to render one's racial salience invisible. There is another dimension of de-racialisation which can be directly contrasted with the repertoire of Afro-centrism. This dimension of de-racialisation refers to the process where those towards the class-minded identity mode define and perceive themselves as 'middle class' rather than Black, and come to espouse racial stereotypes (racial ideologies) about other Black people. In other words, such individuals 'de-racialise' themselves but *re-racialise* other Black people; they 'vacate' the identity of 'Black' in favour of appropriating a middle-class identity. Such individuals towards the class-minded identity mode thus lack the ethnoracial affinity justified through the repertoire of Afro-centrism.

An awkward interchange I had with William, an investment consultant, demonstrates the class-minded de-racialisation. We were discussing how race and class do (or do not) inform his identity. It proceeded as follows:

William: Race is not a big part of my identity. It may matter to some people, but they are far and few between nowadays ... it isn't really a part of who I am.
Ali: You said *isn't* a big part your identity?
William: Right. I don't do [makes inverted commas with his fingers] 'Black' things.
Ali: Black things –
William: I don't listen to the music, what we talked about already – my friends are mostly white, if a book is good, if an exhibition is interesting, I'll read, I'll go, I don't *look* for Black.

The interview with William was one of my first for the research presented in this book, and in hindsight I would have liked to have pressed him more by asking 'If you do not do Black things, do you do white things?' However, at that stage I was not yet confident to clearly disagree with participants who had volunteered their time for this research. What is captured in William's narrative is first a rejection of the idea that 'race' largely informs his identity, as he highlights, it only matters to the racially prejudiced who are 'far and few between nowadays'. Indeed, this cultural repertoire of de-racialisation is even seen in the way that William explicitly claims that he does not 'do Black things', suggesting that there are some cultural performances or tastes which can be seen as *essentially* Black. William thus typifies the de-racialisation cultural repertoire: he *de*-racialises himself, claiming that race does not matter to his own identity, but *re*-racialises other people – he contrasts himself to other 'Black' people who 'do Black things'.

When expressed more vehemently, this de-racialisation/re-racialisation binary can often lead to individuals towards the class-minded identity espousing negative views towards other Black people. In the following two chapters, I explore how this negativity towards other Black people is often expressed by criticising them for not 'assimilating' with white middle-class norms and culture. For the time being, this point can be highlighted by an exchange I had with Keith. Keith was talking about how he had been invited to attend an after-work event in the diverse area of West Croydon for people who wanted to improve their public speaking and interview techniques to make themselves more 'marketable'. He commented,

> So the first person that spoke was fantastic, amazing story, right techniques, engaging the audience and everything. But, he did it with a West Croydon accent. Which meant it was actually quite hard to follow … And I said, it's ok you're all groaning about this is the way you talk in West Croydon, this is fine. When West Croydon person one talks to West Croydon person two, talk however you want. It makes sense for you. But when West Croydon person comes out of the West End to talk to me, and I say I'm finding it hard to follow you because I can't be bothered to listen, but you're trying to persuade me to do something, then you don't care about me, you care about you. I don't care, you've come and talk to me about something, I don't care. You've come here, so I'm not going to make the effort, so I will dismiss you as someone who I can't be bothered to understand. If that's the effect you want, that's fine. But if you've come to talk to me because you want to ask for something, you want me to join you or whatever, then you're missing the point. Why not come and speak in Cypriot, because I can't speak that either!

The boundary Keith deploys here is to do with linguistic capital, an embodied cultural capital seen in people's accents. He contrasts his own refined linguistic capital with the West Croydon accent which he constantly reiterates he cannot understand, nor does he want to bother trying to understand what this person is saying: 'I don't care', as Keith puts it. Admittedly, this boundary is classed inasmuch as it is raced. This speaks to the fact that those towards the class-minded identity mode tend to be disdainful towards the lower classes. However, this disdain does become accentuated when discussing other Black people, largely because those towards the class-minded identity mode (through the repertoire of post-racialism), as I discussed when analysing the class-minded repertoire of post-racialism, construe Black inequality as the fault of Black people themselves.

De-racialisation, browning, Afro-centrism, and cultural lives

As I will highlight in the following chapters, the repertoires of de-racialisation, browning, and Afro-centrism are all central ways that Black middle-class folk organise their cultural lives.

First, we can consider de-racialisation at the class-minded identity mode. De-racialisation refers to such individuals trying to 'downplay' their visual Blackness, see themselves through the lens of being middle class, and often, draw a boundary against other Black and lower-class people. In the following chapters, I thus highlight how this means that individuals espousing the repertoire of de-racialisation have little ethnoracial affinity, consequently showing no predilection towards 'Black' cultural forms. Furthermore, individuals towards the class-minded identity mode use the repertoires of de-racialisation and post-racialism in tandem with each other. Through adopting these two repertoires, such individuals towards the class-minded identity mode often lambast other Black people who do not engage in white middle-class cultural pursuits: they are said to be either culturally myopic or 'playing the race card' in claiming that middle-class cultural spaces are racist.

Second, we can consider the repertoires of Afro-centrism and browning that characterise the ethnoracial autonomous identity mode. While browning is formed around a commitment to resisting white norms of middle-class identity and grounding a positive Black identity, Afro-centrism refers to the belief in one's duty to positively uphold Black diasporic histories, experiences, and cultural forms. One consequence of Afro-centrism – as Gilroy has argued[38] – is that individuals vehemently espousing it often come to reify a difference between Europe and the Black diaspora. Thus, in my research, individuals towards the ethnoracial autonomous identity mode, through their repertoire of Afro-centrism, often remove themselves from traditional middle-class cultural pursuits and spaces that they decode as 'Eurocentric'. On the flipside, such individuals will seek out and support cultural forms and institutions that *do* have a focus on Black diasporic experiences, identities, knowledges, and histories. Lastly, through their repertoires of browning and Afro-centrism, the support of such Black diasporic cultural forms is often justified as a method of resistance to the racial hierarchy; such individuals often use the cultural realm as a space to promote positive definitions and representations of Blackness in a society where Blackness is often devalued.

From the 'what' to the 'why'

My analysis hitherto has focused on describing the triangle of identity. However, I have avoided the question of 'why' people oscillate towards certain identity modes. To be candid, I have not got a complete answer for this question, and neither am I sure that a suitable answer is possible. Drawing from my dataset of thirty-two people, I can make potential hypotheses, but nothing I would determine is close to conclusive. Indeed, while I strongly believe that racialisation aims to fix people to static identities, the triangle of identity shows the power of agency that some have, even in a society that continues to be structured by race.

In terms of economic capital, ethnicity, and age, I am not able to conclusively discern any 'trends' in terms of what pole of the triangle people oscillate towards. For instance, if one was born into a middle-class family, it may be expected that they oscillate towards the class-minded identity mode because their middle-class status is more stable than someone who is first-generation middle class. Nevertheless, of those few people in my dataset who *are* second-generation middle class (Dawn, Ijeoma, Abebi, Benjamin), none of them was towards the class-minded identity mode. By a similar logic, it may be expected that if one is towards the 'upper' end of the middle class (in terms of income), then one may be more disposed towards the class-minded identity mode. However, this too turned out to be false based on my own data. Looking at my three participants who earned over £80,001 annually, then two of them (Thomas and Keith) are towards the class-minded identity mode, and one (Martin) towards strategic assimilation. However, Martin was one of the most vocal critics of the 'myth of racial progress' in my research, being far detached from class-mindedness. Furthermore, I considered whether ethnicity is a factor. For instance, I considered whether those from the West African diaspora oscillate towards the class-minded identity mode. Recent immigrants from the West African diaspora have not faced the same class-downsizing that the Caribbean diaspora faced in earlier generations,[39] which could mean that they have less of an affinity towards working-class culture. However, I found no predilection of 'Black African' rather than 'Black Caribbean' identifying people to oscillate towards one pole of the triangle more than others. Lastly, I considered whether age led to much variation in one's position in the triangle of identity; again, no trend was discernible. Indeed, one finding in my research is that people could belong to completely different generations and yet repeat almost identical narratives. For instance, my oldest and youngest participants, Jacob (in his seventies), and Sarah (in her late twenties), iterated almost identical narratives when they both claimed that white people 'stare' at them in middle-class spaces (as I explore in my next chapter).

One trend worth discussing is gender, although my dataset is too small to discern whether this is incidental. Namely, all of those siding most clearly to the class-minded identity were men (Gary, Harrison, Keith, Thomas, and William); conversely, the majority of those siding most consistently towards the ethnoracial autonomous identity (Abebi, Annabelle, Lawrence, Mady, Morgan, Sarah, and

Toby) were women. My hypothesis, as mentioned before, is that the ethnoracial autonomous identity mode is more common among women, due to the increased expectations for them to assimilate with racialised beauty standards, which offers an obvious target for resistance. Annabelle, an editor of an independent media company, further explained to me how women, by virtue of being subordinate in the gender hierarchy, are also more attuned to spotting the subtleties of inequalities, and hence men will be more likely to adopt 'post-racial views', commenting,

> The thing is, this is again, you must know, you know already, this intersectionality. Because women can recognise how they are oppressed by sex, and they can see the similarities, or aware of it, with sex. Because I'm not just called a Black bastard – you know, whatever epithet, they'll put some 'bitch' in there and all of those things as well. So you feel [pause] you recognise *doubly* how you are oppressed.

An extension of this argument is that class-mindedness is connected to masculinity. bell hooks termed our social formation as an 'imperialist white-supremacist capitalist patriarchy'.[40] It could be that if certain individuals are privileged vis-à-vis the overlapping capitalist (in terms of social class) *and* patriarchal (in terms of being male) systems of domination, then they are more prone to upholding other connected systems of domination (e.g. racial). Nevertheless, this is something to further discern either in my own future research, or from other scholars engaging with my model of Black middle-class identity; qualitative research is never finished or conclusive, and I intend for my research to open up conversations in this area of study.

The use of the theoretical models in sociology

However, while I believe that questioning 'why' people oscillate towards certain poles in the triangle of identity is interesting, this question misses the purpose of using the triangle in analysis. The triangle of identity is first and foremost a theoretical model I am putting forward for understanding Black middle-class identity and culture. I thus use the triangle of identity as any sociologist uses 'theoretical models', as I will now explain.

A criticism that can be put towards my argument presented so far is that the triangle of identity renders the Black middle class static in a way that, therefore, oversimplifies the relationship between repertoires, identities, and cultural consumption. However, at a foundational level, all theoretical models are simplistic, to an extent. As Lamont puts it, 'social life cannot be studied whole, and … knowledge production requires cutting into it with a scalpel that often does violence to it'.[41] When sociologists study the world, we are 'confronted with a mass of hostile evidence',[42] and one of our jobs is to convert this hostile evidence into simplified (yet useful) understandings of the social world. Read this way, theoretical models are[43]

> like a legal argument where a lawyer (researcher) attempts to convince a jury (an academic audience) that something is the case by reference to evidence (often incomplete and contested), narratives about agents (that attribute motives, reasons, and causes) as to why and how something took place (a person was murdered for example). A theory is an argument in which the social theorist strives to convince others about the nature of social reality by the use of evidence, narratives, hunches, concepts, and even material objects as 'exhibits'. … Theories survive or fail depending on their rhetorical force in convincing other social scientists that their accounts of social reality are plausible, if not definitive.

In my research, I argue that the triangle of identity is a necessary, useful intervention for understanding Black middle-class identity. Speaking from my data, constructing this theoretical model of identity allows me to pay attention to two dimensions of Black middle-class life that were not being realised in previous sociological studies.

First is the issue of boundaries *within* the Black middle class. Throughout this chapter, for instance, I have shown how those towards the strategic assimilation and ethnoracial autonomous identity modes draw symbolic boundaries against those towards the class-minded identity mode, referring to them as the 'Black bourgeoisie', or as money-grabbing sell-outs. By comparison, I also analysed how the class-minded identity mode – especially through the repertoire of de-racialisation – is inherently defined via the (spatial and symbolic) boundaries this group draw against other Black people. I also referred to how those towards the ethnoracial autonomous draw boundaries against those towards strategic assimilation, justified by their predilection towards Afro-centrism rather than code-switching. Furthermore, we can also see boundaries being drawn by those towards strategic assimilation against those towards the ethnoracial autonomous identity mode. From his repertoire of code-switching, for instance, Benjamin was consciously aware that the repertoire of Afro-centrism creates boundaries to achieving respectable identities (in the eyes of whites):

> The problem, in terms of cultural capital, with many young Black British people is that what they might want to accumulate is highly contested – are they going to go down the Afro-centric route? If they do, they're going to be dismissed as loonies, yes? And I think they can sort of work out that that's not going to fly in the classroom, they can't really play that card.

Looking at the data, therefore, this is something more going on than simply one unitary Black middle-class identity and pattern of cultural consumption. The triangle of identity is not an abstraction I have produced simply for the sake of 'nuance'[44] or 'distinction',[45] but it is a model that has been guided by the lived experiences of this study's participants. To overlook this internal boundary work within the Black middle class is to overlook a significant dimension of Black middle-class cultural life.

Furthermore, the triangle of identity serves as a useful theoretical model because it helps further demonstrate the link between Black middle-class actions (what people do) and attitudes (what they believe). From the 'attitudinal fallacy' we get the notion that attitudes and actions are the same phenomena.[46] However, the triangle of identity shows two critiques to this fallacy. First, there are circumstances where Black middle-class people have similar attitudes, but different courses of action. For instance, in my following chapter I analyse how those towards both the strategic assimilation and ethnoracial autonomous identity modes decode traditional middle-class culture as 'white' – their attitudes are thus the same. However, those towards the strategic assimilation identity mode consume such cultural forms, while the latter choose to remove themselves from those same forms. Their actions thus differ as they draw on different repertoires to justify their actions, as pinpointed by the triangle of identity. Second, there are times where Black middle-class people engage in similar courses of action, but with different attitudes underlying these courses of action. For instance, those towards both the class-minded and strategic assimilation identity modes consume 'traditional' middle-class cultural forms. However, whereas those towards strategic assimilation are conscious of the 'whiteness' of this culture, those towards the class-minded identity adopt post-racial perspectives of such cultural forms (for example, if Black people are not consuming it, this is because of their myopia rather than structural racism in the cultural field). The triangle of identity, even if it is not perfect, thus helps pinpoint a more detailed understanding of Black middle-class cultural consumption in a way that includes analysis of attitudes and actions.

Perhaps the fundamental thing to remember is that theories do not have to follow a pattern of 'break after break' but can instead be cumulative.[47] Such theories are cumulative by virtue of other researchers putting these concepts to the trial of further empirical research. In this book's next three chapters, I show why I think the tripartite model of identity is useful in studying Black middle-class cultural consumption, and invite readers to build on my explanations.

Notes

1. St John, 2003: 66
2. Mills, 1997.
3. Du Bois, 1967 [1899]; Gunaratnam, 2003.
4. For instance, in the United States, Lacy (2006; 2007) discerns between the lower, middle, and higher Black middle class, depending on economic capital, and Anderson (2011) differentiates between Black middle-class people adopting a 'cosmos' or 'ethnos' code. In the United Kingdom, Rollock et al. (2015) draw a spectrum between Black middle-class people who are 'politically' Black and those who see their Blackness as merely incidental.
5. See Meghji, 2017c.
6. For example, Anderson, 2011; Lacy, 2006; 2007; Pattillo, 2013; Wingfield, 2007.
7. For example, Canham and Williams, 2017.
8. For example, Rollock et al., 2011; 2013; 2015; Wallace, 2015.
9. Lacy, 2006; 2007.
10. Lacy, 2006; 2007.
11. Lacy, 2006: 908.
12. Rollock et al., 2011; 2015; Wallace, 2015.
13. Rollock et al., 2011: 1090; for a discussion of emotional labour, see Evans, 2013; Evans and Feagin, 2012; 2015; Evans and Moore, 2015; Pierce, 2003; Wingfield, 2007; 2010.
14. Wallace, 2018: 467.
15. See Collins, 2004; Fanon, 1986; Fryer, 1984; hooks, 2014.
16. Evans and Moore, 2015: 443.
17. Pattillo, 2013; Rollock et al., 2011.
18. Anderson, 2015: 13.
19. This is not to say that being working class is worse than being middle class. Rather, it is to make the point that the default assumption is that Black people are poor and 'urban'.
20. Skeggs, 1997: 1.
21. See Friedman, 2016; Savage, Bagnall and Longhurst, 2001.
22. Bobo, 2011: 14.
23. Costa, 2016: 508.
24. See Brynin and Longhi, 2015.
25. Bobo et al., 1997: 16.
26. Meghji and Saini, 2018: 681.
27. Frazier, 1957.
28. Frazier, 1957: 131.
29. Rollock et al., 2011; 2013.

30 Moreno Figueroa, 2010.
31 Rollock et al., 2015: 24.
32 Tate, 2013: 224.
33 Anderson, 2011.
34 Anderson, 2011: 197.
35 Gilroy, 1993a.
36 Gilroy, 1993a.
37 See Austin, 2006.
38 Gilroy, 1993a.
39 See Imoagene, 2017.
40 hooks, 2004: 52.
41 Lamont, 2004: 171.
42 Katz, 2015: 135.
43 Turner, 2009: 4.
44 Healy, 2017.
45 Besbris and Khan, 2017.
46 Jerolmack and Khan, 2014.
47 Turner, 2009: 5.

3

White spaces: consuming traditional middle-class culture

It was February 2017, and I was in Somerset House, a famous art gallery, for a photography exhibition entitled *The Eye of Modern Mali*. I recounted the following experience in my fieldwork journal, while the memory was still fresh in my mind:

> I enter the South Wing, take a moment to orient myself and walk toward Sibidé's photography exhibition *The Eye of Modern Mali*. I decide I'd like to go to the bathroom first, so walk towards it, clearly signposted, placed right next to the café. Then I have my first 'interaction' – I'm stopped by a white security guard who has a hand to his ear piece, 'Can I help you?' the security guard aggressively asks – 'Just going to the toilet' I replied, to which he took one more stare at me and walked on. Immediately I suffered the paranoia, common to people of colour, of whether I had just been profiled, or whether the security guard was genuinely asking if I needed assistance. The fact that the bathroom, which was not very far away from us at this point, was right next to the café (which I could logically have been going towards too) made me think (and makes me think) that profiling is not an illogical conclusion.

In sociological language, one may say I experienced a 'microaggression', an act of 'everyday racism used to keep those at the racial margins in their place'.[1] The question of 'Can I help you?' was not an actual offer of help, but was intended to signal to me that my presence was somewhat unwelcome. After all, why would a Brown person be in an art gallery? Many of my participants recounted similar experiences of facing microaggressions in 'traditional middle-class' cultural spaces. This chapter turns attention towards such traditional middle-class cultural spaces, and the ways that these spaces are *made* into 'white spaces' and maintain white middle-class supremacy.

Nevertheless, unlike the prior literature, I go beyond a simple diagnosis of traditional middle-class culture as existing within the 'white space'. Rather, I analyse how those towards the ethnoracial autonomous, strategic assimilation, and class-minded identity modes all draw on distinct cultural repertoires to form different courses of action with regard to traditional middle-class culture.

White spaces: the physical and symbolic

One problem with colour-blind studies of middle-class cultural consumption[2] is that we lose the ability to recognise the overwhelming whiteness of middle-class cultural spaces. This situation is exacerbated by the fact that much recent literature in Britain has turned attention towards how cultural *production* reproduces racial ideologies,[3] or how the 'workforce' in cultural institutions is disproportionately white and middle class, thus constructing issues around racialised–classed gatekeeping.[4] Through this state of the literature, therefore, there is something of a blind spot when it comes to looking at cultural *consumption* from a race and class perspective.

However, race *and* class seem to be essential to cultural spaces that are decoded as being 'middle class'. Overwhelmingly white audiences, with few (if any) people of colour, are a defining characteristic of 'traditional' middle-class cultural spaces[5] – including art galleries, classical music concert halls, film festivals, the opera house, and the theatre. Indeed, many of my interview participants accepted the 'whiteness' of such traditional middle-class cultural spaces as commonplace and everyday. For instance, Miriam, a lawyer from East London, was telling me how she was quite excited that one of her favourite film directors, Pedro Almodóvar, was coming to London to a screening of his new film. Miriam claims that after finding out about this,

> I immediately booked my ticket, just on my own, because I love Pedro Almodóvar, and I want to go and see and meet him. And *I know* there won't be anybody else like me.

Similarly, Benjamin, an academic who lives in North London, made a similar point about being the only Black person in a space of middle-class culture when discussing his partner's interest in classical music. He comments, ever since I met her she will have booked twelve classical music concerts, piano recitals, by the end of September right through to Spring. I don't go to all of them, she'll go with friends, I'll do two or three. A very useful personal insight for the past fifteen years because I go to Covent Garden a lot. And *of course*, it's obvious, it's always obvious to me that [whispers] 'there are no Black people there!'

Miriam's and Benjamin's narratives both highlight how the absence of other Black people, and overwhelming presence of white people, are normal facets of middle-class culture. Miriam talks about how she '*knows*' she will be the only Black person present, emphasising the word to convey her vehement belief. Likewise, Benjamin states '*of course*' there are no other Black people in classical music concert halls – similarly emphasising the phrase to convey strong belief in it. Following Stuart Hall's argument, when people express moments of 'common-sense' – the '*of course*' moments, the '*I know*' moments – they are expressing processes of power and ideology which have become normalised.[6] These narratives of Miriam and Benjamin thus show how the absence of other Black people is a common-sensical, unquestioned, normalised reality of middle-class cultural spaces.

In this line of thought, it becomes convincing to see traditional middle-class cultural spaces as 'white spaces'. The notion of 'white spaces' has been particularly fruitful in US-based sociological studies that highlight how (racialised) social-structural relations have a bearing on spatial relations.[7] White spaces are said to be characterised by 'their overwhelming presence of white people and their absence of Black people'.[8] Key to theorisations of the 'white space' is that it is an *interactional product*, not an a priori state of affairs. People of colour are capable of working out and defining the presence of the white space by empirically examining the space they inhabit – conducting their own 'folk ethnographies' to intelligently work out the present racialised dynamics.[9] Thus, within white spaces, as Anderson comments,[10]

> Blacks reflexively note the proportion of whites to Blacks, or may look around for other Blacks with whom to commune if not bond, and then may adjust their comfort level accordingly; when judging a setting as too white, they can feel uneasy and consider it to be informally 'off limits'. For whites, however, the same settings are generally regarded as unremarkable, or as normal, taken-for-granted reflections of civil society.

Through its current theorisation, 'white spaces' are construed as *physical spaces* that reproduce white supremacy – what Ahmed refers to as a 'sea of whiteness' characterised by the constant arrival and circulation of certain (white) bodies and exclusion of racialised others.[11] My research develops conceptualisations of 'white spaces' through two main ways.

First, my research pays attention to the symbolic level. White *physical* spaces rely on the presence of white folk coupled with the absence of people of colour, and are often maintained through acts of microaggression towards the racialised outsiders. However, focusing on white spaces solely through their physical manifestations runs the risk of 'fixing' race as a static property that people then 'bring' into spaces they inhabit.[12] Contrastingly, the white 'symbolic' space turns towards the cultural forms themselves that are being showcased in these middle-class cultural spaces (for example, what the art is depicting, what the theatre play is about). The middle-class white symbolic space is characterised by *symbolic violence* towards people of colour, involving the ignoring of people of colour's experiences in the cultural form.[13]

Second, my research highlights that while many Black middle-class people may decode certain spaces as 'white', this does not mean that they all partake in the same courses of action. My research thus builds on more unidimensional accounts of Black middle-class interactions in and with 'white spaces', as offered for instance by Anderson.[14] Namely, Anderson argues that if Black middle-class people decode a cultural space (such as a classical music concert hall) as 'white', then 'they consider the activities conducted there off limits for Black people'.[15] I show how this may be true of individuals towards the ethnoracial autonomous identity mode, but it does not hold in the cultural lives of those towards the class-minded and strategic assimilation identity modes. Thus, through using the triangle of identity, I show how individuals' attitudes may be similar, but their *actions* are often radically different. I will first describe these general, often widely agreed 'attitudes' shared by my participants, before using the triangle to show how they engage in different patterns of consumption.

White physical spaces

As highlighted by the previous accounts of Miriam and Benjamin, many of my participants construe disproportionately white audiences as being part and parcel of middle-class cultural spaces. Even though London may be approximately 40 per cent Black and minority ethnic, the city's 'middle-class' cultural spaces make it appear as though London is almost exclusively white.[16] Rather than simply listing all the times my interview participants mentioned the overwhelming presence of white folk coupled with the absence of other Black people in middle-class spaces, it is important to question *how* physical spaces are maintained, or 'kept' white. In this regard, two processes are pertinent to the making of white physical spaces: microaggressions towards those defined as racialised outsiders, and the resulting phenomenological discomfort felt by the racialised outsiders.

One causal effect of the white physical space is to *produce* the subject of the racialised outsider through the performance of microaggressions. Microaggressions 'are small, subtle yet highly damaging everyday incidents which subjugate people of colour'.[17] While microaggressions are acts at the micro level, they ought not to be understood 'solely [as] acts perpetrated by individuals, but … a result of racialized mechanisms … that help reaffirm white supremacy'.[18] Microaggressions thus act as 'the interactional and discursive mechanisms that reproduce the unequal racial order as a normal, and moral, fixture of our social landscape'.[19] As social acts, microaggressions define the racialised outsider in the white physical space, as well as reminding the racialised outsider that their presence within these spaces is construed as 'unnatural'. Microaggressions must be analysed within their situational context. As Anderson comments, microaggressions often occur 'in circumstances where whites do not expect to encounter Blacks. If a Black person is present, whites may assume that he or she does not belong there'.[20] Thus, microaggressions are the interactional cogs used for racial domination; microaggressions *function* as a mechanism to re-establish the racial status quo, which is challenged when racialised outsiders arrive in white physical spaces.

A regular experience my participants recounted was the constant being looked at in spaces of middle-class culture. One narrative I use to illustrate this 'gaze' is Jacob's, who is now retired and in his early seventies, having previously worked in consultancy. Jacob takes an active interest in history, and particularly the history of Black Britons prior to post-war immigration. Thus, Jacob brought up the Chalk Valley Farm History Festival he had recently attended – a festival dedicated to British history that happened to feature no panels on, or researchers of, Black British history. Speaking about this festival, he commented to me, in a downtrodden tone,

> It was *very* challenging. Let me tell you why. Because I'm quite strong as a Black person, and comfortable. But I'd forgotten that *look* that white people give you to tell you 'What you doing here?' erm 'Did you mean to be here? Who are you? What are you up to?' and, erm, I've travelled the world – I'm used to it. But I'd forgotten how it is so [pause] *relentless*.

After making that comment, Jacob then proceeded:

> Jacob: And, erm, [lowers voice] this is anonymous now?
> Ali: Yeah, it is.
> Jacob: I got upset, I just wanted to shout to somebody 'Who are you fucking looking at?!' And obviously, I couldn't do that, it would be wholly inappropriate. Because I got the sense that *they didn't know they were doing it*. They don't, they probably didn't know at all!

Jacob iterates two salient points. First, that you can be accustomed to the gaze – in his instance, having experienced it for several decades – but still be profoundly impacted by it. Second, the perpetrators of microaggressions often do not realise that they are involved in a racialised act, whereas the receiver quite clearly understands these acts as affirmations of whiteness – hence why Rollock et al. refer to microaggressions as 'acts of whiteness'.[21] The gaze is construed as a racialised act because it signals to certain people that their presence is unwelcome and unnatural. Through the gaze, whiteness is made in space, as the racialised outsider has a racial identity 'fixed' into their bodies which is construed as inconsistent with the middle-class space. As Ahmed comments,[22]

> the gaze sticks to you. Sticking out from whiteness can thus reaffirm the whiteness of the space. Whiteness is an effect of what coheres rather than the origin of coherence.

In other words, both the whiteness of the space and the racialised outsider are defined, made, and fixed through and by the gaze. The gaze within the white physical space makes the defined racialised outsider '"stand out" and "stand apart"',[23] while rendering those racialised as white appear normal.

Microaggressions within the white physical space also take more verbal forms. Dawn is a PhD candidate, although she has previously worked in the arts. We were discussing the theme of the white space when Dawn brought up the example of going to an opera house. She claims that while microaggressions may be gendered in these circumstances – claiming her father, as a tall, Black man was more susceptible to microaggressions than herself – she had sometimes been asked in the opera house whether she was one of the singers. After I raised my eyebrows in response, Dawn told me about one of her colleagues – another Black professional – commenting to me, she was talking about how she, erm, how she was at the Royal Opera House, and she went to the toilets – and she was actually a *trustee* – and someone came up to her and said [patronising voice] 'Oh hello, is this your first time at the opera?'

These verbal microaggressions achieve the same function as the silent gaze – to construct and remind the racialised outsider of their peculiar status in middle-class spaces. Dawn's described encounters, similar to Jacob's experience of the gaze, show that verbal microaggressions in the white space do not have to be patent racial slurs; they are often covert, 'liberal' remarks.

Nevertheless, microaggressions can also be much more overt. Walking around the 'highbrow' Mayfair art galleries for my ethnographic fieldwork, as well as busier spaces such as Tate Britain, Tate Modern, and the National Gallery, I became accustomed to being followed by security guards – with especial attention being paid to me as I reached into my rucksack to retrieve my fieldwork journal. Autoethnographically, I saw this treatment as indicative of people within the white space viewing me as a potential violent threat, given the recent attacks by Islamist extremists in London; I was seen as an ideological representation of the Muslim rather than as an individual subject. This 'type' of microaggression, being treated as an ideological representation rather than a subject, was also recounted by my participants. For instance, Sarah was talking to me about how her interests are often decoded as white, and how one such interest, 'indie' music concerts, is decoded as white to the extent that her 'fact of Blackness' leads to her being stereotyped within such spaces. Within this narrative, the fact that Sarah may be at a music concert to consume the music is disregarded, if not seen as too dangerous to believe:

I would go to gigs and actually not being white and being at certain gigs, where you are perceived to be not the right look, can get you into trouble – you can be assumed to be there to deal or something like that. All kinds of stuff like that.

This variety of presented narratives – although only a snapshot of the myriad of microaggressions that my participants recounted – shows how spaces of middle-class culture become defined as white and (re)produce their whiteness. Microaggressions acted towards those defined as racialised outsiders mean that they move with less ease and mobility within the white physical space, and 'if whiteness allows some bodies to move with comfort, to inhabit that space as home, those bodies take up more space'[24] while those moving with less comfort are excluded. The white space is thus constituted through everyday practices of racialised inclusion (to the white middle class) and exclusion (to those racialised as non-white).

Microaggressions within the white physical space, and the possibility of being subject to such microaggressions, often impose a phenomenological discomfort on Black folk. This is well typified by Raymond, an academic with previous experience in IT consultancy. Raymond was talking about how he had worked in an almost exclusively white consultancy firm, and I followed up on Raymond's comment that certain situations in this setting made him feel uncomfortable:

> Ali: So you talked about comfort, it links to another area I want to explore. Some people talk about that similar feeling you were just describing of being uncomfortable when discussing areas that are coded as 'high' culture.
>
> Raymond: Yes, it makes sense [pause]. So yeah, you can go to the Tate and enjoy being part of quite a cosmopolitan audience. Erm, I don't get intimidated by being around loads of white people, I do become aware of how I [pause] it's almost impossible for me to resist acting in a way that makes it easier for white people to engage with *me*. And one of the ways in which I, just today, but you know my voice gets less deep, you know, on occasion, probably on every occasion, that I meet somebody from that erm circumstance. I don't know whether that's just social nerves on my part, or the behaviour, but that's me ... I don't think I, myself am at ease in those environments. I almost always have to think about putting others at ease, other people don't need to think about putting *me* at ease.

Raymond's discussion of the Tate shows that not only are Black folk subject to different treatment within the white space, but there is also a tacit expectation that they must *act* in a certain way in these spaces too. Social action within the white space thus affirms and reaffirms the whiteness of the space. Microaggressions construct the racialised outsider and signal to them that they are in some way unwelcome, or unnatural, in this middle-class setting, which itself can lead to a phenomenological discomfort felt by Black folk moving within these spaces.

White symbolic space

Nevertheless, middle-class culture does not rely just on white *physical* space for its facilitation, but also on white *symbolic* space. In this context, the white *symbolic* space refers to the content of middle-class culture – what the theatre play is about, the story of a book, what an artwork is depicting. Many participants of this study claimed that middle-class cultural forms exclude Black histories, knowledges, and experiences. Coupled with this exclusion of Blackness, middle-class cultural forms were said to be 'Eurocentric', or were accused of only focusing on aspects of whiteness, hence why I theorise the 'white symbolic space'.

The argument being developed here is *not* that there are essential 'Black' experiences which are excluded within entirely separate 'white' or Eurocentric cultural forms. Conceiving of disparate and static Black and white cultural forms simply reifies race through cultural closure.[25] Rather, the argument being made here is that members of the Black middle class are not 'cultural dopes',[26] they practically engage with cultural forms and *decode* the meanings they believe have been encoded within them.[27] Through this practical relation between the subject and object, members of the Black middle class often decode traditional middle-class culture as excluding *what they define as* Black knowledges, histories, and experiences.

The predominant way that my participants decoded middle-class culture as white was through the claim that they cannot 'see myself' or 'our stories' reflected in the cultural form. As an illustration of this point, I was talking with Rosetta, a professional in the third sector, about literature and her admiration for the Nigerian novelist Chimamanda Ngozi Adichie. Without prompt, Rosetta proceeded:

> When you're looking at art, or work, when you're looking at art, or literature, you want to see yourself. I feel though representation is so important, and it's just so much more engaging if you can identify with something personally.

Given that we had not yet talked about art in the interview, our exchange then proceeded as follows:

Ali: So are you into art as well?
Rosetta: I *love* art. I love visiting galleries and stuff. But in some of them – like the one in Trafalgar Square – erm, yeah the National Gallery. I just find it so boring and bullshit [laughs] because it's just like, it's just the same old thing. I don't see myself there.

In this narrative, Rosetta claims representation matters to her in terms of seeing herself in cultural forms, but that this representation is lacking in middle-class culture. Again, we see a Stuart Hall-ian[28] 'common-sense' moment iterated in the interview. Rosetta refers to this situation as 'just the same old thing', suggesting that this exclusion is a regular occurrence that has become accepted as an everyday reality in the middle-class cultural sphere.

The question then turns to what implications the white symbolic space has for members of the Black middle class who wish to consume middle-class culture. Across my interviews, the regular response to this issue was to talk about a lack of experiential connection with the cultural form. Two interview quotes – from Abebi and Martin – help demonstrate this point.

Abebi, a programme manager in her early thirties who lives in South London, was discussing the rise of Black professionals with me. I asked her whether she thinks this is leading to the creation of spaces for specifically *Black* middle-class socialising. Abebi responded that middle-class culture will always have associations with hegemonic whiteness, saying,

> I think the majority of the culture – when I say culture I mean what is determined to be cultural capital so art, music, theatre, things like that – they are obviously focused on the white experience, or focused on white history. Because we are a minority ethnic, we're like 2 per cent in Britain or something, so the large majority – that is their history, that is their background. So, I think if you want to be a cultured middle-class Black individual, and go to all these places, then yes, you're going to feel somewhat out of place, you're not, your history, your experience is not going to be reflected.

In a similar line of argument, I was discussing with Martin, a barrister in his late forties, some of my ethnographic experiences – particularly of struggling to find many Black people in typically Eurocentric art exhibitions such as Tate Britain, Tate Modern, the Mayfair Galleries, Somerset House, and the Royal Academy of Arts. Martin's response was

> I just think that it's what people think they can connect with. And so I think, erm, with a lot of European art it can feel, erm, if you're not familiar with it, and you're not erm, you don't feel you understand the kinda context of it, it can feel quite alienating. And you can feel though your appreciation of it is going to be [pause] *hindered* by not really connecting with it properly, not having the knowledge and the context to fully understand it.

Both Martin and Abebi claim that the issue is not being *necessarily incapable* of consuming and enjoying traditional middle-class culture. Rather, the issue is with people lacking an experiential connection with these cultural forms, stemming from the cultural forms' exclusion of Black diasporic experiences, narratives, and histories. Thus, while Abebi claims that many people will feel out of place given that their representation is lacking in middle-class cultural forms, Martin makes the similar point that one's connection with the cultural form can be hindered by their lack of experiential familiarity with it. At a theoretical level, Martin and Abebi are both claiming that the exclusion of Blackness in the white *symbolic* space is connected to the issue of *recognition*. They both claim that Black people, histories, experiences, knowledges, are not *recognised* in middle-class cultural forms.

Taking a step back, therefore, we can see how *both* the white physical and symbolic space function through mechanisms of exclusion. However, while the white physical space functions through microaggressions, the white symbolic space runs not on microaggressions inasmuch as Black people's 'experience of being ignored and overlooked (which are not cases of aggression per se but of non attention)'.[29] In other words, the white symbolic space relies on a racialised 'recognition gap'.[30] 'Recognition' refers to a state whereby an individual or group believes in the moral worth of another individual's or group's existence and experiences.[31] Recognition of Black folk and 'Blackness' is thus missing in middle-class cultural forms because their experiences, identities, and histories are largely excluded. This lack of recognition of Black folk and Blackness within the white symbolic space is rendered legitimate due to the racial order. Just as microaggressions within the white physical space are made legitimate by a racial hierarchy where whiteness is positioned above Blackness, in the white symbolic space, the lack of recognition of Blackness is legitimised by this same racial order. The lack of Black recognition in the white symbolic space is thus *necessarily interrelated* to the overall devaluation of Blackness within the racial hierarchy.

The political economy of white spaces

Through my discussion of the white physical and symbolic space, we can turn attention towards analysing middle-class culture as *cultural capital*. Cultural capital can be understood as existing in *embodied, objectified and institutionalised forms*, functioning to *curate social, symbolic, and spatial boundaries between particular groups and people*, retaining an *exchange value with other forms of capital*. My analysis hitherto points to the (social) fact that middle-class cultural pursuits, tastes, and practices must be understood through this lens of cultural capital. This is because the discussion of white physical and symbolic space showed how middle-class culture is inherently connected to *white* middle-class boundary making.

First, the physical contours of middle-class spaces are demarcated by whiteness, and the cultural capital thus curates and reproduces *'spatial boundaries'* between the white middle class and raced, classed others. These spatial boundaries are often produced and reproduced through acts of microaggressions from white people towards those defined as racialised outsiders. As I recounted, these microaggressions show the causal 'affective' power of white spaces to cause emotional distress among members of the Black middle class. Second, the symbolic space of middle-class culture excludes or fails to recognise Blackness, thus reproducing *'symbolic boundaries'* against those racialised as Black. Again, this issue of symbolic boundaries and recognition gaps shows how white spaces can *cause* particular racialised emotions[32] on behalf of the Black middle-class person – in this instance, seen in the emergent feelings of non-recognition and being overlooked. Middle-class culture, therefore, cannot be analysed as a colour-blind phenomenon; it functions as a cultural capital that is essential to the reproduction of white middle-class supremacy. Indeed, these middle-class 'white spaces' constitute a cultural political economy, which helps restrict the distribution of cultural capital across the racial hierarchy.

Nevertheless, just because traditional middle-class culture is being used as capital by and for the white middle class, this does not necessarily mean that the Black middle class do not partake in these cultural pursuits; this is only one course of action. Indeed, Black middle-class engagement with(/in) white spaces often involves a deliberate calculation as to whether or not the racialised emotions caused by white spaces are worth experiencing for the sake of accumulating dominant cultural capital. Therefore, I now turn towards analysing how one's position in the triangle of identity largely influences their relationship with traditional middle-class culture.

Traditional middle-class culture in the triangle of identity

As previously analysed, the triangle of identity refers to three Black middle-class identity modes: ethnoracial autonomous, class-minded, and strategic assimilation. The identity mode one oscillates towards considerably influences one's engagement with traditional middle-class culture, which has hitherto been theorised as existing within a white symbolic and physical space.

Ethnoracial autonomous: 'Sometimes I think people look at me more than the art'

Individuals towards the ethnoracial autonomous identity mode are patently aware of the whiteness within traditional middle-class culture, and thus remove themselves from such cultural pursuits. Through their cultural repertoire of Afro-centrism, those towards the ethnoracial autonomous identity mode often dismiss traditional middle-class cultural forms as 'white' or 'Eurocentric', and consequently as 'not for them'.

Mady, a charity consultant in her early thirties, typifies the ideal ethnoracial autonomous identity mode. Since Mady was a child, she has had an interest in the arts. Like many of the other participants who are more 'confident' in their appreciation and understanding of middle-class culture, she had been exposed to such cultural forms as a child growing up in London, where her parents would take her to museums and art galleries. However, Mady recounted to me how she had become less interested in the traditional arts over the past five years; I asked her why, and she referred to Somerset House, where we had previously met. She commented,

> You saw how people were looking at us then? And it is *every* [pause] *single* [pause] *time* [pause] *every single time* … Sometimes I think people look at me more than the art, pictures, whatever. So why would I voluntarily get up and go somewhere where I'm treated like the exhibition myself? I have to ask myself whether it's worth it, whether I actually like it enough to go and be treated [pause], and I think no, I think recently I can't think of any shows, exhibitions, where I've been willing to put up with that for the sake of, you know, 'culture'.

Through Mady's narrative, we can compare the ethnoracial autonomous and strategic assimilation identity modes. Individuals siding towards strategic assimilation often construe their presence in the white space as a challenge to the racial meanings encoded into middle-class culture; such individuals, therefore, consume traditional middle-class culture regardless of the microaggressions they face in 'white spaces'. For instance, Miriam commented to me that art galleries, even if they are running a 'Black-focused' exhibition, will always have majority white audiences if they are in typically 'Eurocentric' or mainstream institutions. However, she comments,

> I feel almost defiant that I am going to these places, that I have a right to be there, I am going to be in there, and stare at me if you want to, I'm used to it!

The differences between the ethnoracial autonomous and strategic assimilation identity modes – illustrated through the accounts of Mady and Miriam – can be furthered with Mady's following narrative. Mady shows cognisance of the situation that Miriam noted – that 'white' institutions will have majority white audiences. However, unlike Miriam, Mady also focuses on the white symbolic space, and how the cultural forms do not speak to her in an interesting way given their focus on whiteness. Mady and I were discussing whether having Black-focused cultural forms in supposedly 'white' institutions will challenge her view that these spaces will have white-majority audiences. We used the example of the Tate Modern's exhibition on the United States's Black Power movement, entitled *Soul of a Nation*, as well as Black Brit Chris Ofili's *Weaving Magic* in the National Gallery, she proceeds,

> So there, how much stuff do they have like this that is about the African diaspora? It happens once a year. So, also, it's, it'll be majority white ... they do not expect us to come to these things, really, and they probably don't want us to. So, tell me, what's the point of having Chris Ofili over in the National, in that room, if the rest of it is not interested in African art or history? ... I think it's good that Ofili's work is there. But my problem is with being *bombarded* with *that* kind of art. That art you were taught and learned about in school – or at least I did, I went to private school so I don't know – but, that kind of history, and European history ... there's always that nagging feeling that it's the same thing you've seen for however many years.

Mady's narrative thus demonstrates the ethnoracial autonomous removal from middle-class cultural pursuits. She first discusses how experiences in the white physical space lead to her having extreme reservations about attending such spaces of middle-class cultural production and consumption. As she comments, 'why would I voluntarily get up and go somewhere where I'm treated like the exhibition myself?' Through the repertoire of Afro-centrism, she then develops her critique to the white symbolic space, claiming that she lacks an interest in the repetitive Eurocentric forms. This is captured in her comment, 'there's always that nagging feeling that it's the same thing you've seen for however many years'. In Mady's narrative, we thus see how through the ethnoracial autonomous identity mode, she comes to remove herself from traditional middle-class culture.

Why consume? Comparing the class-minded and strategic assimilation identity modes

Individuals towards the class-minded and strategic assimilation poles take a different course of action from those sided towards the ethnoracial autonomous identity mode. Those siding toward both the class-minded and strategic assimilation poles consume traditional middle-class culture, although this consumption is incorporated into different cultural repertoires.

The class-minded identity mode, as previously stated, involves adopting repertoires of de-racialisation and post-racialism. Individuals towards this identity mode thus reject that 'race' has any bearing on their life and lifestyle and argue that British society is 'beyond' racism. A consequence of especially the post-racial repertoire is that those towards the class-minded identity mode do not believe that 'whiteness' structures traditional middle-class culture. However, such individuals are happy to deploy 'race' – and particularly 'Blackness' – as being polarised to middle-class culture in various ways. In this respect, while white spaces may cause particular racialised emotions for those towards the ethnoracial autonomous and strategic assimilation identity modes, such spaces are more likely to cause a conceptual verification for class-minded folks; such people use the whiteness of the middle-class space to justify their pre-existing belief that Black people tend to be culturally myopic.

Take, for instance, this comment by William, an investment consultant in his forties, when I asked him whether he tends to socialise with people like himself, followed by a probe on how he defines people 'like himself':

> Yeah, I think it's natural to socialise with people like yourself ... people who like what I like, do what I wanna do, enjoy the activities I enjoy and all that ... things like going to [music] concerts, galleries, upmarket restaurants. And, I dunno, it could be because I tend to socialise with my peers, who are white, but I think lots of Black people are often put off going to these places because it's seen as [pause] it's assumed to be very middle class.

Underlying William's narrative is a distinction between 'middle class' and 'Black'. He contrasts the cultural pursuits of Black people with those cultural preferences of himself, which he labels as 'very middle class'. A logic thus underlies William's reasoning which allows for him to associate certain cultural traits with 'Black people', associate other traits with being 'very middle class', and then claim these traits are incongruous (or are perceived by Black people to be incongruous) with one another. This logic is justified by the class-minded commitment to the cultural repertoire of de-racialisation. As previously explained, individuals towards this identity mode are happy to see themselves as 'race-less' middle-class individuals, but contrast their race-lessness with *other* 'raced' Black people.

A similar logic is deployed by Keith, a chairman of a financial company. We were discussing the issue of heritage, and Keith was making the argument that heritage relates to a variety of factors. He used the example of being a duke – if one was made a seventh duke of a house, he argued, you would invest in your heritage by learning about the first to sixth dukes. This is exactly the same kind of 'heritage' that we talk about in terms of ethnicity, or race, Keith claimed. Already, therefore, Keith was overlooking how racial or ethnic heritage is connected to shared experiences of suffering, struggle, and solidarity (or privilege and domination) arising from racialised processes.[33] Keith continues,

> Heritage is a human condition. It's not a racial point, it's a common condition. Now, people of a similar heritage, have something in common. So they'll talk to each other about things they have in common. So if I like classical music, and I'm half African, I might want to talk to someone about the Nigerian dimension of my life, or the classical music part of my life. So I've got a set of adjectives that matter at any particular point.

Thus, similarly to William, we see Keith 'dissecting' between Blackness – or, as he states, his 'African-ness' – and middle-class cultural practices. The 'adjective' that matters to him at a particular point – being a classical music enthusiast – is seen as disparate to a racialised, or ethnicised 'adjective', namely, being 'half African'. This illustrates the point made in the previous chapter, that those towards the class-minded identity mode, through the repertoires of post-racialism and de-racialisation, construe their own Blackness as merely an incidental adjective.

Through adopting a repertoire of post-racialism, Keith construes middle-class culture as something divorced from racism. For instance, I was discussing with him some of my early research findings that many participants criticise traditional middle-class culture for its Eurocentric or 'white' focus. Answering quite dismissively, Keith stated that this was an issue of self-selection which stemmed from individuals being restrictive in their cultural tastes:

> I see in London people don't do things. They don't go to the Natural History Museum with their children, because they see it as 'not for them', even though it belongs to them! And is absolutely for them! But no one has told them it's not for them. So they must work it for themselves ... There is a lot available – in the whole country, not just London – that people just think is not for them, and don't go for it.

Keith's narrative must be understood in the general context of his commitment to post-racialism. He comments that people decide that certain culture is not 'for them', even though 'no one has told them it's not for them'. In this respect, he counters, for instance, Mady's narrative where she cites quite explicit ways that she has decoded that certain culture is not for her. Even when I pressed Keith on the issue of people not 'seeing themselves' reflected in the cultural form, he was hesitant to go along with this argument, stating,

> One would need to see the data to know it's really true and not a perception that Black people have taken for themselves.

Through the class-minded identity mode, therefore, consuming middle-class culture is important for sculpting a confident middle-class identity. However, within this sculpting of a middle-class identity, a symbolic boundary is deployed between middle-class culture and the cultural tastes and preferences of Black folk. Furthermore, individuals towards the class-minded identity mode construe the (Black) self-removal from middle-class culture through a post-racial repertoire, which dismisses the lingering presence of racism. They therefore tend to believe that many other Black folk are culturally myopic in their pursuits. To this extent, whiteness becomes both hyper-visible and hyper-invisible to those sided towards the class-minded identity mode. It is visible to the extent that such individuals become aware of the majority-white audiences in middle-class spaces, but invisible to the extent that such individuals do *not* construe this situation through an acknowledgement of how whiteness moulds middle-class culture.

This binary of the hyper-visibility/hyper-invisibility of whiteness in middle-class culture is succinctly summarised by Thomas, a CEO in the third sector, when describing his interest in classical music. Using the example of classical music, Thomas points out that certain people are still 'locked into these categories', with many Black people assuming that classical music is not for them, whereas they 'need to look wider than just what's given'. To this extent, Thomas is aware that he is the only Black person present at classical music concerts, but *recasts this as an issue of Black cultural myopia*:

> I love classical music, you know ... and I find the community that likes it as well. And its tiring sometimes as well, you know, because you haven't necessarily got a peer group you can naturally move with and it's because people still are locked into these categories. So you know, I'll go to a concert and I'll be the only Black guy in the whole place – it's like, why? Erm, why are you defined by a particular kind of music? You know, I think Black people need to look wider than just what's given.

In contrast to this class-minded position, those towards strategic assimilation recognise how racism shapes middle-class culture. Thus, while *both* those towards the class-minded and strategic assimilation identity modes consume traditional middle-class culture, the repertoires that this consumption is incorporated into are radically different. This can be demonstrated through Jacob's narrative. Jacob was talking with me about the need to build connections with those (white middle-class folk) who are in 'hiring' positions within the professional world. He comments,

> You have to understand the language they talk, the books they read ... But in order to move within society, certain sectors of society, you've got to know some things, so you can nod and smile rather than look stupid. Americans have a term of code-switching, and it's the ability to code-switch, to go from one ethnic group, one ethnic environment to another, erm, seamlessly. That's where the middle-class cultural capital comes in ... So, coming back to this middle-class cultural capital, for me it's multifaceted, or multi-layered, in terms of what is the simple understanding, the erm the code they use? The metaphors they use? Where do they come from? If you don't know, then you'll have no idea what they're talking about! The second layer is this idea of, erm, being, sounds quite pompous again, being an aesthete, so operas, plays, films, books, literature, paintings – knowing what that means to that society, and to these people.

Within Jacob's narrative, he stresses two cultural repertoires typical to the strategic assimilation identity mode. First, he shows the repertoire of code-switching, that one needs to move between different 'ethnic environments' and not become culturally myopic. Second, Jacob then shows the repertoire of cultural equity, the need to strive to be equal in cultural capital to the white middle class. He claims that one ought to have at least a strategic knowledge of white middle-class culture 'so you can nod and smile rather than look stupid'. Jacob is thus aware that middle-class culture may be used as a capital to maintain *white* middle-class group membership, but he stresses that the consumption of such cultural capital is an anti-racist way for Black folk to achieve and prove their middle-class status in the face of this exclusion.

Characteristic of the strategic assimilation identity mode is thus an acknowledgement that familiarity with traditional middle-class culture is important to navigate the professional, middle-class white world. This is *not* to say that those sided towards strategic assimilation only consume traditional middle-class culture for strategic reasons; many consume it because they like the object of consumption. Yet, even in this act of consumption, such individuals are often aware that their acts *also* carry with them an element of challenging the racial order. This dynamic is well captured in Rosetta's following quote. Although Rosetta recognises the whiteness of middle-class culture, she 'strategically' consumes it through the repertoire of code-switching:

> And then, eventually, I mean, the end, once you get to that certain level anyway you're going to be around a lot of white people. A lot of us find ourselves as the only person of colour in many spaces. So, we've got to learn about a lot of stuff that they do, cultural things – and a lot of the time, get bored, you know. And, yeah, so we also want to make our own version.

Rosetta thus highlights the repertoires of cultural equity and code-switching. She talks about having to 'learn' the codes of the middle-class cultural realm. This code-switching enables Rosetta to fulfil an anti-racist aim to maintain a 'Black presence' in what are often white spaces. Indeed, such individuals towards the strategic assimilation identity mode draw on repertoires of code-switching and cultural equity to stress that without them engaging in white spaces, the links between whiteness and middle classness are going to be reproduced unchallenged. Such individuals therefore construe themselves as playing a game of 'cultural capital catch-up' with the white middle class, as is captured in Danna's narrative presented next.

Danna, an education consultant in her late twenties, was talking with me about the cultural know-how of white middle-class people, and how she had to confront this when she moved from a working-class neighbourhood in Birmingham to the middle-class space of Oxford, where she studied for her degree:

> I felt like I was constantly trying to play catch-up with very rich white people who had gone to museums and had like fifty plus books sitting down in their living rooms, and whose parents were professors! Erm, I found that all of that what mattered culturally, erm what kind of conversations people were having and giving attention. And it was just the whole 'chat' of the people I was around. I just found that really, [pause] really difficult to deal with. [pause] erm, yeah, yeah those are my main things … What I find really quite crap about white middle-class people is the idea that it's not, this idea of accumulating knowledge to brand this shit as your thing that like defines your social status. And not just like I'm enjoying this piece of music because I like music! Or like, I enjoy this book because I like to read books. And like, erm they're like 'Let me tell you about this book', and by *talking* at length about this book, you're being erm, in this intellectual way, erm you're showing that you're intellectual, they're showing something. I just find it incredible.

I then probed Danna, asking her whether she made an active decision to engage more with middle-class culture such that she could better understand 'what kind of conversations people were having and giving attention'. She comments,

> So, I think, erm, I never made the *active* decision 'Oh, I'll go to a museum to fit in'. Even though now, when I look back, that thought was *definitely* in there somewhere. Because I think that, you know, to begin with I was playing cultural capital catch-up.

In Danna's case, we see twice see the notion of 'cultural capital catch-up' – a cognisance of the cultural inequality between Black and white folk, and a semi-conscious attempt to try and reconfigure this hierarchical relationship. However, underlying Danna's narrative is also a belief that white middle-class people only consume and talk about such cultural forms for strategic reasons themselves – as she comments, they do not *really* like the music they are listening to, or the book they are reading; rather, they are using them to signal class status. An almost identical narrative can be seen in the case of Ijeoma, a barrister in her early thirties. Working as a barrister, Ijeoma claimed that demonstrating knowledge of art and artists is a key form of cultural capital required for gaining respect in her social sphere. As she describes,

> Then there's the aspect of [laughing] learning the names of artists and being able to recognise their art – not because I'm interested in them but just because I know that people will expect me to know about them. So, when I go to events and so on I don't seem ignorant. But I actually, I don't care about those bits of art [laughs]! I don't find them *anywhere near* as interesting as I do, like, going to Lekki [a Nigerian market].

Ijeoma then proceeded to say,

> So [pause] what I find really funny about white middle-class culture [laughs] is that it is aspirational in a way that like it wants to pretend it likes a bunch of shit that it doesn't really like. So, you know, 'Oh now I'm educated I'm going to listen to classical music' or 'I'm going to stare at this piece of art and pretend I know what the fuck I'm looking at'.

Similarly to Danna, therefore, Ijeoma highlights how dominant middle-class cultural capital is inherently connected to *white* middle-class boundary making. To this extent, such people towards strategic assimilation are patently aware that 'whiteness' overlaps with middle-class identity and group membership – they thus disagree with the post-racial repertoire of the class-minded folks. However, unlike those towards the ethnoracial autonomous identity mode, those towards strategic assimilation do not simply turn their backs towards this 'white' cultural capital. Rather, through the repertoire of cultural equity, those towards strategic assimilation argue that they need to be familiar with 'white' cultural capital to maintain a strong footing in the professional world. Those towards strategic assimilation thus she construe code-switching and cultural equity as viable anti-racist repertoires for navigating the professional, white-dominated middle-class world.

Three identity modes, three modes of consumption

This section has analysed how three different identity modes lead to different courses of action with regards to Black middle-class consumption of traditional middle-class culture. The most salient difference is between those towards the ethnoracial autonomous and class-mined identity modes. Those towards the ethnoracial autonomous identity mode are cognisant of the white symbolic and physical space; through this recognition of racism, and through their repertoire of Afro-centrism, such individuals thus remove themselves from traditional middle-class cultural pursuits. On the other hand, those toward the class-minded identity mode criticise those who remove themselves from middle-class cultural pursuits, often denying that racism shapes middle-class culture.

A subtler difference exists between those towards the strategic assimilation and class-minded identity modes. While both take the similar course of action – consuming middle-class culture – they do so for considerably different reasons. Individuals toward the class-minded identity mode see middle-class culture through a 'post-racial' cultural repertoire, lambasting other Black people for not consuming such cultural forms. Underlying this class-minded position is a commitment to the repertoire of de-racialisation; such individuals draw a boundary between middle-class cultural practices and 'Blackness'. Such individuals de-racialise themselves, but talk about other Black people who have myopic cultural tastes and practices which are incongruous with middle classness. To an extent, therefore, the class-minded consumption of middle-class culture is used to foster a boundary against these 'other' Black people.

In contrast, those sided towards strategic assimilation are aware of the whiteness of middle-class culture, thus rejecting the repertoire of post-racialism. However, through a repertoire of cultural equity, such individuals consume such middle-class culture. Furthermore, through a repertoire of code-switching, such individuals often stress the need to avoid being ethnocentric and to engage with the 'white space'. Without moving in 'white spaces', then a cultural equity with the white middle class becomes impossible.

So what?

Following the advice of Becker,[34] I like to always ask myself 'So what?' when it comes to discussing my research findings. In the case of this chapter, why should we care so much that different Black middle-class people have different relationships with traditional middle-class culture?

At a foundational level, appreciating the different relationships Black middle-class people have with traditional middle-class culture points to the multiple ways that racism and anti-racism come to shape individuals' lives. Racism clearly has an effect on those siding towards the ethnoracial autonomous identity mode, as they remove themselves from middle-class culture given their disillusionment with the white physical and symbolic space. Racism is 'felt' by individuals towards the ethnoracial autonomous identity mode as they are cognisant of how Blackness and Black people are (mis)treated in traditional middle-class cultural forms and physical spaces. While those sided towards strategic assimilation 'feel' this racism as well, their cultural consumption is also guided by anti-racism. This anti-racism can be seen in individuals adhering to repertoires of code-switching and cultural equity, consuming traditional middle-class culture so that they can establish an equal standing with the white middle class (in terms of cultural capital). Finally, it may appear prima facie that neither racism nor anti-racism influence the cultural lives of those sided toward the class-minded identity mode. However, analysis shows how those sided toward the class-minded identity mode reproduce some of the negative racial ideologies used to describe other Black people, such as claiming that they are myopic in their cultural pursuits and remove themselves from middle-class spaces without justification.

Such analysis of Black middle-class cultural consumption signals how the cultural sphere is far from being race-neutral. Rather – to evoke the language of Omi and Winant[35] – the middle-class cultural sphere becomes a key site for the 'war of position' in our contemporary racialised social system. The institutions producing, and the spaces upholding dominant cultural capital – as well as the *uses* of this dominant cultural capital – are all parts within a system of racial domination. However, just as the cultural sphere can be used for the reproduction of racism, it can also be used to *contest this racism*. In the next two chapters, I attempt to more precisely show how Black middle-class people use middle-class cultural capital for anti-racist purposes, starting with the construction of 'Black cultural capital'.

Notes

1 Huber and Solórzano, 2015: 298.
2 For instance, Friedman et al., 2015a; Savage, 2015a.
3 See Saha, 2016; 2018.
4 See Campbell, O'Brien and M. Taylor, 2018; O'Brien et al., 2016.
5 Traditional middle-class culture refers to those cultural pursuits that social-class studies have defined as 'middle class', measured both by what middle-class people culturally consume, but also the cultural forms of which the middle class are seen as the legitimate consumers (Atkinson, 2017; Bennett et al., 2010; Savage, 2015a). Traditional middle-class culture thus encompasses literary culture, theatre, visual art, opera, and classical music.
6 Hall, 1988.
7 See Anderson, 2011; 2015; Ahmed, 2007; 2012; Lipsitz, 2007; Moore, 2007.
8 Anderson, 2015: 3.
9 See Anderson, 2011; Moore, 2007.
10 Anderson, 2015: 10.
11 Ahmed, 2007: 157.

12　Nayak, 2006.
13　For a discussion of 'lack of recognition' as a form of symbolic violence, see Lamont, 2018; Lamont et al., 2016; 2017.
14　Anderson, 2011; 2015.
15　Anderson, 2011: 212.
16　UK Census, 2011.
17　Rollock et al., 2015: 27.
18　Embrick, Domínguez and Karsak, 2017: 200.
19　Hughey et al., 2017: 329.
20　Anderson, 2011: 256.
21　Rollock et al., 2015: 27.
22　Ahmed, 2012: 41.
23　Ahmed, 2012: 42.
24　Ahmed, 2012: 42.
25　Gilroy, 1993b.
26　Garfinkel, 1967.
27　See Hall, 1980; Meghji, 2017b.
28　Hall, 1988.
29　Lamont et al., 2016: 7.
30　Lamont, 2018.
31　See Honneth, 2012; Lamont, 2018; Lamont et al., 2016.
32　For recent work on racialised emotions, see Ahmed, 2015; Bonilla-Silva, 2019.
33　Gilroy, 1993b.
34　See Becker, 1998.
35　Omi and Winant, 2015.

4

Constructing and using Black cultural capital

I WAS at the curator's tour for the Tate Modern exhibition, *Soul of a Nation*. The exhibition was twelve rooms large, documenting the role that Black artists played in the United States's Black Power movement. The audience included Black and white professionals, a couple of Black families spanning three generations, and tourists from overseas who happened upon the event when they were visiting London.

We were in the ninth room, and the room's theme was 'Black Heroes' – this featured portraits of US Black icons including James Baldwin and Marvin Gaye. This was the only room, the curator told us, where white artists (Alice Neel and Andy Warhol) were showcased in the exhibition. Immediately you could feel the room becoming divided and the atmosphere tense. It was a white person who broke the silence, stating, 'I don't see why you've got to bring attention to their race' because 'lots of white people supported the Black Power movement'. This comment sent a shockwave through the room; every single person of colour had a look of confusion, anger, or bewilderment on their face. One elderly Black lady particularly caught my attention, as she rolled her eyes and sniggered to her daughter and friend. As we proceeded, I overheard her comment 'This is a special exhibition, this is a safe space for Black artists, why can't she accept that?'

Later on the tour, I approached this elderly lady, who I refer to as Sandra. I joked with her, 'I saw you roll your eyes when that person asked the question', to which she replied, in a quiet tone, 'It's that typical white [pause] missing the complete point of the exhibition!' I mentioned that I was doing research into Blackness and middle-class culture, and we carried on talking. Sandra commented that 'This happens all the time', where 'a white person wants to take away from the achievements of Black people'. Sandra further explained that the questioning lady was overplaying the role of white people in anti-racist Black struggle, whereas exhibitions like this are supposed to provide more accurate 'representations of Black struggle and progress'.

This ethnographic episode feeds into two dimensions explored in this chapter. First, Sandra claims that exhibitions like *Soul of a Nation* are intended to offer a 'safe Black space'. To this extent, Sandra points to spaces of middle-class culture which are supposedly 'beyond' the previously analysed white physical and symbolic space. Relatedly, Sandra touches on the issue of how *Soul of a Nation* aimed towards an *authentic* representation of Black experiences and history. To this extent, Sandra points to the existence of 'middle-class' cultural forms which give a proper, authentic recognition of Blackness. In other words, Sandra points to the existence of what scholars have labelled as 'Black cultural capital'[1]: forms of cultural capital that aim to uplift Black folk in the racialised social system.

Black cultural capital

Originally, Black cultural capital was *not* theorised as a specific Black middle-class resource. Namely, Carter theorised the notion of Black cultural capital through her research with forty-four low-income African American youths in Yonkers, New York.[2] Carter argues that Black cultural capital is a *non-dominant* form of cultural capital, only acquiring value within the specific locale and peer groups of these interviewed youths. This Black cultural capital relates to the formation of an 'authentic' racial identity, revolving around stylistic manners, deployed as a boundary against other racialised groups.[3]

Black cultural capital was then theorised in studies on the Black middle classes in the United States. Whereas Carter's formulation defined Black cultural capital as non-dominant, Banks[4] and Grams[5] argue that many Black middle-class individuals engage in cultural pursuits which mediate dominant cultural capital through a prism which heightens ethno-racial affinity. For instance, while going to 'mainstream' museums and art galleries qualifies as 'dominant' cultural capital, Black cultural capital involves a preference for the work of Black artists, or Black-led art institutions.[6] The production and consumption of such Black cultural capital is used to ascribe legitimacy to Black knowledges and histories in middle-class spheres, while also helping to produce positive depictions of Black identity through associating 'high culture' with Blackness.

This US-based research has influenced recent British studies on the Black middle classes and Black cultural capital. Drawing on interviews with Black middle-class families, Wallace defines Black cultural capital as the 'contextually acquired knowledge, tastes and styles that index expansive possibilities attached to being middle class and the looming liabilities of being racialised ... in British society where middle-class identity is often synonymous with whiteness'.[7] Wallace thus highlights how Black cultural capital is a cultural resource garnered and used by the Black middle class for *anti-racist purposes.*

Within this book, I further demonstrate the anti-racist dynamics of Black cultural capital, and how Black middle-class folk pursue Black cultural capital to *uplift Black people of all class backgrounds.* To begin with, it is important to highlight how Black cultural capital provides a resistance to dominant 'controlling images' of Blackness.[8]

Attacking controlling images

Black middle-class consumption of Black cultural capital only makes full sense when we contextualise the cultural sphere. As became salient in my previous chapter, the cultural sphere is not immune to the racialised social system but is in fact *a key area of social space for the reproduction of the racial hierarchy.* In this line of thought, many of my participants pointed out that while Blackness is often excluded in middle-class cultural forms, when Blackness *is* present, it is often represented in stereotypical ways, such as through the lens of urban or underclass culture, knife crime, drug delinquency, and so on.

For instance, I went to the Roy Williams theatre play *Soul* at Hackney Empire, about the life and death of Marvin Gaye. The play was followed by a question-and-answer session about 'diversity in the arts'. In this session, one person in the audience claimed that she submitted a play to a white-majority production company about two Black middle-class women growing up in London; the play was rejected on the basis that the story was 'really about white people' and that the play should be rewritten so that the two main characters are both white, or to make it 'more urban'. I remember people muttering, disapprovingly, before another person recounted an almost identical experience – they had submitted a play about Black youths growing up in London, only to be told that the play 'was not urban enough' because it lacked stories of drug use and petty criminal activity. Triangulating these ethnographic findings, I had interviewees repeat near-identical narratives. Talking about the representation of Black Britons in literary culture, for instance, Miriam commented to me,

> It's all knife crime – yawn – sorry we need something else for *us.* Not all of us are just hanging out with kids stabbing each other all the time!

Now, a post-racial sceptic may say that these are all isolated events; the two playwrights may have coincidentally encountered bigoted editors, while Miriam simply is not reading the right books. However, we must contextualise these narratives in the context of a growing body of literature that highlights how, within Britain, the cultural industries increasingly use a 'rationalising/racialising' logic, where gatekeepers argue that cultural forms produced by, or focusing on the lifeworlds of, racialised minorities will only have market success if they reproduce dominant racial tropes.[9]

One of the main functions of Black cultural capital is to resist and roll back these controlling images of Blackness that are promoted through dominant cultural capital. In this regard, Black cultural capital is inherently connected to a politics of Black representation.

Black cultural capital, Black representation

Following Stuart Hall's advice,[10] it is useful to think of the politics of Black representation on two levels: basic and advanced. 'Basic' representation, on the one hand, aims towards increasing the number of Black cultural producers, such as writers, artists, and playwrights. 'Advanced' representation, on the other hand, involves an *authentic* exploration and representation of Blackness and Black diasporic lives.

Miriam captures the dynamic of 'basic' representation when discussing classical music and opera. She begins by talking about how she is due to attend a performance of an all-Black orchestra called Chineke!, before proceeding to discuss the South African opera singer Pumeza Matshikiza, whose performance she had just attended:

> they're an all-Black orchestra but there won't be any kind of jazz; they're playing a completely classical programme: Dvorak, Hayden's Cello Concerto in C, and the guy who won young musician of the year, the cellist – he's gonna be starring. The only difference is, they're an all-Black orchestra. And I'm going to that, and I'm really pleased there's more of that stuff now ... And there's also a Black opera singer from South Africa, she's absolutely amazing, Pumeza Matshikiza, who's just come. So do you see what I said to you earlier about Black orchestra, Chineke!, here's another one, she's just burst out into the opera world. So [pause] *good*! So [pause] we, *we* can claim opera. Do you see what I mean? So, the more people kinda start to do this, even if they just become an aberration, it

means people like me can grab on to them and embrace it. So if people say to me 'Why are you listening to opera?' I can say 'Look at her singing it, and she looks just like me!'

Miriam highlights how 'basic' representation can legitimise the presence of Black *consumers* of said culture. The very presence of Black producers of middle-class cultural forms enables her to say, 'Look at her singing it, and she looks just like me!' – her occupation of the symbolic and physical space becomes more legitimate. To this extent, Miriam is not concerned with the content of the culture; she explicitly mentions 'there won't be any kind of jazz', implicitly making the point that they are not performing so-called Black music.[11]

Nevertheless, it is through the advanced form of representation that forms of Black cultural capital become key (cultural) resources for contesting the racial hierarchy's controlling images of Blackness. In advanced representation, the cultural form represents Blackness in an authentic manner. In Du Boisian terms, the cultural form focuses not on Blackness as an object – that is, as a set of debased ideological representations – but on Black *souls*.[12] By focusing on Black souls, the cultural form interrogates some dynamic of Black existence without succumbing to dominant, negative representations of Blackness.

Throughout my ethnographic work, I regularly encountered this advanced representation. Towards the beginning of my research, I visited the photography exhibition *Made You Look*, curated by Ekow Eshun and focusing on Black masculinity and dandyism, showcased in the Photographers' Gallery. Through visiting this exhibition, and from talking to other visitors and reading the noticeboard where visitors can write small reviews, it was immediately apparent that many Black consumers were decoding the exhibition as a resistance to the stereotypes of Black men as aggressive. Examples of some of the reviews on the noticeboard read

You captured the Black essence, fragility, power, and beauty of my people.
Now I await the women.
This empowerment is so relevant. We need more representations like this.
Reminds me of so many beautiful men I have known. These lovely souls.

Some of my interviewees had also attended this exhibition. Daniel, for instance, stated to me that he struggled to find other exhibitions which worked so effectively towards dismantling racial stereotypes. Similarly, Miriam commented about this exhibition, it was absolutely fascinating how just photographs of Black men from different countries, from different socio-economic backgrounds, expressing their pride through their dress and that kinda thing. And not in any aggressive way, or hyper-masculine way, but just being themselves. And I thought I just wished that everybody in the country could just come in and say 'Look! It's just some guys wearing suits, just being themselves'. And there's no agenda, they're not angry, they're not criminals, or they're not – do you see what I mean – mentally ill, they're just them.

My interviewees, and many people visiting the *Made You Look* exhibition, thus acknowledged the advanced representation that the exhibition accomplished. It was curated by a Black artist, and all the work was from artists of the Black diaspora – however, what was given most credit was how it deconstructed the idea of Black men as hyper-aggressive.

Skipping forward a few months, I was at Somerset House to visit a photography exhibition focusing on Mali in its immediate years of independence. The exhibition, entitled *The Eye of Modern Mali*, was two rooms large, featuring photographs taken by the Malian photographer Malick Sibidé, with a joining playlist created by Ghanaian-British Rita Ray. As one of the songs came on – Ziboté by Ernesto Djédjé – I heard one of the exhibition visitors make a noise of joy; I turned to her, and she commented, 'I grew up around this music!' I talked with this visitor, Mady, and (as you can tell by now) ended up recruiting her as an interview participant. At the exhibition, she remarked, 'It's so nice to have stuff like this, Africans, Black Africans, happy, dancing, enjoying themselves. Not all the poor children and poverty you always see on the TV and the TV adverts.' From Mady's point of view, the exhibition had *positive* racial meanings: the people photographed were not simply portrayed through the lens of poverty, and the exhibition, she later observed, celebrated emancipation from colonialism. Similarly to visitors to the *Made You Look* exhibition, therefore, Mady praised the exhibition primarily through its advanced representation.

Taking a step back, we can then question what Black cultural capital with this 'advanced representation' does. Given that studies of British (middle-class) cultural capital are rarely intersectional, we are often presented with the view that middle-class cultural capital functions to reproduce material inequalities,[13] or to sustain middle-class symbolic boundaries.[14] However, if we look at Black middle-class experiences, then we can see that forms of *Black* cultural capital are being used to contest the racial hierarchy; the cultural capital is thus being used to *challenge* rather than reproduce inequalities. Furthermore, this contestation to the racial hierarchy is predominantly *ideological*. The concern of such Black middle-class folk is *not* to garner equal levels of cultural capital to the white middle class; rather, the cultural capital is being used to contest the system of images, stereotypes, and representations that continue to subjugate Black people.

Anti-racist connections and practice

Indeed, looking even closer, we can see that many Black middle-class people use Black cultural capital not only for an ideological battle, but simply as a coping mechanism for living in a society that is inherently racist. In this respect, the Black cultural capital is an anti-racist resource in that it constructs a phenomenological buffer between the Black middle-class individual and the wider racial structure within which they are positioned. This dynamic is captured in participants' narratives, where they draw a distinct connection between their own individual storylines and the stories being presented in the content of the Black cultural capital. For instance, Rosetta was talking with me about how she had recently seen Nigerian author Chimamanda Ngozi Adichie give a public lecture at the Southbank Centre. Interestingly, Rosetta explained her hesitancy with the subtle anti-Christian messages in Adichie's writings, but did not let this anti-religiosity get in the way of connecting with her work:

> Rosetta: And also, also for me, I'm usually, I don't know if she's spoken about it outright, but I can just sense a lot of anti-Christian, like, undertones in what she says, what she writes, and obviously as a Christian I'm uncomfortable with that. But I still appreciate her work. Just like, putting Nigerian authors on the map. It's just so important. Writing about our experiences of race, in the West. Is just amazing.
> Ali: Is that something you're quite concerned with culturally?
> Rosetta: Yeah definitely. Like reading her books was so comforting, I was like 'Oh my gosh, this is my life! I totally know what you're talking about!'

Rosetta's connection with the writings of Adichie is realised in her comment 'Oh my gosh, this is my life! I totally know what you're talking about!' In contrast to the previously analysed white 'symbolic space', therefore, Rosetta points to the existence of forms of Black cultural capital where Black folk do feel recognised and do feel as though their stories are validated. These forms of Black cultural capital, as Rosetta highlights, are essentially *comforting*.

One of my other interview participants, Ijeoma, had also seen Adichie speak at the Southbank Centre. Aside from liking Adichie's novels, Ijeoma also mentioned liking the works of another Nigerian author, Chinua Achebe. This led me to question whether she has a preference for Nigerian authors. She clarified that she has a preference for Black diasporic authors in general, but did proceed to discuss why Nigerian authors and stories take her interest:

> There's something about reading a book and, like, them mentioning food you've grown up with, or places you don't necessarily know – because I've never lived in Nigeria – but are familiar sounding because you've heard your parents talking about them. I like that familiarity which is something that I've never really got from reading English literature. Whereas with this stuff it was really good.

Ijeoma thus develops the point made by Rosetta. Black cultural capital fills an experiential void left by dominant 'white' cultural capital; as Ijeoma claims, the writings of Achebe provide her with a 'familiarity which is something that I've never really got from reading English literature'. In a similar style of argument, Dawn used music to discuss with me how she builds a connection with certain cultural forms through her fact of being racialised as Black. She commented on how gospel music had been important to her grandparents when they moved to the United Kingdom in the Windrush generation, saying that she now has a predilection for this music because of the memories and histories it evokes:

> So for me, when I listen to gospel music, that's where I guess, something happens. Stirs inside of me. Just because I think of that music as part of the African diaspora. And I think of my [pause] it means something to me. I hear it and I hear the history of my people, of slavery, of everything that has happened since. And, erm, I think that's where, but I mean that's not really reflecting on my own experiences, that's I guess me connecting with my experience of some epigenetic level. But I'd say that is the closest thing of where I would consume something and it would be like 'Yes, this is me', and because I [pause] I like to sing – rather than saying I can sing – and if I'm singing back to them, then it feels as though there is something that connects me to other generations before and to the whole diaspora, and to the continent.

As Dawn argues, through music she feels 'something that connects me to other generations before and to the whole diaspora, and to the continent'. Within the music, therefore, Dawn speaks to the past and present diaspora, she evokes collective memories and histories 'of slavery, of everything that has happened since'. Importantly, Dawn qualifies that this does not necessarily involve reflecting on her own lived experiences, but instead she talks about a connection at an 'epigenetic level' where she is connected to others in fact of their being racialised as Black.

The three narratives of Ijeoma, Dawn, and Rosetta thus highlight another salient anti-racist feature of Black cultural capital that has hitherto 'slipped under' the radar of sociological analysis. It is fairly straightforward to see how the Black middle class *use* cultural capital to contest ideological dimensions of the racial hierarchy through promoting positive imagery and representation of Blackness and Black people. However, such Black cultural capital also enables individuals to draw a connection with cultural forms, to connect with other members of the diaspora, and, ultimately, to achieve a feeling of comfort and belonging in a racialised social system that relies on producing a constant threat towards the existence of Black people.

Indeed, sometimes, consuming Black cultural capital is simply geared towards learning more about these 'threats' to Black people, and learning ways to ameliorate them. To this extent, Black cultural capital serves as a cultural resource that enables the Black middle class to deal with racism – both in *defensive* and *offensive* ways.

Defensively, Black cultural capital helps members of the Black middle class learn how to cope with everyday acts of racism. This can be demonstrated in the case of Dawn. Dawn was telling me how, when she was working for an arts company, the manager had made a covert racial remark towards her. The manager had asked everyone on the team to recommend someone to fill a vacant position, and all the team apart from Dawn recommended a white British person. Dawn recommend someone that the manager construed as having a 'foreign-sounding' name, and Dawn describes how her manager went into much more detail to scrutinise her recommendation compared to the other team members' choices. Eventually, the manager stated that she did not want to take Dawn's recommendation because she could be accused of tokenism (i.e. favouring her only Black team member). When I asked what Dawn did in response to this, she commented,

> So what I did with this person is I just got angry for a week, and then was like 'Argh!' and then I just had to wait, let it calm down in my mind, *read a lot*. I read Audre Lorde's text on Black women and the uses of our anger, and

> I spoke to her afterwards. And I said – 'Look, we need to have a conversation about this. Because what you said [pause] did this, and that's not ok.'

In Dawn's case, we thus see how she uses a text, Audre Lorde's *The Uses of Anger*,[15] to better strategise what course of action to take in response to a problem she has encountered. Dawn puts Lorde's text, existing as a form of Black cultural capital, to use in building effective strategies of anti-racism. This anti-racism is *defensive* in that it helps Dawn cope with microaggressions and teaches her what to do when confronted with such everyday acts of white ignorance.[16]

In terms of Black cultural capital enabling an *offensive* anti-racism, we can turn to the narrative of Catherine, a doctor in her early thirties. Catherine was telling me how through her twenties she became more aware of issues of racism in British society, and how she used books and magazines to learn more about these issues and how to confront them. I asked whether her parents had taught her about these issues and how to cope with them. She then compared the teachings of her parents and grandparents as 'defensive' strategies with the more 'offensive' strategies she has gained through reading:

> I think every individual of colour has the teachings of parents, grandparents, and so on. But this is something that, erm, I say it was kind of like a defence. So what they were teaching me was almost like [pause] how to defend myself *mentally* from what the world was going to be like, for me, as a Black woman. But it wasn't necessarily a mechanism teaching me to be like 'This is how you now need to go and like teach others and educate others and like campaign for, against, x, y, z.' Whereas I think in my latter stages, and how I am now, it's a lot more about trying to get involved in things, trying to get involved in certain conversations, discussions, educating people on certain topics, areas, talking about why that offends me, et cetera, et cetera. So, therefore, less of a defence, more on the – well not on the offensive like going out there, beating up people [laughs] – but you know what I mean? Like being more proactive [pause] about the issues. So I started reading more articles, more books and things that tackle those kind of issues. So, erm, James Baldwin, which is excellent, Gal-Dem, Jezebel, erm, I just finished *Bad Feminist* by Roxane Gay who is an African-American, English scholar. Yeah, I've got *Invisible Man*, also about the Black experience in America, it was going to be my next book to read but I'm like 'No! it's literally all you've been reading about!' So yeah,

yeah, I try to get a better grasp on the type of philosophies and ideologies in this field, so I can explain myself better when I talk to people about it.

Catherine, therefore, like Dawn, uses texts to learn about the world and the problems she encounters, and puts these cultural forms to *practical use* in confronting racism. These two cases show how the consumption of Black cultural capital is not always geared towards proving oneself as a cultivated consumer (as in Bourdieu's Distinction model)[17]; the consumption of Black cultural capital is aimed towards *learning about the racialised social system which construes Black folk as inferior, and learning ways to navigate, and dismantle this system.*

If we can spot three anti-racist uses of Black cultural capital by looking at my participants' general narratives, then the matter becomes even more nuanced when we bring the triangle of identity into the equation. Through the triangle of identity, we particularly gain insights into how those towards the strategic assimilation and ethnoracial autonomous identity modes use Black cultural capital for slightly different anti-racist missions.

Black cultural capital in the triangle of identity

As may be expected, Black cultural capital is not of concern to those towards the class-minded identity mode. This is captured in participants making claims such as 'I don't *look* for Black' (William, when discussing his cultural preferences), or 'Black culture doesn't really interest me' (Harrison, when I asked him about London's Black cultural capital scene). To this extent, Black cultural capital is more so in the interests of those towards the strategic assimilation and ethnoracial autonomous identity modes.

First, a salient difference exists in how those towards the strategic assimilation and ethnoracial autonomous identity modes construe the status of white consumers of Black cultural forms. Namely, those siding towards strategic assimilation are more open to increasing white engagement with Black cultural forms. Conversely, through their repertoire of Afro-centrism, those sided towards the ethnoracial autonomous identity mode are more dismissive towards white engagement with Black cultural forms. This difference becomes important in differentiating between the anti-racist missions of those towards the strategic assimilation and ethnoracial autonomous identity modes. Namely, the former use Black cultural capital as a means to promote inter-racial solidarity, while the latter use Black cultural capital to challenge the so-called cultural capital deficit model.

Dominic's approach to white consumers of Black cultural forms illustrates the ethnoracial autonomous identity mode. Dominic had iterated several times in the interview that white middle-class people had little idea about the content of Black cultural lives – he mentioned this with regard to how television, art institutions, and publishers exclude authentic Black narratives. Central to Dominic's argument was a repertoire of Afro-centrism, which led him to a form of cultural essentialism whereby there are 'Black things' that *only* Black people can understand. When the moment arose, I therefore asked him,

> Ali: You talked about Black cultural life and content, and how white middle class have an inability to comprehend it?
>
> Dominic: So white folk, can certainly enjoy reggae, grime, garage, hip hop, why not? The question is, however, do you understand the sentiment or the lives that are being expressed in the song, in an empathetic fashion? Or is it just, you know, a fad … I mean the book sales, they exist. People buy a variety of books. James Nolan's book on Jamaica or erm, you know, Zadie Smith's books on UK and London. They're all good intellectual books, intelligent reads on diverse life. Does that lead you to be better able to have a better dialogue with other people? No! Because they are not in our setting! White settings are pure, they are not diverse. So how can they say 'I read in a book last week blah blah blah, what do you think?' when there's no one to say what they thought of other than them! So where's that expansive conversation coming from?

As can be seen in Dominic's narrative, he critiques the ability of white consumers to properly engage in so-called Black cultural forms because of their white 'pure' settings. Dominic makes the point that white folk will always read cultural forms through their own 'racial frame'.[18] Dominic's issue with such consumption is that because white middle-class people, according to him, show little diversity in their close social-capital networks, they have little ability to engage in meaningful discussions about Black music, literature, and arts.

This ethnoracial autonomous criticism of white consumers is also replicated by Morgan. We were discussing Chinua Achebe's *Things Fall Apart*,[19] a novel exploring the beginnings of colonial rule in a Nigerian village. I recalled how in an English class in secondary school, where I was the only non-white person present, all my classmates treated the story as if it were a comedy about African tribalism. I made the point that when I re-read it more recently, the anti-colonial messages were extremely clear, but my schoolteacher had failed to effectively tease these out. Morgan and I were hence discussing how conceptual schemes impact the way people read culture, and how the 'white racial frame'[20] is one such conceptual scheme. Morgan commented,

> You can only see it through the screen of your experience. And that has to be expanded for you to see more things, to see things differently. Erm, so, yeah, is it the case that a British person who has gone to school in the last twenty, thirty years, who then reads *Things Fall Apart*, reads *White Teeth*, reads you know *The God of Small Things*, you know, is going to read it through the lens of 'Britain had Empire and the Empire was awesome, there are non-white people in the world but not many of them, and they've, they screw up their own countries' – is that likely? Yeah! Probably! [laughing]. It's the case!

Both Morgan and Dominic, therefore, take issue with the projection of the white racial frame on to Black cultural forms. From a critical race perspective, Morgan and Dominic demonstrate the belief that people within the racialised social system are 'racially socialised' – including white people.[21] This racial socialisation means that those on top of the racial hierarchy will, more often than not, perceive the world through the lens of their superiority. According to Morgan and Dominic, this is no different in the case of white folk approaching Black cultural forms. Indeed, underlying their narratives is an Afro-centrism which reifies a separation between 'white' and 'Black' cultural forms, specifies a concrete preference for the latter, and asserts the *inability* of those racialised as white to engage with 'Black' culture given their present and historical role in racial domination.

Those sided towards strategic assimilation, however, have a more open approach towards white consumers of Black cultural forms. Such individuals believe that culture should never be stratified by race, and that central to an effective anti-racism is an inter-racial appreciation of different cultural forms. This difference between the ethnoracial autonomous and strategic assimilation identity modes can be illustrated in Dawn recalling a disagreement with her father. In this narrative, Dawn represents the strategic assimilation identity mode, while her father is sided more towards the ethnoracial autonomous identity mode. Dawn was recalling how she had been at an anti-Tory demonstration in London, and how reggae music had been playing at the protest. She proceeded,

> And I thought about how [pause] my dad always thinks of reggae that has been co-opted by the mainstream, and reggae that's being made by white people as well, as being completely devoid of any, any erm, real sentiment, and real political message – which is what it was created for in the first place. And he said that is an abomination. But actually, I think that time, in that protest, it was white leftists who were really listening the words. And the people dancing to it were also. So, I think it's about how you engage with certain concepts, and whether you can listen, how much you – I guess it comes back to what we talked about at the beginning, how much you can listen about feeling guilty that this is critiquing *you*, being able to see beyond that, being able to say that this is actually about a situation that affects everybody, and I don't gain if somebody loses. And those people were able to see that, in that context. And so, I [pause] I think it is about that being able to be self-reflexive, and being able to hear things without constantly putting up walls. I think that happens on all sides, but I think it's harder when you're in a position of power to do that. Because it really involves acknowledging that you have some of that power. So, I wouldn't say my dad's critique is right, necessarily.

Unlike Dominic and Morgan, therefore, Dawn points to a concrete example where she believes that white folk are meaningfully engaging with a Black diasporic cultural form – in this case, reggae. It could be argued, therefore, that in Anderson's language, Dawn follows more of a cosmopolitan 'cosmo' code – emphasising the gains we achieve from cultural fluidity – compared to Dominic and Morgan's more Afro-centric 'ethnos' code.[22] Dawn realises the importance of reggae to convey a racialised, political message and sentiment. This is seen in her talking about how white consumers of reggae often must confront that the music is talking about the exploitative powers of whiteness. However, Dawn uses the example of the anti-Tory march to show how white people are capable of confronting this dynamic, and they are able to authentically engage with the cultural form beyond the myopia of a white racial frame

Dawn's comment that we should aim towards not 'constantly putting up walls' shows how she believes that authentic cultural fluidity is not just important to broaden one's cultural knowledge but is important to anti-racism more generally. Indeed, I have hitherto focused on how those towards strategic assimilation adopt a cultural repertoire of code-switching; Dawn's narrative also suggests that *white people too* ought to code-switch, to familiarise themselves with diasporic cultural forms, as this may help them confront their position of privilege.

Constructing and using Black cultural capital

Similarly to Dawn, Edward talked to me about the importance of increasing the empathy of white consumers of Black cultural forms. Edward is an academic who also works in the arts. We were discussing the *Women Artists: A Conversation* exhibition I had attended at the Fine Art Society. I identified the work of only one woman of colour in the exhibition – Phoebe Boswell – whose piece was a collection of WhatsApp messages she had received when travelling around Scandinavia, many of which explicitly exoticised her Black hair and dark skin. Altogether, it takes five to ten minutes to read these messages in their entirety. Spending a couple of hours in the exhibition, I found that white consumers skimmed through this piece of work, spending a minute browsing it, before spending much longer looking at what appeared to be mundane portraits. The only Black person who I saw attend this exhibition, however, spent a much longer time appreciating the work of Phoebe Boswell. Given that Edward was familiar with the exhibition I was talking about, I asked him what he thought about my experience. He commented,

> That's interesting, that you're kind of mapping people's experiences in terms of how long they spend with the work. There's kind of a double fold to that story. One is that, you know the white consumers, maybe they weren't invested in the same way. But I often find that really, really strange. I feel it's very weird that a lot of white audiences don't feel they can enter a work, when it's a Black subject. They're like – that's a Black experience, it's not my experience. So suddenly [pause] it becomes this kind of barrier to, erm, identification. Like 'That's not for me.' So we get this really dangerous essentialism, erm, the work becomes ghettoised, culturally [laughing] and that work then becomes purely for a Black audience. And that is important – because that work is, that identification is important – but what's important for me is that it should be able to kind of speak beyond. So it's not like if I ever see a work of a Chinese artist I can't engage with it! 'I can't do that because it's China!' It's like, you know. I find that really interesting how that, erm that's become, often becomes entrenched.

Similarly to Dawn, Edward acknowledges the importance for Black people to consume Black cultural forms, but he also qualifies that we need to avoid cultural essentialism. The narratives of Dawn and Edward thus shed light on the differences between the strategic assimilation and the ethnoracial autonomous identity modes. Those siding towards strategic assimilation use *inclusionary* boundary work: they try to use cultural forms for inclusive means (in this case, creating meaningful inter-racial dialogues). Contrastingly, those sided towards the ethnoracial autonomous identity mode use these Black cultural forms as a (Black) *cultural capital* to draw a symbolic boundary against white folk.[23] Through a cultural essentialism justified via a repertoire of Afro-centrism, those towards the ethnoracial autonomous identity mode hold that white consumers have an inability to correctly and authentically engage with Black cultural forms because they have been racially conditioned by their whiteness to see the world through the lens of their racial superiority. Black cultural forms are thus recast as existing *for* Black people. Indeed, not only do those towards the ethnoracial autonomous identity mode attempt to draw symbolic boundaries against white folk through consuming Black cultural forms, but this cultural consumption also enables them to draw *spatial* boundaries against such white people. I will now explore this dynamic by discussing 'Black spaces'.

In the previous chapter, I analysed white physical spaces of traditional middle-class cultural production and consumption, such as art galleries, music concert halls, and opera houses. In contrast to these *white* physical spaces, many members of the Black middle class seek out Black-led or Black-owned physical spaces which showcase Black cultural forms. The Black Cultural Archives (BCA) in Brixton was the most popular example used to demonstrate such a 'Black space'. While those sided towards the strategic assimilation and ethnoracial autonomous identity modes both recognised the importance of 'Black spaces', the two clusters differed in the extent to which they were fully comfortable moving *predominantly* within such confines.

As previously analysed, the strategic assimilation identity mode involves a repertoire of code-switching. This code-switching is connected to the repertoire of cultural equity, where individuals towards the strategic assimilation identity mode realise that they need to move and socialise within the white middle-class cultural sphere if they are to establish legitimate middle-class cultural membership. Consequently, such individuals often have an affinity towards Black spaces, but warn against people becoming too comfortable in one space. Raymond demonstrates this well, when he talks about how in London it is easy to get too comfortable in Black spaces, and how he himself realised this danger and thus started to code-switch more:

> In London, I mean there was *so much* that you can do in the cultural scene [pause] that in a way I think there's a danger of just being *too comfortable* in being in spaces that are dominated by – to me – Afro-Caribbeans, or it might be Africans and Caribbeans, because I started hanging around

with lots of Ghanaians and Nigerians as well. So [pause] and there are certain ways of being Black, especially if you're relatively well off, that you know you do have a little bit of cultural cache, there are places for that. But [pause] you've got to get out more, so I realised that, and started making more time for the Tate, RA [Royal Academy of Arts]. Yeah, that was quite important for me.

The strategic assimilation repertoire of code-switching is thus captured in Raymond's narrative, as he comments on the dangers of 'being too comfortable' in Black cultural spaces. Other participants, such as Kwadwo and Edward, made similar arguments, claiming that if 'Black culture' is to be taken seriously in the mainstream, it has to be produced and consumed in mainstream institutions – even if such institutions are essentially white. Using the example of places like New Beacon Books, the BCA, and the Bernie Grant Arts Centre, such participants claimed that they were incredibly important for meeting like-minded Black people with interests in literature and the arts, but they lamented that such spaces had limited anti-racist potential in the grand scheme of things, given that they were ghettoised from the mainstream. This dynamic of strategic assimilation is succinctly summarised by an ethnographic participant I talked to when visiting the Tate Britain exhibition about Black Britons in 1960s–70s London: *Stan Firm Inna Inglan: Black Diaspora in London, 1960s–70s*. As this participant, who I will call Roy, commented,

> It's great that we're here. Because we, if my parents came here when they were my age, they wouldn't see this. But now, this is here, in the most famous museum in the country. We don't have to be afraid to hide anymore, we don't have to limit ourselves to South London or our own small communities, *we* can be in places like this, reaching out.

In fact, I used the very same exhibition at Tate Britain to talk to Julia, a journalist, about her cultural preferences and 'Black' and 'white' spaces. Julia mentioned that when she goes to spaces such as Tate Britain, she will be the only Black person present (or one of few). I asked her whether this makes her feel uncomfortable. In response, Julia made the point that having a Black social network encourages her to code-switch, avoid ethnocentrism, and be culturally omnivorous:

> Literally all my friends are Black, my family are Black, so I'm always around Black people when I'm not in these situations [at art galleries]. So I'm not

like desperate to look for Black people or something, and, actually, we're in England, we're a minority, so if we're only going to take interest in our own cultures then we're going to miss out on basically, almost everything, and there won't be much for, culturally speaking, much to do whatsoever.

In direct contrast to this, participants towards the ethnoracial autonomous identity mode claimed that these very same Black spaces are essential in anti-racist struggles. They argued that such institutions create spaces where Black cultural forms can be appreciated *beyond* simple discussions of racial identity. Especially in literature and the arts, cultural forms produced by Black people are often assumed by critics to only have meaning vis-à-vis 'Blackness'.[24] Having Black spaces, those towards the ethnoracial autonomous identity mode stress, creates a locale where the work of Black cultural producers can be discussed vis-à-vis Blackness and race, but *also* where the cultural form itself can be appreciated and praised. As Daniel commented to me on the BCA in Brixton,

> I see great value in it. Because what I see is that when you traditionally put a [pause] the problem is that Black work doesn't get as much credit as it should do, and so in order to be able to build the confidence and give you that credibility, erm, if you create your own space and you value it accordingly within that own space, it gets the attention that it requires ... Hence the reason I feel that spaces for Black is important. Then it expands your realms of possibility, it expands your mindset in terms of what you can do, what's acceptable, what you're inspired to do and take from there. So yeah, I definitely think it's important to see things where people who look like you and are doing great things [pause] and they're *not* just always doing something about them being Black, you know, other stuff too, other good stuff.

Daniel thus highlights the importance of Black cultural spaces to ascribe recognition and legitimacy to Black cultural producers. Such individuals towards the ethnoracial autonomous identity mode do not believe that having Black cultural forms in 'mainstream' institutions will have any anti-racist gains. Given this predilection towards Black spaces, individuals towards the ethnoracial autonomous identity mode do not exhibit the fear of 'over-comfort' that is seen in the strategic assimilation identity mode. In fact, I posed the question of over-comfort to Mady, when she was discussing how she prefers to move within Black spaces. Our conversation proceeded,

Ali: Some people talk about being *overly* comfortable in those situations?
Mady: But that doesn't make sense to me. It's back to what I said earlier, if people don't want us in certain places then we won't be put off 'culture', we'll go to places we are welcome, where we are among our own.

Earlier in this book, I discussed how the ethnoracial autonomous identity mode involves a rejection of the repertoire of code-switching. This rejection of code-switching towards the ethnoracial autonomous identity mode, in favour of a repertoire of Afro-centrism and browning, is concurrently visible in such individuals' cultural lifestyles as they discuss the Black space. As typified between my exchanges with Daniel and Mady, Black cultural spaces do not only offer 'safe' spaces for the appreciation of Black cultural forms, free from white racial frames; such spaces also offer a context for the appreciation of cultural forms where people are cognisant that they are 'welcome'. At the ethnoracial autonomous identity mode, such Black cultural spaces are said to offer a space outside the confines of negative racial ideologies and frames, while performing their own anti-racist role in ascribing legitimacy and authority to Black cultural producers and consumers. Black spaces thus offer locales for Black middle-class folk to consume culture *outside of the confines of the white symbolic and physical space*.

Different identity modes, different racisms and anti-racisms

These differences between individuals towards the ethnoracial autonomous and strategic assimilation identity modes offer insights into how the two identity modes engage in different forms of anti-racism. Again, this is important for appreciating the various *uses* of Black cultural capital.

Towards the ethnoracial autonomous identity mode, Black cultural capital is predominantly being used to challenge the 'cultural capital deficit model'. As scholars have regularly noted, by virtue of their Blackness, Black people's cultural capital is often deemed to be worth less than whites'.[25] Within this context, especially when it comes to dominant cultural capital, the white middle class are seen as the most 'legitimate consumers' while Black folk are seen as the most *illegitimate* consumers. Indeed, it is through this logic, as I have previously shown, that microaggressions and acts of non-attention are made legitimate to Black folk in mainstream (white) middle-class cultural spaces.

In contrast to this, those towards the ethnoracial autonomous identity mode, on the one hand, challenge the deficit model in two main ways. First, they redefine who is the 'proper' consumer of certain middle-class cultural forms (that are additionally racialised as Black). Through critiquing the white racial frame, they create a circumstance where they – as folks racialised as Black – are the legitimate consumers of certain cultural forms; their symbolic mastery outweighs that of the white middle class. Further, they argue that the white racial frame *prevents* white folks from ever having legitimate authority over these cultural forms. Second, and relatedly, through attempting to (symbolically and spatially) exclude white consumers, those towards the ethnoracial autonomous identity mode attempt to create networks of Black folks to produce, value, and legitimise the circulation(s) of Black cultural capital.

On the other hand, those towards the strategic assimilation identity mode use Black cultural capital in a much more inclusive way. Black cultural capital provides a (cultural) space that can promote inter-racial dialogue and solidarity; it can help whites learn about their position of racial dominance and the experiences of people of colour, and can therefore encourage white people to work towards a more racially equal society. In a twist of logic, one could argue that those towards strategic assimilation actually want white folk to adopt a repertoire of code-switching and to become more culturally omnivorous, arguing that cultural eclecticism is one way to battle racial prejudice. In rather general terms, it thus appears as though those towards the ethnoracial autonomous identity mode are more so anti-racist 'radicals', and those towards strategic assimilation are more so anti-racist 'reformists'.

Nevertheless, while we pay attention to the anti-racist uses of Black cultural capital, it is always important to remember the straightforward point that anti-racism is only being pursued *because of racism*. Indeed, once we pay attention to the triangle of identity, the dynamic of how racism shapes Black middle-class cultural lives becomes more salient. Namely, as I argued, those towards the strategic assimilation identity mode often worry about becoming overly comfortable in Black spaces. This warning against over-comfort is *necessarily* tied such individuals' cognisance of the requirement to engage with white spaces to maintain equal standing with the white middle class. Racism thus remains lingering behind the cultural repertoires of the strategic assimilation identity mode; individuals towards this identity mode emphasise the repertoire of code-switching, and therefore reject *only* moving within Black spaces, *because they realise that the white middle class are still the primary custodians of power*. Those sided towards strategic assimilation are thus affected by racism in displaying a hesitancy in the extent to which they can be ethnocentric in their cultural pursuits. Furthermore, focusing on the ethnoracial autonomous identity mode, it is through 'feeling' racism that many towards this identity mode turn to Black spaces. Such spaces are said to offer safe contexts outside the reach of the racial hierarchy. Even when it comes to Black cultural capital, therefore, we must appreciate how Black middle-class individuals' cultural consumption is being shaped by a constant interplay between racism and anti-racism.

This link between Black cultural capital, racism, and anti-racism is also visible in how Black middle-class folks use cultural consumption to contest the polarisation of Blackness and Britishness. Turning to this discussion of culture, race, and nation, we again gain insights into how cultural capital becomes a key cultural resource for contesting a racialised social system that runs on the fuel of anti-Blackness.

Notes

1. See Banks, 2010a, b; Grams, 2010; Meghji, 2017b; Wallace, 2017; 2018.
2. Carter, 2003.
3. Carter, 2003.
4. Banks, 2010a, b.
5. Grams, 2010.
6. Banks, 2010a; Grams, 2010.
7. Wallace, 2017: 916.
8. Controlling images can be understood as ideological collective representations used to subjugate people of colour (Collins, 2004; hooks, 2014; Meghji, 2018; Wingfield, 2007; 2010).
9. See Saha, 2016; 2018 for a discussion of this 'rationalising/racialising'. A similar argument has been developed in art and theatre criticism by Cosentino, 2000; Fusco, 1999; Goddard, 2015; Peacock, 2015, among others.
10. Hall, 1996.
11. See Rose, 1994 for a problematisation of 'Black music'.
12. Du Bois, 2007 [1903].
13. For instance: Hey, Grimaldi-Christensen and Savage, 2017; Reeves and de Vries, 2018; Savage, 2015a; Wakeling and Savage, 2015.
14. For instance: Atkinson, 2017; Bull, 2016; Bennett et al., 2010; Chan and Goldthorpe, 2005; 2007.
15. Lorde, 1997 [1981].
16. Meghji, 2018; Mueller, 2017; 2018.
17. Bennett et al., 2010; Bourdieu, 2010.
18. Wingfield and Feagin, 2012.
19. Achebe, 1996 [1959].
20. As Feagin (2009: 3) argues, the white racial frame refers to 'an overarching worldview, one that encompasses important racial ideas, terms, images, emotions, and interpretations' that reproduce white supremacy; see also Feagin and Elias, 2013; Wingfield and Feagin, 2012.

21 Bonilla-Silva, 2017a; Feagin, 2006; 2009.
22 Anderson, 2011.
23 Further demonstrating that one of the functions of cultural capital is to draw spatial and symbolic boundaries against other social groups.
24 See Chambers, 2012; Hall, 2005.
25 See Anderson, 2011; Rollock, 2012a; 2013; Yosso, 2005.

5

Revisiting race and nation: double consciousness, Black Britishness, and cultural consumption

SINCE MOVING to London in 2016, I found that the Senate House Library provided a good sociological writing climate. It was fair to say that I had become quite familiar with the space surrounding the Senate House and got into a standard routine of working until lunch time, grabbing a sandwich to eat in the park, working until the late afternoon, and hopping back on the Piccadilly line to go home. Little did I know that each day I was going to the Senate House Library, I was moving through a space that was rich with Black British culture and history.

Indeed, the theme of space has been running through this book so far. I considered how the symbolic boundaries of middle classness often lead to the construction of white middle-class physical spaces, also showing how members of the Black middle class create their own physical cultural spaces as a means of solidarity and resistance. In this respect, my work implicitly connects with the longstanding interest social theorists have had in space and place. Looking back at this literature, a common theme is that the production of certain spaces is needed for the reproduction of wider social-structural relations.[1] However, we can take the matter even more critically. For instance, how do social-structural relations prevent certain spatial imaginaries? How do hierarchies make sure that certain spaces get social meaning, while the social meaning of other spaces is erased? Why – simply put – did I have to spend ten pounds for a Black history tour to find out that down the road from the Senate House Library in 1943, Learie Constantine (a Black British cricketer) was not allowed to stay in the Imperial Hotel, leading him to take court action aspiring to radically challenge the London hotel colour bar?[2] Why did I have to go on this Black history tour to also find out that the space I had been inhabiting – the Senate House – had a plaque of Mary

Prince, a pioneering anti-slavery activist in nineteenth-century England, hidden away around the back of the building? If anything, these instances point not to the production of social meaning into space, but rather to the non-production of social meaning into space; they demonstrate exclusions of meaning that are justified through larger social-structural relations.[3]

These non-productions of meaning, I argue, stem from the overall devaluation of Black Britishness that inflicts the British racialised social system. Scholars such as Kapoor have referred this devaluation in terms of a doxic British 'racial amnesia',[4] Joseph-Salisbury refers to it as 'white amnesia',[5] and Stuart Hall simply calls it a 'profound historical forgetfulness'.[6] Syntax aside, the semantics could not be clearer. An erasure of Black Britishness, and Black British histories, is an integral part of British racial hierarchisation. This chapter contextualises my participants as not just Black, nor just Black and middle class, but rather as Black British middle-class subjects. Through this contextualisation, I look at how the participants construe the 'British' aspect of their identities and use cultural consumption as a means of resistance to this 'profound forgetfulness' that plagues the British racial structure.

The changing same. But different?

It has been more than twenty years since Gilroy commented that 'today's racist ideologies render Blackness and Britishness mutually exclusive social and cultural categories'.[7] The 'Go Back Home' signs that greeted previous colonial subjects arriving in Britain have simply been painted on the side of vans.[8] The Thatcherite policies of turning British citizens from former colonies into undesirable immigrants in the 1980s now translates into the deportation of people from the Windrush generation back to Caribbean countries (in some cases, these people are being deported to Caribbean countries within which they have no ancestry).[9]

Over the long durée, therefore, it seems legitimate to argue that Britishness and British citizenship have always been equated with whiteness: race and nation have been, and continue to be, inseparable. Within sociological literature, the conflation between whiteness and Britishness became a salient issue of study in the 1970s and 1980s.[10] Especially with the rise of the putative 'new conservatives' in the 1980s, scholars focused on the 'new racism' which defined the British nation as the white nation.[11] However, just like torn jeans and sportswear, this 'style' of 1980s racism has also become fashionable in our present day. Thinking about 'Brexit Britain', for instance, both Bhambra[12] and

Hunter[13] comment that the dominant frame which inspired Britons to vote to leave the European Union was a white 'purging' of the nation. While popular media often frames this political happening in the context of Islamophobia and xenophobia against Eastern Europeans, anti-Blackness is still ingrained in this racialised definition of the nation-state. Thus, in the aftermath of the EU referendum result being announced, it was not just EU nationals and visible Muslims who were threatened in acts of street racism; Afro-Caribbeans were subject to such acts as well.[14] Thus, the same polarisation between Blackness and Britishness which was central to the cultural racism of the 1980s still rears its ugly head in contemporary times. Perhaps this is a striking example of Bell's concept of racial realism – the notion racial progress is but a myth.[15]

We can play around with this concept of racial realism to interrogate the notion of 'social change'. Perhaps a key difference between the racial structure of the 1980s and our present day (2018) is that a Black middle class has both emerged and solidified in our economic order.[16] Simply put, therefore, it seems obvious that there has been some form of (racialised) social change between the 1980s and 2010s. However, through the concept of racial realism we get the notion that racial progress is not simply a 'linear affair', and instead it is often accompanied with 'shifting mechanisms reproducing changes in racial inequality'.[17] If the polarisation of race and nation has been a constant feature of the British racial structure for the past half century, then it seems more prudent to say that when it comes to race and racism, social change is often accompanied by social stability.

Nevertheless, in my research I found that resisting this 'stability' of the polarisation of Blackness and Britishness was a key facet of many of the participants' cultural lives. I want to use this chapter to tease out what these cultural resistances and contestations to the polarisation of Blackness and Britishness can tell us more generally about Black middle-class identity, British post-racialism, and the general (US)Americanisation of Blackness. We can approach these cultural resistances through the lens of Du Bois's concept of double consciousness.

Say it loud: I'm Black (British) and proud
Double consciousness and Black British identities

More than 100 years ago, Du Bois put forward the concept of African American double consciousness: 'this sense of always looking at one's self through the eyes of others'.[18] Many scholars have interpreted Du Bois's concept of double consciousness as a theory of *identity*. Thus, scholars have highlighted how Du Bois used the notion of double consciousness to 'reflect the tension he believed Black Americans experience as they negotiate two "unreconciled" identities: their status as Americans and their status as Blacks'.[19] Through this lens, double consciousness becomes an identity strategy used by those racialised downward as 'a survival mechanism in which the racially oppressed learn through time not to show their real selves to the dominant'.[20]

It is especially through this lens of double consciousness as an analysis of *identity* that the participants of my study perceive their Black Britishness. However, owing to the fact that these participants are also middle class, this identity of Black Britishness is perhaps not only one of 'double consciousness' but something much more plural. This notion of further pluralising Black identities from simply a 'doubled' consciousness was evoked by Gilroy, when he proclaimed,[21]

> it doesn't seem productive to try to transplant or reinvigorate the old ideas so that, for example, being a Black European ... could be considered analogous to what being an American and a 'Negro' meant when Du Bois was writing *The Souls of Black Folk* and speculating about the constitutive power of the 'color line'.

In this ethos of thought, when Rollock et al. were analysing Black middle-class identity, they proposed that[22]

> the Black middle classes are living through not a double consciousness (as Du Bois has famously theorized) but instead through a set of multiple consciousnesses as they move back and forth the class and race divides within different social spheres populated by audiences and actors of varying race and class backgrounds.

Approached this way, 'Britishness' becomes important to the identities of many of this study's participants, in a way that it is co-articulated along with gender, race, and class. Britishness thus becomes incorporated into such participants' 'multiple consciousness' as they move within and through different areas of social space. Through this multiple consciousness, the 'British' aspect of my participants' identities often becomes more or less salient in different interactional spaces. This is well captured in an interchange I had with Abebi when we were discussing how she construed her identity. To begin with, Abebi says quite firmly that she identifies as 'Nigerian':

> If someone asks me where I'm from, I'll say I'm Nigerian – even though I was born in England ... I feel if a white person asks, or non-Black person 'Where are you from?', they can see I'm Black, they can probably hear from my accent that I'm from London or I'm British, so I therefore assume that the question they're asking is really 'Where are your parents from?' or 'Where's your heritage from?'. So my answer to that, I don't say London because that's not what they're asking, I say Nigeria. Erm, however, if a Nigerian person asked me that, I'd say I'm Yoruba or I'm from Lagos. I'd say this information because they already know I'm Nigerian. So, I think for me, my answer depends on who is asking. However, I don't think I can ever remember a time where I've answered that with 'I'm English', or 'British', I don't personally view myself as British.

As we can see, depending on the interactional encounter ('my answer depends on who is asking'), Abebi construes her identity in different ways. Indeed, from this quoted encounter along, Abebi's position seems similar to the Nigerian-descended people living in Britain encountered in Imoagene's research, where such people often have an ambivalence towards the 'British' aspect of their identity.[23] However, right after this quote, I asked Abebi why she does not identify as British, to which she then revised her position:

> So for me, to identify as a British person is not just to live here but also means the cultural elements of being British. And I love living here, and I've loved growing up here, but the things I've been brought up with, and culturally I've always been African. Maybe it's Black British, because now if I compare myself with someone born and raised in Nigeria, actually we have a different view of things. So maybe I'm more Black British, or British African, but there's definitely that African element of it which shapes who I am.

On reflection, therefore, Abebi does incorporate Britishness into her identity within a larger set of identity 'consciousnesses'. In a similar stream of thought, Dawn pointed out her frustration with being classified as a 'second-generation West Indian immigrant, not a Black British person who can identify how she wants to'. After Dawn claimed this, our conversation proceeded,

> Ali: Right. I mean you talked about being Black British?
>
> Dawn: I think it depends. I don't know if it's the same as everyone. For me it shifts depending on where I am, who I'm speaking to, erm, and, what time of day it is [laughs]. No, it depends on the situation ... I think that Black British is something that goes down, sometimes, well here [in Britain]. I can't say Black British in France – they don't accept that as a concept. And in America, they, erm, I've been called African American with a British accent [laughing] – so you know, I don't, I don't. If you're Black you're African American, they don't accept that England has Black people! And this isn't everybody, you know, but, yea. And when I was in France, they'd be overwhelmed when I said I was Black and from Britain. And they ascribed me with Britishness which meant either Dick Van Dyke or the Queen [laughs].

Similarly to Abebi, therefore, Dawn shows how the 'British' aspect of her identity is interactionally specific – 'it shifts depending on where I am, who I'm speaking to'. As Dawn claims, the British aspect of her identity becomes more salient particularly in the British context, whereas when she travels to France or the United States, identifying as 'Black British' becomes construed as problematic or nonsensical. In this respect, Black Britishness becomes a form of racialised 'national repertoire' – it becomes a group categorisation that is available to be taken up by the Black diaspora within Britain.[24]

In terms of Black Britishness as a 'structure of feeling',[25] or as a racialised national repertoire, this means that as an identity Black Britishness constantly evolves as its surrounding racial structure develops. Compared to previous research on Black British identity as provided by seminal writers such as Stuart Hall,[26] Paul Gilroy,[27] and Claire Alexander,[28] many of my participants claimed how being 'Black British' in our current historical juncture – with increasing immigration from West Africa – involves an increased mixture of 'West African' and 'Caribbean' iterations of Blackness and Black culture. For instance, Martin described this changing pan-ethnic, racialised nationality of Black Britishness as such:

> Being Jamaican was very much lined up with that first generation of being Black British. ... Increasingly, for a number of reasons, as you'll know, recent census shows the British Black community is increasingly a community with a West African accent, a West African heritage, its future is essentially going to be carried by people of West African heritage. And,

as a result, there's an adjustment that every Black British person needs to make as you make a jump from Caribbean dominated, kinda sense of what it means to be Black British to a West African dominated sense.

Martin claimed that this 'shift' in what it means to be Black British was itself an identity motivated by the fact that Black Caribbean and African people tend to live in close social and spatial proximity to one another. However, not all of my participants grew up in neighbourhoods with lots of other Black people in London. Neither did these participants go to schools with many other Black children. In these cases, the 'script', or repertoire of Black Britishness was not as clearly accessible to them, and they had to find other means to work out what Black Britishness means to, and for, them.

Ijeoma, for instance, grew up in an area of North London that was majority white, also going to a majority white elite school. This meant that Ijeoma relied on her family as a source for discussions on Black identities and histories. However, Ijeoma's problem was that her mother and grandmother – with whom she lived – did not explicitly talk about these areas of Blackness with her. This was not because Ijeoma's mother and grandmother did not have any affinity towards Blackness – as I have described in terms of the class-minded Black middle-class identity mode. Rather, it is because they had lived most of their lives and gone to school in Nigeria, where they were not racialised as a minority. In this context, they did not have to learn about 'Black history', because it was simply presented as national history. As Ijeoma explains,

> I think my parents' generation and the older generations take it for granted that they know about history. Because they have never been an ethnic minority, they were born and raised in Nigeria, everyone knows about the history, everyone is aware of those things, because it is like a habit ..., and then, yea, within Nigerian history, I think you just take for granted that you know your history and your kids will know. I mean it's, I don't know Yoruba either [laughs] – so they didn't even get as far as teaching the language, let alone the actual history of our tribes and so on. And now they're really frustrated I don't know it! I'm just like, 'Where did you expect me to pick it up from?' [laughs].

Not only did Ijeoma therefore not have an interactional setting for discussions around Blackness, but she claims her problem was deepened by the fact that she was the first in her family to be distinctively 'Black British'. Given that Ijeoma was not learning about Black Britishness in her school, and lacked interactions with other Black Britons, this constrained her ability to take up the national repertoire of Black Britishness. As she comments,

> And I don't really think it's ever really occurred to my mum that I wouldn't learn stuff about Black history, and also, you know, to my mum and to my grandma, Black British history is not our history. Because we're not, because we're not really Black British; we're Nigerians who live here. I'm the only person, my generation and younger, we're the only ones who are Black British. So that's not something they would have been able to teach me, because they wouldn't have known about it.

In response to this, Ijeoma took it on herself to teach herself about Black history and Black Britishness. However, to begin with, she mentioned that Black history was most commonly accessible through a US-centric perspective. She describes first encountering Black history in school:

> The first time we learned about Black history in any form was on my G-, was it my GCSE, no it was AS-level history course, we did American civil rights, that was the first time I'd done any form of Black history at all.

This sparked a curiosity inside Ijeoma's mind, leading her to seek out 'Black literature' in her spare time. Again, this literature was mostly US-focused:

> I would seek out bits of history – so I read *Roots* by Alex Haley, and I read various books. So I would read things, I read things like that. That's the kind of literature I would read. But never, I think, maybe it's just a lot easier to find literature that relates to Black American history, so I never actually read anything about Black British history ... I've had to consciously think about what being Black means to me. I need to be a lot more clued up about what being Black and British is.

After moving to Brixton in South London, having graduated from Oxford, Ijeoma claimed that institutions such as the Black Cultural Archives (BCA) helped her learn more about Black Britishness. She recalled attending events run by the BCA – such as Black Britons in the First World War – as well as these institutions' events (such as on Rastafarianism in Britain) to help contextualise and associate herself with Black Britishness.

Double consciousness: from identity to epistemological second sight

I have described Ijeoma's narrative at length because I believe it points to another aspect of Du Boisian double consciousness beyond simply a focus on identity. Of course, the identity aspect is still present – as Ijeoma claims, she needs to 'be a lot more clued up about what being Black and British is', and she tries to work this out through learning more about Black British history. However, Ijeoma's narrative also points to the Du Boisian concept of 'second sight' – another key component of double consciousness. This second sight involves Ijeoma's realisation of the exclusion of Black British narratives from mainstream cultural production – as she claims, 'it's just a lot easier to find literature that relates to Black American history, so I never actually read anything about Black British history'; indeed, Ijeoma has to go out of her way and attend courses at the BCA to help her learn about these excluded narratives. I argue that the 'Black Britishness' of many participants of this study enables them to acquire a second sight to effectively critique the British racial hierarchy.

Inspired by Du Bois's work on double consciousness,[29] there has been a resurgence in sociologists paying attention to the 'second sight' of racialised minorities living in Britain.[30] As Virdee comments, this second sight commonly refers to how racialised minorities have historically possessed[31]

> a form of privileged epistemological standpoint which allowed them to see things as they really were, equipping them to expose the inequities of a system because they experienced it most directly and powerfully.

Expanding on this concept, Meer shows how this 'second sight' thus involves 'a way of seeing things that escapes the notice of the majority … serving as a means to probe deeper meanings and contradictions of a racialised experience and providing the resource for transformative change'.[32] From Du Bois's first theorisation of African American double consciousness, through to its contemporary use for discussing 'racialised outsiders' more than 100 years later, there has therefore been an underlying theme and use to this concept. Namely, double consciousness stresses that those who are racialised as minorities within their respective nations come to understand the workings of inequality within that nation in a way that often escapes the notice of the majority. Being 'Black British' constitutes a form of double consciousness in this regard. Being racialised 'downward' enables Black Britons to understand the fundamentals of what it means to be British, and how British identity itself is not just a box you tick on a citizenship or census form, but itself an 'imagined' state of being that amalgamates with ethnicity and race (and consequently ethnic and racial domination).[33]

The Black British 'second sight' encountered in my research involved critiques of British post-racial ideology. Within sociological literature, there is a growing cognisance that post-racial ideology is becoming increasingly globalised with similar international compositions (for instance, by containing components such as the 'myth' of racial progress, equivalence between anti-racialism and anti-racism, and culture of racial equivalence).[34] However, what this extant literature also needs to contend with is that the United States possesses a form of racial gravity; post-racialism in many nations – including Britain – often works by geographically displacing racism on to the United States: 'racism exists over there, not here'.[35] Indeed, this geographical displacement of racism was even propagated by some of my participants who were towards the class-minded identity mode, as they adopted the repertoire of post-racialism. Keith, for instance, talked about a conversation he had with another Black professional colleague:

> we were talking about race relations in America compared with race relations in the UK. There are almost no parallels. So we were busy demonstrating to one another there were no parallels. And [friend] said 'There are no doors in this country than I cannot go through'. And it is true. As I sit here – there are no doors one cannot go through.

In contrast to this class-minded position, other participants of this study used their second sight as Black Britons to effectively criticise the view that Britain was a post-racial utopia. Indeed, this second-sighted critique of British racism was often framed around a critique of the (US)Americanisation of 'Blackness' and racism. This critique can be teased out in the case of Morgan, as we were discussing a predilection he has towards Black British literature. Referring to the recent Hay Literature Festival, Morgan commented,

> So, people within that space are dominated by white people, most of the people on the ground are white women, most of them are upper middle class, most of them went to a handful of universities, and act accordingly. So just a very brief example of that being attending a panel at the Hay Festival, and hearing the head of Bloomsbury defend her record of

publishing, erm, well defend the fact that they have published very few people of colour who are British, by saying well they published Maya Angelou, or Toni Morrison, or something like that, and failing to see that you know, that isn't publishing Black British history [laughing]. That's just publishing Black people from America. Black people in Britain and Black people in America are not the same [laughs] you know? This is kind of the myopia we deal with.

Morgan's prescient remark, 'Black people in Britain and Black people in America are not the same [laughs] you know? This is kind of the myopia we deal with', was replicated across other participants' critiques of British post-racialism. Throughout my ethnography, for instance, many of the folks I talked with would make an especial effort to support art with a focus on Black Britishness as a means to contest the (US)Americanisation of all race-related phenomena.

For instance, on the first Black history walk I attended, we were guided around the Bloomsbury and Soho areas of London. At one stage of this walk we were in the British Museum, waiting for an elderly lady and her daughter to go to the bathroom. I spoke with one lady, who I will refer to as Melinda, about whether she was enjoying the tour, and we got on to the theme of Black British history. Melinda commented that she has had an interest in Black British history since her teens, but twenty years later she now only sees African American history and achievements being regularly presented in the United Kingdom. She comments that this helps racism in Britain 'go under the radar' while the legacies of Britain's racist history are simply forgotten. Especially now Melinda's niece is in secondary school, both Melinda and her sister have been actively working with the school to improve their Black History Month, given that for the past years the school celebrates Black History Month through focusing on the civil rights movement in the United States, highlighting figures such as Malcolm X and Martin Luther King Jr, and pop-culture icons such as Beyoncé and Mariah Carey. Melinda's complaints were twofold: that Black British history was excluded, and that the current Black supposed 'role models' were all in the same industry and not related to what she called more 'intellectual' pursuits. Attending these Black history walks, along with attending events and courses at the BCA and Bernie Grant Arts Centre, Melinda claimed, not only helped her satisfy her own desire for culture exploring Black Britishness, but helped her spread this knowledge with her family, friends, and other Black Britons. Indeed, I had an almost identical interaction with Sandra, the aforementioned woman who was also on the curator's tour of *Soul of a Nation* in the Tate Modern. In this case, Sandra claimed that while cultural institutions are interested in exploring racism in other national contexts (in this case, the United States), 'We are some way off having our stories included in this space.'

One of my interview participants, Dominic, formed a similar critique of the *Soul of a Nation* exhibition. In a similar frame to Sandra, he argues,

> All these institutions are very comfortable with things from abroad. They are. So everyone can wallow in the American context, the Black American experience, very comfortably and very arrogantly from afar. But really, we had a Black arts movement in the UK! And it was vibrant for many years, and challenging, and provocative. I don't see any major exhibitions about that. There was something in Nottingham recently, which was done as a retrospective. But, it didn't travel anywhere. It didn't come to London any size. So, again, we can do the American story quite comfortably with big size and scale, but let's not have *ours* on display for too much.

Our conversation proceeded,

> Ali: And from a personal experience, is it frustrating to have little amounts of art which explores the Black experience *in Britain*?
> Dominic: So yes, personally I think it's extremely sad and an indictment on our society, an indictment on our middle-class custodians of power, that we are still having the same conversations over and over again – in an unrelenting fashion. ... why are we having problems with the content? – because white, white middle-class professionals have *no idea* about Black cultural life and content. So how would they make judgements on it?

These collected narratives all point to a similar dynamic of Black British second sight. The Du Boisian principle of second sight is that the racialised minority is epistemologically able to realise their society's hierarchies in a way that escapes the perception of the dominant.[36] In this case, Morgan, Sandra, Melinda, and Dominic all appreciate that there are specificities to both British racism and to Blackness in Britain, and contrast their epistemological standpoint with others who do not possess such a second sight, whether that be literature gatekeepers, art curators and institutional boards, white teachers, or simply 'white middle-class professionals' in Dominic's narrative.

Double consciousness, identity, and second sight in the triangle of identity

It seems as though double consciousness influences Black British middle-class identity in two predominant ways, therefore. On the one hand, double consciousness is reflected through the lens of identity, where Blackness and Britishness are seen as two disparate components of one identity, separated by historical and present social processes of national, racialised exclusion, rendering the Black Briton a 'familial stranger' in their own land.[37] On the other hand, double consciousness is embodied in the second sight that many Black Britons have that enables them to see beyond the veil; through being racialised as Black, but nationalised as British, such Black Britons acquire a second sight that allows them to criticise contemporary British racism.

Taking a closer look at the participants of this study, it appears as though these two aspects of double consciousness carry different salience for different participants, depending on their position in the triangle of identity. While those towards strategic assimilation often display Black British double consciousness in terms of identity management, those towards the ethnoracial autonomous identity mode display double consciousness in terms of second sight. This has significant implications for both clusters' practices of resistance, everyday anti-racism, and cultural consumption.

Double consciousness and strategic assimilation

Underlying the strategic assimilation identity mode is a form of double consciousness where individuals construe Blackness and Britishness as two disparate parts of their identity that need to be brought into harmony with one another. One way this harmony is achieved towards the strategic assimilation identity mode is through consuming cultural forms that synthesise what are construed as traditional British and traditional Black diasporic cultural elements. This cultural preference adds a new layer to the research on strategic assimilation as a Black middle-class identity mode. Whereas previous research focuses on how those involved in strategic assimilation move between, and culturally consume, in both white and Black spaces,[38] my research demonstrates how many *also* seek out cultural and social spaces that supposedly contain elements of both the Black and white worlds.

Miriam demonstrates this strategic assimilation position. Miriam and I were discussing the recent BAFTA awards, and the success of what were decoded as

'Black films'. Miriam pointed out that all these films – *Moonlight*, *Hidden Figures*, and *Fences* – were focused on the African American experience. In contrast to these US-centric films, she claimed she had recently been to a British film festival called 'Shakespeare Shorts' – independently made short films based around Shakespearean plays. She proceeded,

> Miriam: And at least two of them were erm made by Black people. But you know, they were brilliant. One of them was SBTV erm Jamal Edwards, they did a whole rap around Shakespeare's Globe, telling the story of the Twelfth Night. And that was superb. And then, also, there was one called *Dear Mr Shakespeare* with Basha, who performed in the white House in front of Obama actually – he's a British Dominican – *Dear Mr Shakespeare*. And that was superb – about Othello, he was playing Othello, it was brilliant. But again, it was great. But you had to know a bit about Shakespeare to understand what's going on, but that was so good, and you know, the two Black films in particular, I believe, would resonate with Black teenagers. It's people they know, people they respect, people they think are cool, just talking about Shakespeare, so it will open minds. It shows that culture isn't fixed by what race you are, and that we can have these conversations across these fixed categories. It was really good.
>
> Ali: So there's almost a [pause] personal significance to this, Shakespeare kind of –
>
> Miriam: [Interrupts] Yeah, exactly. It shows me that 'liking Shakespeare' doesn't mean you are or are not a certain level of Black. It shows me that, also, that being Black doesn't mean you have to not like things like Shakespeare. And that we can have this cultural conversation, being 'Black' or, erm, 'person of colour' but also appreciating the culture of here, where we belong.

Interestingly, Thomas[39] also had a narrative involving a synthesis of what is decoded as 'Black' diasporic culture with Shakespeare. In Thomas's case, he was working on a project where children from a school in Jamaica come to England and perform a Jamaican interpretation of a Shakespearean play. About his motives on working on this project, he commented,

> I also wanted Jamaica to be taken more seriously on the planet, so connecting with the Great British icon is interesting, because that's better than just

saying 'Here is a reggae band' or 'Here's some other stereotype'. So, you know, it's a nice way of kinda still having that conversation in the world about my identity and my culture, and at the same time addressing the mainstream.

I introduce these narratives from Thomas and Miriam, not only because they are both about Shakespeare, but because they highlight the anti-racist aims – and drawbacks to anti-racism – underlying the double consciousness of strategic assimilation. On the one hand, the anti-racist aims of this strategic assimilation double consciousness are clear, and again they are guided by the repertoire of cultural equity. In this instance, the repertoire of cultural equity is iterated in Miriam's claim that she does not believe Blackness constrains one's ability to engage with a traditional highbrow cultural form ('culture isn't fixed by what race you are … being Black doesn't mean you have to not like things like Shakespeare'), and Thomas's quest for 'Jamaica to be taken more seriously on the planet'.

However, despite their anti-racist conscious efforts, this strategic assimilation course of action ends up reproducing the racial structure in certain ways. In particular, this strategic assimilation 'synthesis' of putative Black and British cultural forms seems to give more value to the latter, and consequently demonstrates an uneasy relationship with so-called Black culture. The incorporation of the 'British', or the 'Shakespeare', seems to work as a cultural component that 'uplifts' the Black component. Straightforwardly, this is seen in Thomas's seeming polarisation between 'respectable' Shakespeare and 'stereotypical' reggae; he asserts that engaging with Shakespeare is a better way to give a positive portrayal of Jamaica, rather 'than just saying "Here is a reggae band" or "Here's some other stereotype"'. While Miriam is not as overtly dismissive of Blackness as Thomas is, there is still an element of her narrative that shows some limitations to an effective anti-racism. Namely, Miriam talks about how these Shakespeare films performed through rap music 'would resonate with Black teenagers', helping to 'appreciat[e] the culture of here, where we belong'. In this case, Shakespeare is construed as the universal 'culture of here, where we belong', whereas rap is implicitly relegated to a more particular cultural form for Black folk.

Perhaps this is where the 'middle class' aspect of Miriam's and Thomas's identities becomes especially pertinent to discussion too. Namely, as cultural theorists have shown, because of the 'over-proletarianisation'[40] of Black people in Britain, historically what has become 'Black culture' – including rap, mentioned by Miriam, and reggae, mentioned by Thomas – in Britain has acquired a necessary association with working-class consciousness and struggle.[41] Miriam's and Thomas's narratives tap into this historical formation of Black culture; adding something traditionally highbrow, such as Shakespeare, into the cultural form allows for the 'Black' culture to be upwardly mobile into the realms of respectability. Of course, this position is in tension with the desire of those towards the ethnoracial autonomous identity mode to uplift Blackness and Black culture independent of white confirmation.

Afro-centrism and the second sight of the ethnoracial autonomous

Those towards the ethnoracial autonomous identity mode espouse a double consciousness based around an epistemological second sight. Here, rather than Blackness and Britishness being two components of one's identity that need to be holistically articulated, those towards the ethnoracial autonomous identity mode use their Black Britishness to critique the veneer of British post-racialism. Such individuals thus use cultural consumption again as a means of resistance to the racial structure, as they seek out Black British cultural forms, and support Black British cultural producers, with the aim of uplifting Black British history and increasing awareness of Britain's past and present racial projects.

This ethnoracial autonomous, double conscious second sight was particularly salient in my conversation with Dominic. Dominic was talking about becoming a grandfather, and given his repertoire of Afro-centrism, he was inspired to keep diasporic histories and cultures alive in his family tree. This led him to particularly pursue an interest in Black British art, and he makes an especial effort to attend art exhibitions about, and to collect art exploring, Black Britishness. After I commented on his art collection, he replied,

> I buy too many pictures! I haven't got enough wall space for pictures, I haven't got enough walls. And I've bought three recently – it's not good! I do. But I try really to get a sense of the Black British story. The Black British imagery, where possible. Not overly 'poppy', but, but I have a sense [pause] let me show you my worry. My worry is that as the white structure negates our presence and stories, we too also do that by default. What I mean by that – because I can see your question-mark frown – what I mean by that is erm, our schools will bombard us with white stuff, white writers of stories, white writers of history, white perspectives of history, the lot. If you do Black history, so called, it starts with slavery

– who wants to know about that story? And, erm, any other stories are about empire. So, so you end up with having no sense that there is another side, another dimension, another shared history to explore. You spend your time doing, therefore, your A-levels on the same narrow band of knowledge, because it has been passed on. You go to university, and you *might* stumble upon a book, or some characters, but that is somewhat late in the day – but that's the only time you may have. And *even then* you might find, as my daughter did, that lecturers aren't keen to explore race-related topics, even if it's in psychology, because it's uncomfortable. So where is the knowledge base going to come from? We need to feed our people, that they have stories, and they have a presence, and there is a dynamism that is beyond racial tension.

Immediately, a difference can be seen between Dominic's narrative and the narratives of those closer towards strategic assimilation. Those towards strategic assimilation, on the one hand, are concerned to uplift Black cultural forms via synthesising them with other 'traditionally' British cultural forms that are given more value and recognition within the white symbolic space. On the other hand, those towards the ethnoracial autonomous identity mode are not concerned with white recognition as such; in fact, as is captured in Dominic's narrative, the absence of white recognition is taken as a starting point: 'My worry is that as the white structure negates our presence and stories, we too also do that by default.' Indeed, Dominic's comment that 'We need to feed our people' itself speaks to the ethnoracial autonomous repertoires of Afro-centrism and browning, that recognition of Blackness and Black Britishness must be achieved through Black resistance itself, and the burden of achieving recognition thus largely falls on the shoulders of Black folk.

Another subtle difference underlies the strategic assimilation and ethnoracial autonomous iterations of Black British double consciousness. Namely, on the one hand, towards strategic assimilation, there is a reification of Blackness and Britishness as two identities in conflict, and an underlying desire to articulate these facets of identity into a reconciled whole. This is why Thomas talks about 'having that conversation in the world about my identity and my culture', and Miriam says that 'It shows me that "liking Shakespeare" doesn't mean you are or are not a certain level of Black.' On the other hand, those towards the ethnoracial autonomous identity mode are less concerned with an identity reconciliation, and more so with a resistance to the erasure of Black Britishness, thus speaking to the more general difference between the strategic assimilation repertoire of code-switching and the ethnoracial autonomous repertoire of browning. This ethnoracial autonomous resistance is further demonstrated in an exchange I had with Toby, when discussing literature.

When discussing literature, Toby did not construe Black Britishness as a doubled consciousness (Blackness 'and' Britishness) in need of a holistic articulation, but as a historically constituted singular identity in itself, requiring constant acts of resistance to processes of erasure and exclusion. Discussing his interest in Black British writers, he proceeded,

> There is a reason why my shelf is like this, yes? Zadie Smith, check. [Malorie] Blackman, check. And classics – Selvon, James, Lamming – again, yes, they're there. They give me something different, differences to reflect on. I am a book worm – so I read a lot – but these reflections on race and society in Britain [pause]. They are invaluable to me, Black Brit, my parents could have been living a street away from Selvon! The reflections need to be known as our history, because even come October [Black History Month] I'm not sure this is talked about at all. [laughs] Very British – polite, 'We don't talk about that! No way!'

On the very same theme of British literature, Dominic also commented,

> I would be [pause] *horrified* [pause] yeah, I'll use that word, it's a nice word, if my kids had no idea that there were engaging titles by African, Caribbean, and Asian writers – South American writers as well. Which, in the UK, is easy to do ... This speaks to the fact that our stories are not of any relevance.

In both Toby's and Dominic's cases, therefore, we see the support of Black British cultural forms as a means of resisting the racial structure. In these cases, the racial structure involves both devaluation of Black Britishness (as Dominic claims, 'This speaks to the fact that our stories are not of any relevance'), as well as the exclusion of Blackness from the national repertoire of Britain (as Toby claims, 'The reflections need to be known as our history ... I'm not sure this is talked about at all'). Towards the ethnoracial autonomous identity mode, therefore, the consumption of Black British cultural forms gets tied to the repertoire of browning: the anti-racist desire to resist and reconfigure the racial structure.

Black Britishness, cultural capital, and symbolic boundaries

I want to conclude this chapter by reflecting on how this discussion of Black Britishness, and Black British cultural forms, feeds into discussions of cultural capital and symbolic boundaries. This discussion is important to recognise some of the underlying similarities across the cultural lives of many of this study's participants, regardless of their differing cultural repertoires.

Throughout this book, I have been engaging with the notion of cultural capital as a cultural resource used to reproduce material inequalities and/or to curate boundaries between different social groups.[42] Through this chapter's discussion, it is undeniable that many of the participants of this study – regardless of whether they oscillate towards strategic assimilation or the ethnoracial autonomous identity mode – use cultural capital as a resource to curate symbolic boundaries around Black Britishness. As Lamont and Molnár clarify, symbolic boundaries are concerned with 'conceptual distinctions made by social actors to categorize people ... also separat[ing] people into groups [which] generate feelings of similarity and group membership'.[43] Through this definition, it is evident that participants of this study are using the consumption of Black British cultural forms to generate feelings of Black British group membership. This is why, throughout this chapter, we have seen participants drawing links between Black British cultural forms with inclusive language such as 'We', 'Us', and 'Our'; Dominic claims that supporting Black British cultural forms enables him to challenge the way that '*our* stories are not of any relevance', Miriam claims that '*we* can have this cultural conversation, being "Black" ... also appreciating the culture of here, where *we* belong', and Toby talks about Black British literature being '*our* history' (emphasis added in all quotes). While my constructed triangle of identity pinpoints some differences in the repertoires and strategies of action across my participants, there is a foundational similarity in how they use Black British cultural forms as a means to draw an inclusive boundary with other Black Britons – both past and present.

One of my participants, Lawrence, commented to me that the very fact that you have to add 'Black' as a precursor to certain things – such as 'middle class', or 'feminist' – signals that the phenomenon by default excludes Blackness. We can think about Black Britishness in this same way. Why does 'Black' need to be added as a precursor to British, and what does the 'Black' do to the meaning of 'British' once it is added? I can only agree with Lawrence that the 'Black' is still added because it is a racialised category that is seen to exist outside the confines of authentic Britishness; the fact that many of this study's participants were concerned with drawing boundaries around Black Britishness highlights a wide recognition of this reality. The Black racialised outsiders of the British imperialist core from almost 100 years ago retain their status as racialised outsiders in the twenty-first century; they remain a focal point of comparison from which authentic 'Britishness' can be imagined, practised, and made as white.[44] While previous research has suggested that one way for racialised minorities to 'become' more British was by becoming middle class,[45] this chapter has demonstrated the existence of a Black middle class who still recognise racialised barriers to national group membership. This speaks to the inevitability and omnipresence of racism – even in domains of social space that appear to be non-racial. It is this theme of the inevitability and omnipresence of racism that I now want to expand on.

Notes

1 See Lefebvre, 2004; Soja, 1980; 1989.
2 See Hill, 2018.
3 de Sousa Santos, 2001.
4 Kapoor, 2011.
5 Joseph-Salisbury, 2018: 6.
6 Hall, 2016: 145.
7 Gilroy, 1993a: 58.
8 Jones et al., 2017; Solomos, 2003.
9 Bhambra, 2017; De Noronha, 2018; Hall, 2016.
10 CCCS, 1982.
11 For instance: Gilroy, 1982; 1987; 1993a, b; Hall, 2016; 2017a; Virdee, 2014a.
12 Bhambra, 2017.
13 Hunter, 2017.
14 Parveen and Sherwood, 2016.
15 See Bell, 1980.
16 Although there are suggestions that creating this Black 'bourgeoisie' was a central aim of Thatcher's 1980s government as it attempted to reproduce the capitalist system. See Daye, 1994.
17 Ray et al., 2017: 149.
18 Du Bois, 2007 [1903]: 34.
19 Lacy, 2007: 251. Of course, this shows that Du Bois (2008 [1920]) rightfully demonstrated how 'American' identity was racialised as white, as argued in the *Souls of White Folk*.
20 Stanfield II, 2011a: 233.
21 Gilroy, 2010: 152.
22 Rollock et al., 2011: 1088.
23 Imoagene, 2012; 2017.

24 On national repertoires and the cultural construction of available group categorisations see Lamont, 1992; Lamont et al., 2016; Lamont and Molnár, 2001.
25 Williams, 1977.
26 Hall, 1996.
27 Gilroy, 1993a, b.
28 Alexander, 1996.
29 Du Bois, 2007 [1903].
30 For instance, Meer, 2018; Meghji, 2017a; Rollock et al., 2011; 2013; 2015; Virdee, 2014a; 2017.
31 Virdee, 2017: 2403.
32 Meer, 2018: 7.
33 Brubaker, 2009. On the impossibility of race and ethnicity without racial and ethnic domination, see Bonilla-Silva, 1999; Emirbayer and Desmond, 2015; Goldberg, 2009.
34 See Costa, 2016; Meghji and Saini, 2018; Song, 2014.
35 For example, see Gilroy, 1993b; Lewis, 2012 and Telles, 2006.
36 In this regard, Du Bois's work on double consciousness is foundational for contemporary work examining 'white ignorance', and how perception is influenced by one's position in the overall racial structure. See Bonilla-Silva, 2012; Meghji, 2018; Mills, 2017; Mueller, 2017; 2018.
37 Hall, 2017b.
38 For instance, Anderson, 2011; Lacy, 2006; 2007; Rollock et al., 2015.
39 I perceive Thomas as lying at the boundary between the strategic assimilation and the class-minded identity modes.
40 Wright, 1989.
41 Gilroy, 1993a; 1998; Hall, 1993.
42 Drawing on the cultural sociological tradition of Michèle Lamont. See Lamont, 1992; Lamont and Molnár, 2001; 2002; Lamont and Lareau, 1988; Pachucki, Pendergrass and Lamont, 2007.
43 Lamont and Molnár, 2002: 168.
44 Virdee, 2017.
45 Gilroy, 1998; Lorimer, 1978; 2003.

6

Race, class, and culture in the British racialised social system

ONE TEXT I often turn to in my sociological writing is Becker's *Tricks of the Trade*.[1] As Becker claims, one question that sociologists must continually ask themselves is simply 'So what?'[2] I use this chapter to address this 'so what?' question – or as Du Bois puts it, 'the meaning of all this' question[3] – looking both backwards and forwards. I look backwards by reviewing how the data presented in this book makes contributions towards the micro field of Black middle-class studies, as well as to large areas of sociology including the sociology of race and class, cultural sociology, and critical race theory. I look forwards by examining the paths that my work opens for future research.

Black middle-class identities and cultural repertoires

One of my main aims in writing this book has been to encourage us to think about the complexities and diversities within an understudied social group in Britain – the Black middle class. Prior to my research, British Black middle-class identity was understood through the lens of strategic assimilation.[4] This former research emphasised how Black middle-class people will 'switch' identities such that they assimilate with white middle-class norms in the public sphere.[5] Furthermore, the extant literature on Black British middle-class cultural consumption has a unidimensional approach, focusing exclusively on 'strategic anti-racist cultural consumption'.[6] I sought to broaden our understandings of Black middle-class identity and cultural practices beyond this current literature, putting forward the model of a triangle of Black middle-class identity modes. Through focusing on three Black middle-class identity modes – ethnoracial autonomous, strategic assimilation, and class-minded – I hoped to pinpoint how and why Black middle-class people show diversity in their identities and cultural consumption in a way that juggles between the reductive nature of racialisation and the openness of individual agency. Through theorising this triangle of Black middle-class identity, I also intended to show how Black middle-class identity and cultural practices are tied to practices of racism and anti-racism, as I now review.

Strategic assimilation

I argued that individuals towards the strategic assimilation identity mode adopt repertoires of code-switching and cultural equity. Through the repertoire of code-switching, those towards strategic assimilation often switch identities when around white middle-class people. Such individuals consciously seek to become 'palatable' to the white middle class to establish legitimate middle-class cultural membership. This commitment to code-switching interrelates with the repertoire of cultural equity, the desire to be equal to the white middle class in levels of cultural capital. Such individuals towards strategic assimilation thus make sure to consume traditional middle-class cultural forms to avoid exclusion from the white middle-class milieu. Nevertheless, because of their commitment to code-switching, individuals towards strategic assimilation do retain an ethnoracial affinity, and thus also make sure to consume culture they decode as 'Black'.

Racism and anti-racism both affect how individuals towards the strategic assimilation identity mode construe their middle-class cultural membership. First, the presence of racism can be seen in the way that such individuals 'switch' identities when around the white middle class. Such individuals only 'switch' identities because they realise that one needs to become palatable to the white middle class to gain middle-class cultural membership. Individuals towards strategic assimilation thus perform a range of emotional labour such that they can *prove* their middle-class status, while they avoid being positioned according to negative racial ideologies (such as Black people being aggressive). Nevertheless, by virtue of engaging in this emotional labour and challenging racial stereotypes, individuals towards strategic assimilation also can be said to be engaging in everyday anti-racism.[7] This everyday anti-racism involves micro performances which show how dominant racial ideologies – such as Black people being uncultured, all being lower class, and being aggressive – are merely representations, not reality.

Racism and anti-racism also affect the cultural consumption of those siding towards strategic assimilation. First, such individuals claim there are racialised barriers to the consumption of traditional middle-class culture. This criticism is often formed around the point that traditional middle-class cultural spaces tend to be dominated by white audiences and producers, with Black people being made to feel uncomfortable in these spaces through acts of microaggressions. At a more symbolic level, middle-class culture is produced not just in 'spatially white' places but in symbolically white places too, by excluding authentic Black narratives, histories, and knowledges in the cultural forms. To this extent, individuals towards strategic assimilation show how there are barriers to the consumption of traditional middle-class culture, and therefore that such middle-class culture is not equally distributed across the racial hierarchy. While the *white* middle class are construed as the 'legitimate' consumers of middle-class culture, this legitimacy is not afforded to the *Black* middle class. Nevertheless, such individuals towards strategic assimilation adopt the anti-racist repertoire of cultural equity. They do not remove themselves from middle-class cultural spaces they decode as 'white' because they strive towards establishing not just an economic but also a cultural (capital) equality with whites. Thus, we see their anti-racist contestation of the distribution of cultural resources across the racial hierarchy. This anti-racist contestation is also seen in such individuals' support of middle-class culture with a focus on Blackness, which I will now turn to in discussing the ethnoracial autonomous identity mode.

Ethnoracial autonomous

Individuals towards the ethnoracial autonomous identity mode adopt cultural repertoires of browning and Afro-centrism. Through the repertoire of browning, those towards the ethnoracial autonomous identity mode attempt to resist white norms of middle-class identity, stressing that people ought to be 'proud' that they are Black. Unlike individuals towards the strategic assimilation identity mode, therefore, individuals towards the ethnoracial autonomous identity mode do not 'switch' identities when around the white middle class. Indeed, such individuals argue that this code-switching leads to inauthenticity and reproduces the racial structure within which whites are deemed more acceptable and respectable than Black folk. Browning is thus connected to the repertoire of Afro-centrism. Individuals towards the ethnoracial autonomous identity mode adopt a repertoire of Afro-centrism, believing that they have a duty to positively uphold Black diasporic histories, experiences, knowledges, and identities.

Anti-racism is salient in the cultural lives of the individuals towards the ethnoracial autonomous identity mode. First, they make an especial effort to support Black cultural institutions (such as the Black Cultural Archives (BCA)) and Black cultural producers to show that Black folk have a legitimate claim to 'middle-class culture'. This support of Black cultural institutions and producers can be read through an anti-racist lens: those towards the ethnoracial autonomous identity mode are responding to the unequal distribution of middle-class cultural capital by *creating their own avenues to garner such resources*. Furthermore, those towards the ethnoracial autonomous identity mode also have a preference for cultural forms which give authentic representations of Blackness. To this extent, individuals towards the ethnoracial autonomous identity mode, similar to those towards strategic assimilation, use their cultural consumption to support *positive* imageries of Blackness, thus challenging the negative ideological representations of Blackness common in the middle-class cultural realm.

Nevertheless, it is important to appreciate how the anti-racism practised by individuals towards the ethnoracial autonomous identity mode stems from their cognisance of continuing racism. It is therefore necessary to highlight how racism affects the cultural lives of those towards the ethnoracial autonomous identity mode. Such individuals, unlike those towards strategic assimilation, *do* remove themselves from traditional middle-class cultural spaces. This self-exclusion stems from the individuals' beliefs that such cultural spaces and 'capital' are not intended to be consumed by them, and thus they have no interest in what is essentially a Eurocentric, white middle-class practice of distinction. To this extent, we must appreciate how individuals towards the ethnoracial autonomous identity mode restrict the flows of their *dominant* cultural capital by excluding themselves from the white middle-class milieu. Once again, this is not construed as problematic by individuals towards the ethnoracial autonomous identity mode, as their practices of anti-racism are built around the assumption that they can create their own systems of valuation outside the reach of white middle-class norms. However, such self-exclusion is heavily criticised by those towards the class-minded identity mode.

Class-minded

Individuals towards the class-minded identity mode adopt repertoires of de-racialisation and post-racialism. Through the repertoire of post-racialism, such individuals believe that racism is no longer a significant issue in British society. Through the repertoire of de-racialisation, these individuals see their Blackness as merely an incidental skin colour and not as an identity they display any political or moral affinity towards. They therefore identify as 'middle class', rather than 'Black', and often construe these two group memberships as incongruous. Such individuals thus often de-racialise themselves, but *re-racialise others*; they internalise and reproduce negative ideologies (stereotypes) of Blackness to distinguish themselves from other Black people.

It is through their cultural repertoires of post-racialism and de-racialisation that we see how racism comes to affect the cultural lives of individuals towards the class-minded identity mode. First, such individuals confidently assert and 'feel' their middle-class cultural membership. However, such individuals use their middle-class cultural membership as a way to distinguish themselves from other Black people. Therefore, they contrast their respectable identities with the 'common', urban identities of other Black people. This can be demonstrated by such individuals comparing their middle-class manner of speaking (linguistic capital) with the 'common' accents of others. Such individuals also argue that their middle-class cultural membership means they become involved in cultural pursuits which are polarised to the interests of Black people, thus creating a division between middle classness (within which they claim cultural membership) and Blackness (within which they do *not* claim cultural membership). Not only do such individuals state how these middle-class cultural practices are polarised to the interests of Black folk, but they also lambast other Black people for unnecessarily excluding themselves from such cultural spaces. They argue that other Black people are either myopic in their cultural preferences or simply 'playing the race card' in calling these spaces 'white'. To this extent, those towards the class-minded identity mode are influenced by racism in that they *reproduce negative racial ideologies* of Black folk – such as Black people being uncultured – while also reproducing post-racialism, which allows for the reproduction of racism through denying its very existence.

Bringing discussion back to the extant literature on Black British middle-class identity and culture, I hoped to make two thematic developments. First, my research shows how strategic assimilation is only one mode of Black middle-class identity. Focusing only on strategic assimilation overlooks the experiences of those who believe we are beyond racism and thus see no need to 'switch' identities (those towards the class-minded identity mode), and those who contest the idea that one must assimilate with white norms (those towards the ethnoracial autonomous identity mode). Second, my research goes beyond the idea that all Black British middle-class people consume middle-class cultural capital with a 'Black' focus. Instead, my research also shows the existence of Black middle-class folk (those towards the class-minded identity mode) who, through their repertoires of de-racialisation and post-racialism, show no predilection towards 'Black' cultural forms. Similarly, I show how individuals towards strategic assimilation may have a predilection towards 'Black' cultural forms, but through their repertoires of code-switching and cultural equity, also make sure they are competent in 'traditional' middle-class cultural spheres.

Beyond Black middle-class identity and culture

While this study has sought to develop our understanding of Black middle-class identity and culture, this micro case also connects to much grander sociological subfields: the sociology of race and class, cultural sociology, and critical race theory.

The sociology of race and class

Perhaps one of the largest contributions of this book is the premise that class works differently for differently racialised people. Indeed, scholars have made this claim in the context of Britain's Black and brown working class.[8] Such literature highlights how Black and brown workers historically and presently have been below the status of the white worker – both in terms of objective location in the labour market, but also in terms of institutional access, for instance, access to trade unions, and in terms of the moral worth they are ascribed by the State.[9]

My work shifts the perspective slightly by focusing on how middle classness works differently for Black and white people. This is incredibly important for understanding that 'middle-class privilege' is not a given for Black folk, and that middle-class privilege is much more easily realised by white people.[10] Some of the former literature on the Black middle class has shown this in the field of education studies. Thus, whereas from the Bourdieusian tradition[11] we get the notion that educational systems are made for the middle class, research has shown that Black middle-class students are negatively stereotyped by teachers, leading to underperformance and lack of attention being given to such students.[12] In this case, while being middle class ought to bestow a class privilege on the Black middle class to accelerate through educational systems, instead racism works as a gravity to prevent such ascension.

My research signalled that racism constrains middle-class privilege in a variety of ways. Since the introduction of 'social capital' analysis in sociological theory and methods, scholars have noted that social class often relates to 'who you know'.[13] Recent class analysis, as expected, highlights that those in professional occupations maintain closer ties with other people in professional occupations – indeed, it is such networks that allow for the transmission of class privilege across (or, more accurately, 'within') certain social groups.[14] However, when we discuss Black employment in Britain, we have to acknowledge that the Black middle class has emerged relatively recently – in the 1990s.[15] Before the 1990s, equal opportunities laws simply were not effective in their ability to fight institutional racism.[16] From the 'Windrush generation' in the post-war era through to the 1990s – which is only one generation away from the time I am now writing this book – Black people in Britain were thus largely downpressed into the lower areas of Britain's economic order.[17] Compared to the typical professional worker uncovered in quantitative class studies, therefore, the average Black professional in Britain is going to have a network with much greater class heterogeneity. As I have highlighted, the majority of this study's participants are first-generation middle class – their immediate family members are working, or lower class, as well as some of their childhood friends. Dawn, despite herself being second-generation middle class, explained this reality to me towards the beginning of our interview:

> I did a BBC survey thing. And, it said I was firmly working class. So I was like 'Oh okay!' And it was all based on my social capital. So like, how many nurses you know, do you know any this that and the other, and I was like 'Oh!' But at that time I was living in Paris, I was working in the Louvre, I was travelling all over the place, working as a lecturer – so I was like, how the hell am I working class?! I didn't mind, but I just found it really interesting. So I'm just wondering what middle class really means. Does it really *work* for Black people? Because I'm always going to know people who do those kind of blue-collar jobs. And, and when it asked that question – what do your parents do? Well my parents have done everything!

Therefore, Black middle-class people, because of the inability to escape history, are often much closer to the working class than a typical (white) professional worker. Their social networks are not as homogeneously middle class as those of the white middle class, and consequently such Black middle-class people do not necessarily have a ready-made network of privilege that they have access to. A large reason for this reality is, as I mentioned, simply history: most of Britain's Black middle class are first-generation middle class. Yet, we already know this will have further economic consequences, given recent findings that those who are first-generation middle class face a 'class pay gap' compared to those who are at least second-generation middle class.[18] However, on top of the 'class pay gap', those in the Black middle class also face a 'racialised' wage gap shown to exist in professional occupations, and Black middle-class women will additionally face a gender pay gap.[19] All of this is to say that when looking at the objective location and circumstances of Britain's Black middle class from a quantitative perspective, the notion of 'middle-class privilege' seems ambiguous, at best.

Beyond these quantitative arguments around wages and social networks, there are also qualitative dimensions to the ways that (middle-) class privilege works differently for Black people. This harks back to my approach to social class outlined in the first few pages of this book; classes have economic foundations, but they also have to be made through cultural and symbolic boundary drawing. This means that 'class' is not something you constantly possess and can hold on to throughout your life. Especially for Black folk, being middle class becomes highly situational, and one's middle-class status is often capable of being taken away. Elijah Anderson refers to these situations as 'n****r moments' – where the colour line is quickly drawn through interactional encounters, and the Black professional 'is powerfully reminded of his or her putative place as a Black person'.[20] As Lawrence mentioned in an earlier quote presented in this book, a person can have copious amounts of economic capital; 'However, put them in a different context and they will realise that they have *no* class.' All of the microaggressions recounted through this book signal the ability of the racially dominant to temporarily take away the middle-class status of Black professionals.

This ability of Black professionals to have their class status taken away from them speaks to the wider social process that middle-class spaces and organisations are additionally racialised as white. A large reason why Black professionals encounter microaggressions in art galleries, the opera house, and even in their workplaces, whether that be a law firm, a newsroom, or a financial company, is simply that Black people are not seen to 'belong' in those spaces. As Purwar declares, such Black professionals – by virtue of moving in middle-class spaces – become reified as 'bodies out of space'.[21] However, given that the majority of studies on Britain's middle class retain a colour-blind approach,[22] we still have a limited understanding of the implications of middle-class spaces in fact being white middle-class spaces. From the research presented in this book, a particular implication is that we need to shift how we think about the use of middle-class 'cultural capital'. Namely, we cannot only equate middle-class cultural capital as a resource used to curate a boundary around the middle class, with the middle class then gaining a monopoly over this resource.[23] Such analysis overlooks the racialised barriers to the effective consumption of middle-class cultural capital – signalled through, for instance, my discussion of white symbolic and physical spaces. Indeed, through my analysis of 'traditional' middle-class culture as white, I showed that what we often think of as middle-class cultural capital is really used as means for sustaining *white* middle-class supremacy.

An implication of middle-class spaces being racialised as white, as I have explored elsewhere, means that such spaces have their own 'racialised interaction order' instilled in ways that reproduce white supremacy and privilege.[24] Through this interaction order, Black professionals have to learn rules for action in (white) middle-class spaces to 'pass' as respectable. One such rule is not to be 'racially closed' – that is, not to become friends with the only other Black person within the space (if there are any). For instance, both Catherine and Ijeoma attended the same college at Oxford and started university at the same time; they both said to me how in their first days they made an especial effort to not talk to each other because of the racialised interaction order instilled in this white space. Their comments were almost identical to Raymond discussing the rules for Black professionals at networking events, when

> You find yourself in a room and you're *not* the only Black person in the room, there's another Black person in the room and you know there's something about that person, you cannot go and talk to them, you can't be seen to just be sticking together.

Again, this points to a difference in how middle classness works differently between white and Black people. Racialised interaction orders are constructed such that they burden Black folk, while whites do not have to think about them at all. Indeed, this highlights Frankenberg's notion of white privilege as involving obliviousness to their privilege – having the ability to not have to reflect on their social structural advantages.[25] Simply put, therefore, this book has shown that if middle-class identity and culture are the (research) question, then colourblindness is most certainly not the answer. It is this issue of middle-class culture, and cultural sociology more generally, that I now want to discuss.

Cultural sociology

The cultural capital approach (the 'sociology *of* culture') is sometimes seen to be at odds with the cultural repertoires approach ('cultural sociology').[26] My research shows how such a division is uncalled for. Particularly through my triangle of identity, I show how the consumption of cultural capital is often incorporated into cultural repertoires. Thus, those towards the ethnoracial autonomous identity justify their preference for diasporic cultural producers and cultural forms through their repertoires of browning and Afro-centrism; those towards strategic assimilation justify their consumption of traditional middle-class culture through the repertoires of cultural equity and code-switching; and those towards the class-minded identity draw on repertoires of post-racialism and de-racialisation, consuming traditional middle-class culture as a means to separate themselves from other Black people.

This is not to say that *all* consumption of cultural capital is guided by fully conscious, strategic, and deliberately planned courses of action in cohesion with agents' chosen cultural repertoires. Rather, it is to stress that cultural consumption can be more or less consciously incorporated into cultural repertoires. Thus, when we see the strategic assimilation repertoires of cultural equity and code-switching, and see such individuals consuming cultural capital they decode as 'white' to maintain an equal standing with the white middle class, we can see on the one hand how cultural consumption is *very consciously* guided by deliberately chosen repertoires. On the other hand, when we look at the class-minded repertoire of de-racialisation and these individuals' confident consumption of traditional middle-class culture, the link does not appear to be as conscious. It takes a dose of the sociological imagination, including the rigorous analysis of transcripts and analysis of boundary work, to show how such class-minded people pursue de-racialisation, constructed through contrasting themselves to other Black people.

Through showing the link between cultural repertoires and cultural consumption, my work also contributes to studies of class cultures. As social science moves towards more 'big data' studies,[27] my research shows that large-scale quantitative surveys will not give us proper depth in analysis of social classes and cultural consumption. Thus, large-scale surveys – such as the recent Great British Class Survey[28] – can show us that certain people in certain economic locations and trajectories consume the same forms of cultural capital. However, when bringing race(ism) into analysis – as I do – the picture becomes more complicated than simply asserting 'people in X economic location show a preference for Y cultural forms'. For instance, if we look at individuals of both the class-minded and strategic assimilation identity modes, then they both regularly consume traditional middle-class cultural forms. However, their reasons for this consumption are incongruous with one another: while those towards strategic assimilation are struggling for cultural equity in what they believe to be a racist society, those towards the class-minded identity are often distinguishing themselves from other Black people. Showing us *what* people consume does, therefore, not reach the important sociological question of *why* people consume what they do; it is this 'why' question that qualitative sociology is well placed to analyse. In a time when we are influenced by 'impact-led' agendas, and quantitative social science is deemed more 'fundable',[29] my research thus shows how the sociology of class must retain its commitment to qualitative analysis if it wishes to remain critical.

Furthermore, given that my research shows that people may consume the same cultural capital for radically different reasons, I also argue that we need to increasingly focus on the *phenomenology of consumption*. Admittedly, this move is being made in British social class studies, where analysis is increasingly focusing on how working-class people see their consumption of middle-class culture as illegitimate, while middle-class professionals are cast (by themselves or by the lower classes) as the 'proper' consumers of middle-class culture.[30] Current research is thus moving towards an analysis not only of what different classes consume, but of the confidence they have in their own cultural consumption. Nevertheless, my research brings the additional focus of race and racism to these discussions of the phenomenology of cultural consumption, which have hitherto remained colour-blind.

Through focusing on the phenomenology of consumption, my research also brings a new perspective on debates over the 'cultural omnivore', another cultural process that has been analysed largely through colour-blind goggles. Broadly, British sociologists have pinpointed how especially the middle class no longer consume only middle-class cultural forms but a range of cultural forms, including 'popular' media, and how the lower classes also have increased consumption of traditionally 'middle-class' cultural forms.[31] One identified trend in this research is that while cultural consumption, through the rise of 'omnivores', seems to be more fluid in terms of social class, the class hierarchy is still rigidly reproduced through these streams of cultural capital. Namely, working-class consumers often see their consumption of middle-class cultural forms as unauthentic, or lacking in some way, while the middle class are still deemed as the 'proper' consumers, and are also said to even bring a more nuanced understanding of popular media, too.[32] In other words, through distinct phenomenologies of consumption, the middle class – despite increasing class cultural eclecticism – still maintain a monopoly over certain forms of cultural capital.

My research shows that unlike the white middle class, certain Black middle-class people see it is a necessity for them to be culturally omnivorous to balance their racial and classed identities. Given the emergence of 'Black culture' within working-class confines – as discussed in the former chapter – this means that many Black middle-class people must necessarily be cultural omnivores if they wish to engage with what they decode as elements of Black cultural expression. This cultural omnivorous-ness is captured in Raymond talking about his son:

> You know when my son was born, the first thing, the first piece of music was Vivaldi's *Four Seasons*, the second thing that he heard was Dizzee Rascal's *Maths + English*, in the hospital.

However, we must note as well that Black middle-class people are also required to be versed in traditional middle-class cultural capital – such as classical music, mentioned in Raymond's previous quote. The Black middle class face a 'deficit of credibility', the default assumption is that they are lower class, and they must strenuously work to show otherwise.[33] As I recounted in this book, one way that Black middle-class people overcome this lack of credibility is by gaining a symbolic mastery over traditional middle-class cultural forms, hence why Ijeoma talks about 'learning the names of artists and being able to recognise their art ... So, when I go to events and so on I don't seem ignorant', and why Dawn talks about learning 'the codes, and I learn the practices' when moving in middle-class cultural institutions. These collated narratives thus symbolise a different kind of cultural omnivore to what we typically see in the sociological literature. Namely, such Black middle-class folk are not omnivores by choice, inasmuch as (from their perspective) by necessity.

In terms of a new perspective to what we typically see in sociological literature, I argue that cultural sociology also increasingly needs to focus on micro cultural spheres of social space where whiteness is not the default or normative background. In other words, I believe we need to go beyond the universal 'cultural capital deficit' approach to studying Black people in Britain.[34] This deficit model argues that the cultural capital Black individuals have is inherently devalued by virtue of their ethnoracial membership. Of course, in many cases this deficit model rings true, and it speaks to the ongoing structural presence of racism.

However, in my research, I showed certain cases where members of the Black middle class challenge this deficit model. Many of my participants often talked about how they were the 'proper' consumers of middle-class cultural forms which focused on Blackness (for instance, cultural forms that focused on elements of Black diasporic history). When I attended a James Baldwin literature course at New Beacon Books for my ethnographic work, for instance, there was only one white person present (out of around twenty people). A social class survey may have coded this four-week, after-work course as 'middle class', but the consumers were almost exclusively Black. Indeed, a large part of this course was framed around using Baldwin's writings to understand contemporary British anti-Blackness – the white person barely muttered a word over the entire course; Black people were cast as the legitimate consumers, they were cast as the people with the most symbolic authority. The current research is not well placed to analyse these instances, because analyses of middle-class culture hitherto have largely neglected the question of race. To this extent, therefore, my research shows that there are cultural spaces where the white middle-class consumer is not construed as the 'proper' consumer, even though the cultural form may be construed as middle class given the findings of previous social-class surveys. Cultural sociology needs to further research such cultural spaces where Black individuals' symbolic mastery of cultural capital is deemed superior to whites', to further flesh out how the cultural sphere is used as a key site for resistance to the restricted flows of dominant cultural capital.

Critical race theory

You may have realised by now that part of the reason my work makes contributions to race and class, and cultural sociology, is because of my insistence to keep talking about the presence and effects of racism. While I do not believe that the identities and actions of the participants of this study are only determined by racism (and anti-racism), I think that to analyse their actions, identities, and attitudes without a central focus on racism and anti-racism is a grave error; as Mills puts it, 'in a racialized society people will continue to have racialized experiences'.[35] However, this 'racism' I am concerned with showing is not just to do with individual acts of prejudice and bigotry, but a structural, system-like phenomenon. In this regard, I am indebted to the work of critical race theorists, who understand racism as involving the unequal distribution of societal resources across a constructed racial hierarchy.[36] At first sight, the very presence of a Black middle class seems to complicate this critical race structural understanding of racism; after all, by virtue of being middle class, the Black middle class are relatively privileged in their possession of economic resources. My research brings a new critical race perspective towards structural racism by turning to the cultural field, and to the unequal distribution of cultural resources.

In particular, my research pointed to the unequal distribution of middle-class cultural capital across the racial hierarchy. Once again, I analysed this through the lens of the white physical and symbolic space. In such analysis, I showed how, through the reproduction of racial ideologies and creation of white institutional-cultural spaces, the white middle class have spaces 'sheltered' from 'diversity' despite the fact that they are based in one of the most 'diverse' British cities (London) where Black and minority ethnic (BAME) people make up just over 40 per cent of the city's population.[37] Indeed, while there is a burgeoning literature on the multicultural conviviality of *working-class* spaces,[38] my research shows that this conviviality is *not* being realised in middle-class cultural spaces, which still serve to maintain white middle-class supremacy. To this extent, my research demonstrates how the construction of traditional middle-class cultural spaces are examples of how the white middle class are able to protect their cultural resources (cultural capital) from more equal redistributions across the racial hierarchy.

Furthermore, critical race theory is concerned with the durability of the racialised social system – the mechanisms that allow for its reproduction, and the micro, meso, and macro forms of anti-racism that attempt to challenge the racial system. My research highlighted how the middle-class cultural realm itself involves 'controlling images'[39] or ideological representations of Blackness that reproduce the total racialised system. Characteristic of the white symbolic space, as I showed, was a reproduction of stereotypes about Blackness and Black people within traditional middle-class cultural forms – Black people appear as criminals, urban and dangerous, as delinquent 'folk devils' at best.[40] Yet my research also pointed to the anti-racist actions many Black middle-class folk take against this situation. Thus, I mentioned how many Black middle-class people support and consume cultural producers and forms that give authentic representations of Blackness. These authentic representations are very much supported as a form of 'counter-framing' to the dominant controlling images of Black people in the racialised system.[41] Similarly, I showed how many Black middle-class folk consume particularly Black *British* cultural forms as a way of contesting the British racialised social system's attempts to erase their existence. In this respect, my research pays attention to the 'everyday anti-racism'[42] practised by Black middle-class individuals at the micro level, in a way that is indubitably connected to the wider racial structure.

Still on this issue of the micro, I have also attempted to show how the wider racial structure has a bearing on the everyday lives, emotions, and feelings of this study's participants. Through this focus on the everyday, I have attempted to flesh out the critical race perspective that while 'racism has a material foundation, humans cannot live of bread alone – that is, race cannot exist without an emotional bond'.[43] Throughout this book, an implicit theme has been loneliness and isolation: stories of Black middle-class people being the only Black person at their workplace, the only Black person in an art gallery or a music hall. From these described situations, it seems peculiar that people would use the existence of the Black middle class to justify the existence of post-racialism: if you are the only Black person, or one of few Black people, in a given middle-class space, then to what extent is this racial progress and to what extent is this simply – as Shirley Chisolm put it – bringing one folding chair to the otherwise all-white table? One of my interviewees, Martin, captures this dynamic well when he talks about the isolating experience of being the only Black person in the professional workplace:

> that sense of just not having somebody who is going through a similar experience to you, or your doubts about whether people are judging you a certain way, having to kind of go through that journey on your own, *day in day out*, it can become very lonely ... For some people it won't be *hostile, overt* racism that drives them out, it won't be erm anger at a system that's against them [pause] it's just loneliness.

Looking forwards: sociological developments

In the spirit of Martin's comment, it is perhaps an apt moment to claim that sociologists do not work alone, we are not – by design of the academy – lonely. This is because no one does sociological work in a vacuum; we engage with each other's work, through the very act of citation we engage with writers – past and present – meaning that despite the 'acceleration' of the academy,[44] sociology, and academia more generally, is an inherently collaborative enterprise. With this in mind, I wish to briefly describe two ways that my work presented in this book can serve as a foundation for future research.

First, there is the issue of the triangle of Black middle-class identity. As I have reiterated throughout this book, this triangle of Black middle-class identity is a theoretical model. By that I mean that it is a model I think helps us to understand the social world, and to understand Black middle-class identity and culture better, relative to the rival theoretical models that are currently available (for instance, strategic assimilation and strategic anti-racist cultural consumption). This by no means implies that I think the triangle of identity is the 'final word' on Black middle-class identity and culture. By absolute contrast, I think the best way to test the accuracy of theoretical models and claims is for them to be constantly put to trial in empirical research.[45] As Bourdieu and Wacquant put it, 'theory properly conceived should not be severed from the research work that nourishes it and which it continually guides and structures'.[46] To this extent, I believe the best way for the triangle of identity to be judged is simply through other researchers seeing its applicability (or lack of) in their own research projects.

I am particularly interested in seeing how the triangle of Black middle-class identity works in British contexts not examined in this book. First, my research is almost exclusively based in London – a city, as I mentioned, that is over 40 per cent BAME, and a city that has the largest population of Black middle-class people in Britain.[47] The opportunities to be ethnoracial autonomous in London, surely, far outweigh the ability to be so ethnocentric in a city where you are one of few Black people in an overwhelmingly white city. This speaks to the wider need for sociologists of race to study race, racialisation, and racism in cities that are not ethnoracially diverse, but very ethnoracially homogeneous.[48] Second, I am interested in how the triangle of identity works in Britain beyond the Black-white binary. There is literature which highlights how some middle-class British South Asians adopt repertoires of code-switching, similar to my analysis of strategic assimilation.[49] Further, there is also research which demonstrates middle-class South Asians adopting a cultural repertoire of post-racialism, akin to the class-minded identity mode.[50] I therefore believe it to be likely that my theoretical triangle of identity may find empirical weight in the study of non-Black ethnoracial groups in Britain.

I also believe my triangle of identity can be tested outside the British context. Outside this book, I have argued that the Black middle class face similar situations in the United Kingdom, United States, South Africa, Brazil, and Mexico.[51] Thus, despite some of these countries being 'white majority', 'Black majority', or founded on mixed-ness and racial democracy, Black middle-class people still face the problem that Blackness is understood through the lens of a lower-class identity, while middle classness is understood in its connection to hegemonic whiteness.[52] Given these similarities in experiences, it would be interesting to see how the triangle of identity works outside Britain, and whether it finds empirical weight in these different nations. For example, the Black middle class in the United States is considerably larger than in Britain.[53] It could therefore be, on the one hand, that the ethnoracial autonomous identity mode is more popular in the United States, as there is potentially a greater presence of social and cultural spaces free from white influence. On the other hand, South Africa is a Black-majority country, so it could be that the class-minded identity mode is more dominant in South Africa where there are greater attempts to symbolically separate the Black middle and lower classes.

This widening, and testing of the triangle of identity thus connects with the sociology of race, class, and space (both at the local level of London and at national levels). It would also be interesting to look at the Black middle class more broadly in urban processes that are often seen to be class-based, such as gentrification. In one of my very first interviews, Samuel and I met in Brixton, and he described how Black professionals were supporting institutions like the neighbourhood's BCA to assert some 'staying power' against white gentrification. Much later in my research, another interviewee – Martin – told me about his experiences as a 'Black gentrifier' in Brixton. Martin claimed that being a Black gentrifier is phenomenologically different to being a white one, because you inherently build a connection with the (Black) people you are supposedly gentrifying:

> what we noticed is that when we walked around Brixton for the first few years we lived there, we were part of the community as Black people, other Black people noticed you, they see you, they respond to you. You respond to them. Whether it's a nod in the street, because it's your neighbour, when my mum came to stay with us, kids would say 'hi auntie, hi grandma, hi mummy' – it's your mum, as a West Indian woman on the road, right? They notice you, what you're doing, right? I got to know them. But the impression you have is that for the middle-class white person, our counterpart, my colleague at work who lives on the same street, he would not have that connection … So, as a Black professional person, you have a, in a context of gentrification – what we might call gentrification – your role is slightly different [pause] whether you want it to be or not. Your presence is different, whether you want it to be or not. We're almost like a, like an anomaly. We're almost like a bridging presence. And if you've got this race dimension that accompanies it, or cultural dimension, because you're coming in with a very similar culture, sometimes one generation away from being identical to the people who you're supposedly gentrifying, you have a different cultural context and relationship with those people, culturally, partly because you're, the differences between you, the class differences, are there but they are ameliorated by other great similarities.

In a context where much literature on British gentrification universalises the experience of white middle-class gentrifiers to the middle class as a whole,[54] I think a study on Black middle-class gentrifiers can enrich our understandings of the inclusive (or exclusive) symbolic boundaries that Black middle-class folk draw towards (or against) the Black working class in urban spaces such as Brixton. Indeed, we could even use the triangle of Black middle-class identity to examine whether people of certain identity modes are more inclined towards 'inclusive' forms of gentrification than others. For instance, do those towards the class-minded identity mode show a preference for living in 'white neighbourhoods'? Do those towards the ethnoracial autonomous and strategic assimilation identity modes move to Black neighbourhoods that are being gentrified (such as Brixton) to maintain some Black 'staying power'? These are all questions that extend the research of this book in various ways, highlighting the reality that sociological research is never finished but constantly develops as our we enter our work into collaborative dialogues with the research of others.

On racism, resistance, and social change

It is true that sociological research is always developing, and the reason for this is that social processes are also continually developing, adapting, and evolving. This is evident in the case of racism, captured in what Malcom X used to tell his followers: 'racism is like a Cadillac, they bring out a new model every year'.[55] I want to finish this book by reflecting on Malcom X's comment, tying links between racism, resistance, and social change through the perspective of my study on the Black middle class.

First of all, we have to admit that the very existence of a Black middle class is evidence of social change in Britain. In 1971, quantitative sociologists claim that 0 per cent of Black women and 1 per cent of Black men were in professional occupations.[56] Indeed, prior to the emergence of a distinctive Black middle class in the 1990s, the racial structure was reproduced through this exclusion of Black and brown folks from sections in the economy – the (coloured) glass ceiling was thus a mechanism to reproduce the unequal distribution of economic resources across the racial hierarchy. Social change is thus undeniable.

However, as Ray and Seamster put it so aptly, 'change and progress are not synonymous'.[57] In this context, racial progress and social change are by no means the same thing. The emergence of a Black middle class, while certainly being evidence of social change, is not itself a sign of racial progress. A large reason why is because, to carry on with Ray and Seamster's argument, racism is a 'fundamental cause', whereby 'although the historical mechanisms reproducing inequality change, basic relations of sub- and superordination are remarkably stable'.[58] In this context, a Black middle class clearly exists, but this chapter (and the book in its entirety) has highlighted multiple ways that this Black middle class are still subject to various forms of racially based inequalities despite their privileged class location.

Furthermore, viewing racism as a fundamental cause of inequalities 'shifts our focus from attempts to measure "progress" to instead show how social structures influence patterns amidst relatively superficial changes'.[59] Thus, it is true that a Black middle class emerged in the 1990s and consolidated in the second decade of the twenty-first century. Yet, in this same period, we also see the rise of a new group of people – wealth elites – monopolising economic and institutional resources.[60] In other words, the very time where the Black middle class was growing and consolidating was the very same time where the middle class, as a whole, were losing economic and institutional power.[61] Furthermore, this new wealth elite are not racially mixed by any means. We know, for instance, that only 2 per cent of FTSE 100 directors are British BAME, with more than half of FTSE 100 companies having no BAME board members at all.[62] We also know simply from the most recent UK Census (in 2011) that as a percentage of their overall ethnoracial group, around twice as many white folk work as senior managers and officials (12 per cent) compared to Black folk (6 per cent). What we see, therefore, is just what Ray and Seamster state – relatively superficial change.[63] This is because while the Black middle class consolidates, we still have a situation whereby 'sections of the labour market are reserved for whites only'.[64]

In the midst of this (albeit relatively superficial) social change, this book has also highlighted how members of the Black middle class are largely aware that they have not broken free from the effects of racism. Indeed, one reason I used qualitative methods in this project was to capture the everyday acts of resistance that many of these Black middle-class folk perform against the wider racial structure. Through this lens, we do not only see the ubiquity and the fundamental cause of racism, but also the ubiquity of anti-racism. Wearing an expensive outfit, speaking in a refined manner, learning the names of famous artists, and reading Shakespeare all become actions that can be (at least partially) understood as acts of resistance against the absence of racial progress. Even actions that would pass under the radar to the casual onlooker – such as the Black middle-class person withholding from making a critical remark from fear of being labelled as aggressive – become micro acts of resistance at the emotional level aimed to challenge wider racial structures and ideologies.

By means of an overview, to believe that the Black middle class are 'beyond' racism because of their economic status is spurious. If anything, the experiences of the Black middle class *confirm* racism; they show that attending an elite higher education institution and making a lot of money do not enable one to transcend racism. This racism they face, moreover, is much more than individual prejudice. Rather, the racism they face speaks to a general structure – a racialised social system – which relies on the unequal distribution of societal resources across a constructed racial hierarchy. While my work is one of few studies in Britain to investigate how racism affects those who many claim are 'beyond' racism – the Black middle class – I believe it can open further debates about race and class in Britain, and how British society remains far from a post-racial utopia.

Notes

1 Becker, 1998.
2 Becker, 1998.
3 Du Bois, 1967 [1899]: 385.
4 Rollock et al., 2011; 2015; Wallace, 2015.
5 Rollock et al., 2011; 2015; Wallace, 2015.
6 Wallace, 2017; 2018.
7 Lamont and Fleming, 2005.
8 For instance, Gilroy, 1982; 1998; Hall, 1993; 2016; James, 1963; Jones, 1949; Ramdin, 2017; Sivanandan, 1976; 1985; Virdee, 2000; 2014a, b; 2017.
9 For the past, see Gilroy, 1982; Sivanandan, 1976; 1985; Virdee, 2000. For the present, see Bhambra, 2017; Bassel and Emejulu, 2017.
10 And even then, middle-class privilege works best for those who are at least second-generation middle class, as uncovered by Friedman and Laurison's work into the class pay gap. See Friedman, Laurison and Miles, 2015b; Laurison and Friedman, 2016.
11 Bourdieu and Passeron, 1990.
12 Rollock et al., 2015.
13 Butler and Robson, 2001; Li, Savage and Warde, 2008; Putnam, 2001.
14 Savage, 2015a.
15 Robinson and Valeny, 2005.
16 Solomos, 2003.
17 See Brown, 1984; Robinson and Valeny, 2005.
18 For instance, relative to those who had a parent in higher managerial or professional occupations, those with parents from lower tiered occupations earn on average £11,200 less per year in finance; £9,440 less in media; £8,830 less in law; and £5,050 less in medicine (Friedman, Laurison and Miles, 2015b; Laurison and Friedman, 2016).
19 See Clark and Drinkwater, 2007; EHRC, 2016; Khattab, 2016; Li, 2015; Li and Heath, 2008.
20 Anderson, 2011: 253.

21 Purwar, 2004.
22 Atkinson, 2000; 2004; Benson and Jackson, 2013; Bridge, Butler et al., 2012; Butler, 1997; 2003; 2007; Butler and Hamnett, 1994; Butler and Robson, 2001; 2003a; Hamnett, 2003; Jackson and Butler, 2015.
23 Atkinson, 2017; Bennett et al., 2010.
24 Meghji, 2018; on interaction orders (racialised and otherwise) see Goffman, 1983; Rawls, 2000; Rawls and Duck, 2017; Rosino, 2017.
25 Frankenberg, 1993.
26 For example Alexander, 2003; Lamont, 1992.
27 Silva, 2015.
28 Savage et al., 2013.
29 Maxwell, 1992; Wiles, Crow and Pain, 2011.
30 Atkinson, 2017; Bennett et al., 2010; Bull, 2016; Silva, 2008.
31 Chan and Goldthorpe, 2005; 2007; Friedman, 2012; Warde and Gayo-Cal, 2009; Warde, Wright and Gayo-Cal, 2007; 2008.
32 For instance, Atkinson, 2017; Friedman et al., 2015a.
33 Anderson, 2015: 13
34 For example, Rollock, 2012a; 2014; Yosso, 2005.
35 Mills, 1998: 66.
36 See Bonilla-Silva, 1997; 2017a; Hughey, Embrick and 'Woody' Doane, 2015; Ray et al., 2017.
37 UK Census, 2011.
38 Gilroy, 2004; Jackson, 2019; Neal et al., 2013.
39 Collins, 2004.
40 CCCS, 1982.
41 On counter-framing, see Feagin, 2009; Wingfield and Feagin, 2012.
42 Lamont and Fleming, 2005.
43 Bonilla-Silva, 2016: 243.
44 Carrigan, 2015.
45 Wacquant, 2004b.
46 Bourdieu and Wacquant, 1992: 30.
47 Rollock et al., 2015.
48 Nayak, 2007; 2011.
49 Archer, 2011.
50 Meghji and Saini, 2018.
51 Meghji, 2017c.
52 Meghji, 2017c.
53 Landry, 1987; Rollock et al., 2015
54 Atkinson, 2000; 2004; Benson and Jackson, 2013; Bridge, Butler and Lees, 2012; Butler, 1997; 2003; 2007; Butler and Hamnett, 1994; Butler and Robson, 2001; 2003a; Hamnett, 2003; Jackson and Butler, 2015.
55 Quoted in Lipsitz, 1998: 182.
56 Robinson and Valeny, 2005.

57 Ray and Seamster, 2016: 1364.
58 Ray and Seamster, 2016: 1362.
59 Ray and Seamster, 2016: 1364.
60 Cunningham and Savage, 2015; Hey, Grimaldi-Christensen and Savage, 2017; Savage, 2015b.
61 Savage, 2015a.
62 Parker, 2016.
63 Ray and Seamster, 2016.
64 Bhopal, 2018: 142.

Appendix: Building a reflexive case study of the Black middle class

I WANT to use this section in the Appendix to reflect on two main issues. First, I wish to outline in more detail the 'case-study logic' underlying my research on the Black middle class. Second, I want to give my two cents on reflexivity and the 'across difference' debate within qualitative research, given that I am a non-Black person of colour researching with Black people.

Casing and the case-study logic

Perhaps one thing that stands out from this research is that I go from thirty-two interviews and a set of ethnographic observations, through to macro claims about the British racialised social system. Given that I used such qualitative methods, I faced the issue common to qualitative sociology of defining 'what we can say about what we've found out in our research'.[1] I want to use this section of the Appendix to flesh out the epistemological foundations of my research, which leads me to argue that my interviews and ethnographic work provide me with deep insights into the experiences of Black middle-class people living in the British racialised social system, and that the accuracy and reliability of my research lies in the wider scholarly community engaging with the premises of my research findings.

Within sociology journal articles and books, it is common to have a reflection on the authors' methodology fairly early on. Indeed, even in this book, I made a brief note to my methodology in the opening chapter. The reasons why we do this are quite clear. Importantly, it was the rise of 'Black sociology' in the early twentieth-century United States, where we see methodology chapters becoming institutionalised and prerequisites for research papers; the Atlanta School of

Appendix

sociology in the United States, founded by Du Bois, made such methodological reflections a prerequisite to resist the growing sociological literature that was simply being conducted to reproduce the (racial) status quo.[2] In other words, reflecting on methodologies was inherently linked to the sociological practice of 'disciplinary reflexivity',[3] where there emerged a wide recognition that we need to share our ways of collecting and analysing data to put our research to the trial of sociological discourse.

While appreciating this history of disciplinary reflexivity, I think it also beneficial to have an extended discussion of methodology *after* the presentation of one's research. This is because readers can then look backwards: they know the book's central arguments, they know the book's intended contributions, and they can now use this extended discussion of methodology to question the extent to which the methodology uses an epistemological framework that allows for such arguments and contributions to be made.

Case studies: analytical frames and subjects

In fact, this delay in presenting the methodology until the end of the book also reflects the general nature of (especially qualitative) sociological enquiry. Especially with case-study researchers, the logic of our method becomes more apparent to us as our research progresses. Qualitative research is often 'messy',[4] whereby 'one begins with multiple hypotheses and is confronted with a mass of hostile evidence'.[5] For case-study researchers, this means that often 'what the research subject is a "case of" may not be known until after most of the empirical part of the project is completed'.[6]

Key to the case-study logic is a split between the 'analytical frame' and the subject.[7] The analytical frame refers to a larger class of events (for example, 'war'), the subject is the empirical case that the study primarily focuses on (for example, the Korean War).[8] To discriminate between the analytical frame and subject, it is useful to reflexively ask of one's research 'what is this a case of?'.[9] In my research, this division between frame and subject became quite apparent as my research developed: while my subject was Black middle-class cultural lives, my analytical frame was the British racialised social system. As outlined throughout this book, this means that my research on Black middle-class cultural lives was more broadly '*a case of*' racial hierarchisation and the unequal distribution of cultural resources across this racial hierarchy.

The case-study logic involves two epistemological consequences. First, I rejected a *sampling logic*.[10] A sampling logic involves studying a predetermined

143

number of, and deliberately 'representative' selection of, participants. This form of sampling is focused around being able to understand descriptive trends across a given population (for example, occupational distributions of the Black middle class). However, as you can tell by now, my work is not about descriptive questions of the Black middle class inasmuch as 'asking how or why questions about processes'[11]: how do Black middle-class people resist racism through cultural consumption, why do different Black middle-class people have different patterns of cultural consumption, how do these different patterns of cultural consumption each lead to different forms of racism and/or anti-racism? Thus, I deployed a case-study logic whereby I had no predefined 'number of interviewees' to reach before I started data analysis; instead, I stopped my fieldwork at a pragmatic moment where I believed I was capable of making *logical inferences* in my research.

It is the use of *logical* rather than *statistical* inferences that is the second epistemological commitment in case-study research. Statistical inference involves inferring the properties of an overall population from a given study – it is thus necessarily connected to the 'sampling logic' maxim to study a representative sample of a given group.[12] Logical inference, contrastingly, is 'the process by which the analyst draws conclusions about the ... linkage between two or more characteristics in terms of some explanatory schema'.[13] Logical inferences thus bear similarities to Peirce's notion of 'abduction'.[14] Abduction, and logical inference, relate to the production of *tentative explanations* which can be further tested in empirical research. Case-study logic, with its focus on abduction, thus provides a 'looser generalization'[15] than quantitative logics; the aim is to use the 'force of example'[16] to build explanations about the social world, and to then invite other scholars to critique and develop your explanations.

My research thus involves logical inferences despite the lack of a 'representative sample'. The logic I ascribe to in my research is that 'empirical cases, studied in depth, lead us ... to important social processes and the details of social organization that produce them'.[17] Studying Black middle-class cultural lives enables us to learn more about the racialised social system in Britain. Just as Archimedes only needed to step in the bathtub once to achieve his 'Eureka!' moment, displaying the grander theory that the volume of water displaced is equal to the volume of his body he had submerged, sociological case studies too can be forceful as individual examples of social facts. Qualitative sociology thus aims not to conjure 'statistically representative' information, but rather, as Becker argues, it treats research as a part of a grander mosaic, whereby 'each piece added to a mosaic adds a little to our understanding of the total picture'.[18]

Judging case-study research

Given this outlined epistemology, judging the quality of a case-study project therefore goes beyond commenting on the representativeness of a sample and the ability to draw statistical inferences from this sample. Rather, the value of case studies is realised within, and through, wider sociological dialogue. As Becker's aforementioned comment signals, we work together as sociologists to all add pieces of a mosaic, aiming to collaboratively construct a 'total picture'.[19]

Given that the value of case studies is realised within their relational position within the total discipline, it is useful to think of evaluative concepts such as 'accuracy' and 'validity' through this qualitative, collaborative prism. Indeed, the notions of reliability (stability) and validity (accuracy) are useful for qualitative sociologists, so long as we re-contextualise the meanings of the terms from their quantitative bases.[20] Within the qualitative domain, validity ought to be understood not through notions of generalisability and representativeness. Rather, this validity first refers to *interpretive validity*, that is, how accurately the researcher interprets their participants' narratives and ethnographic observations.[21] Second, this validity refers to *theoretical validity*, that is, how accurately the researcher goes from what participants do (for example, a student throwing a pen at a teacher) to the grander class these actions are representative of (for example, student resistance to authority).[22] Given that there is no objective criterion for how accurate one's interpretive and theoretical interpretations are, we must realise that validity, reliability, and 'rigour' are concepts that we work towards, and never fully realise in practice.

Given that we work towards and never fully realise concepts such as validity, I argue that the judgement of qualitative sociology often relies on the author engaging with both an actual and a counter-factual audience. Flyvbjerg's comment relates to this issue when he discusses the role of the reader in the overall process of qualitative research[23]:

> Readers will have to discover their own path and truth inside the case ... readers are invited to decide the meaning of the case and to interrogate actors' and narrators' interpretations to answer that categorical question of any case study, 'What is this case a case of?'

If the reader is part of the overall validity value of one's research, then qualitative researchers can achieve 'better' research if they always write with the audience in mind. If one's writing involves rich descriptions of methods, and of how interpretations and inferences were formed, then the wider academic community are better placed to understand how the research findings interrelate to the overall research practice.

In my research, following a case-study logic meant that my data analysis was committed to the mission of 'link[ing] the empirical and the theoretical – to use theory to make sense of evidence and to use evidence to sharpen and refine theory ... to produce theoretically structured descriptions of the empirical world that are both meaningful and useful'.[24] This involved adopting an interactive research design in my data analysis.[25] This interactive design stresses a constant back-and-forth between theory and data, but also constantly triangulating one's research question, methods, data, concepts, and literature review with one another. The whole research process thus ceases to be a series of isolated tasks (coming up with a research question, deciding your methodology, doing the research, constructing theory, writing up), but rather a process whereby each of these parts are interlinked. Pursuing an interactive research design meant that my data analysis began from the moment I started my research. My original research question was 'How does racism affect the Black middle class?', which I intended to answer through the lens of the racialisation of middle-class cultural capital. As I began my fieldwork, it was evident that I needed to change my research focus to how racism *and anti-racism* affect Black middle-class cultural lives, given that so many participants formed narratives around resistance, and re-articulations of traditional middle-class culture. As my research progressed, I also realised that I ought not to only focus on 'cultural capital', but that I also need to focus on cultural repertoires to cut to the core question of why certain participants valued certain forms of cultural capital more than alternate forms, and what they were doing with this cultural capital.

As my fieldwork progressed, my data analysis accelerated. I decided to code my transcripts (on Atlas-ti) to easily spot similarities across different interviews. This meant that I would transcribe and begin coding the interviews as I conducted them. My use of early coding meant that I spotted emerging themes – such as how Black middle-class people face microaggressions in middle-class cultural spaces – and then further explored these themes in interviews and ethnographic observations. When coding my interviews, I began with very broad concepts based on interviewees' narratives. For instance, many participants talked about traditional middle-class culture as being a 'white space'. Thus, I simply coded this *in verbatim* as 'white space'. On re-reading transcripts and re-coding towards the end of my fieldwork, it was apparent that participants were using 'white space' to refer to two interrelated things – first, a physical space dominated by white people, and second, a symbolic space dominated where the cultural forms focus on white experiences. Thus, I used my interactive design, and constant comparative coding, to split the code 'white space' into 'physical white space' and 'symbolic white space'.

My coding was thus 'thematic' in that I used it to identify themes across my research. Thematic coding enabled me to see how people often iterated similar narratives and experiences despite being different in terms of ethnicity, age, or gender – thus providing individualised windows into the reality of the same racialised social system. Coding also enabled me to spot correlations between emotional responses to particular situations. For instance, the emotive state which I coded as 'feels uneasy' was regularly present when participants mentioned the 'white physical space'. Through my coding I could thus form logical inferences, presenting examples of participants having similar experiences and narratives, and then using this similarity to form understandings of macro phenomena such as racism, anti-racism, and cultural hierarchisation.

A specific way that coding helped benefit my data analysis was in constructing the triangle of identity. Coding enabled me to see how participants would draw on similar cultural repertoires throughout their interviews, to the extent that by the time I finished interviewing my thirty-two participants it was quite clear that there were three 'clusters' of Black middle-class identity. Thus, certain interviewees would regularly talk about code-switching and establishing a cultural equity with the white middle class; this became theorised into the strategic assimilation identity mode. Others regularly talked about de-racialisation and post-racialism – in terms of how they understand their own identities, and how they understand social inequalities – which became theorised into the class-minded identity mode. Lastly, others would regularly draw on repertoires of 'browning' and Afro-centrism in their interviews, regularly talking about how they 'resist' white norms, and how they stress 'Black pride' to their selves, friends, and family; this became theorised into the ethnoracial autonomous identity mode. Having coded participants' cultural repertoires, I was thus able to re-read the interviews to see how there was a rough consistency between people's cultural repertoires and their cultural consumption. Thus, code-switching was often mentioned in the context of justifying the consumption of 'white middle-class culture'; post-racialism and de-racialisation were often used to justify a lack of affinity towards 'Black' cultural forms; Afro-centrism was often used to justify a preference for Black diasporic cultural producers. To this extent, therefore, coding helped me to impose a theoretical model – built from participants' narratives – that became central to my research findings.

Similarly to my interviews, I also analysed my ethnographic data holistically. When I began my ethnographic visits, I entered spaces and simply sought to note down as many details as possible.[26] As time went on, I was able to see repeated findings, for instance that the visitors in traditional middle-class cultural spaces were overwhelmingly white, janitors and cleaners in these spaces were often Black, and Black people visiting art galleries or theatre productions based on diasporic experiences often came as families with educational motives. Indeed, I even discerned the existence of a 'racial time',[27] whereby it would take much longer to see a white person in a 'Black institution' (such as the Black Cultural Archives) compared to seeing a Black person in a 'white institution' (such as Somerset House). Through consistently hunting for a 'logic' underlying these repeated findings, I was able to move from description to analysis. In fact, I followed the ethnographic maxim that rigorous, thick description necessarily morphs *into* analysis, as you end up describing particular mechanisms and social processes at play.[28] My reasoning was that if the same realities kept occurring in particular spaces (such as audiences of traditional middle-class cultural spaces being white), then these realities are more likely to be ingrained into the logic of these spaces rather than being mere coincidence.

Reflexivity in the research process

I have argued that the value of qualitative, case-study research is often confirmed externally from the wider community of sociologists. An important implication of this, as I argued, is that as case-study researchers, we present a thick description of our data analysis to show how logical inferences were made. However, this 'thick description' of data analysis must inevitably be tied up with a description (and practice) of reflexivity, which I now turn to. However, the form of reflexivity I am endorsing stretches beyond *only* commenting on my individual position in the research process. Restricting reflexivity to such descriptive comments on one's individual location leads to a form of sociological narcissism.[29] As Bourdieu comments,[30]

> sociologists must first avoid the temptation of indulging in the type of reflexivity that could be called *narcissistic* ... because it has its own end and leads to no practical effect.

Instead, the reflexivity I imposed on my research was three-headed, divided between the individual, disciplinary, and scholastic.[31]

Appendix

Individual reflexivity

Especially within 'Black sociology', standpoint theory, and Black feminist thought, there was a turn within qualitative sociology to recognise that the position of the individual researcher within structures of power was inherently connected to the eventual research findings.[32] Such methodological debates have given rise to discussions over researching 'across difference', essentially questioning whether differently gendered and racialised researchers (e.g. men, or white people) can conduct meaningful research with those gendered or racialised otherwise (e.g. women, or Black people). Within this across-difference debate, the focus has largely been on a Black/white binary, mostly considering the question of whether 'insiders' (Black people) are better positioned than 'outsiders' (white people) to conduct research with Black people/on Blackness.

In the reification between insiders and outsiders, I find myself in a peculiar space. As a British South Asian, it is evident that I am racialised downwards in comparison to whites, especially due to Islamophobia.[33] However, we are also in a historical juncture where the previous 'political Blackness' that united diasporas from South Asia, Africa, and the Caribbean is fractured.[34] To this extent, in my research I cannot see myself as an 'insider' (a member of the 'Black middle class'), nor as a complete outsider (in terms of not being white).

My individual reflexivity thus casts light on the capricious definition of insiders and outsiders. Indeed, in his autobiography Du Bois highlighted the pernicious logic behind defining people as 'insiders' simply because of their racialised identities, commenting on his study on Black ghettoisation in Philadelphia that he 'became painfully aware that merely being born in a group, does not necessarily make one possessed of complete knowledge concerning it'.[35] Similarly, Nayak argues that defining someone as an 'insider' because they share an ethnoracial identity with their research participant(s) 'fixes' race as a static, over-determining essence to both the researcher and researched.[36] Contrastingly, Nayak shows how in his research he has 'been multiply positioned as Asian, Black, British, Indian, Scouse and, rather less ceremoniously, '"that Paki"'; he argues this is evidence of 'the ontological insecurity of all race markers'.[37]

Thus, rather than reifying myself as an insider or outsider, I found that through my individual reflexivity in the research process I was often able to achieve 'moments' of insider-ness, and moments of outsider-ness. The fact that these were 'moments' highlights how qualitative research involves a constant shift in positions and positionings from the researcher and researched.

My insider moments were often predicated around participants' drawing a boundary between 'us' and whiteness. For instance, I was discussing with Toby, a solicitor, how discourse on racism is often limited in white circles, which has a significant impact in the professional workplace. Toby commented, 'Well, you know how white people can get when you point it [racism] out.' Similar boundary drawings can be seen in a conversation I had with Miriam after our interview:

> Ali: I've been asking people at the end – when I sent you the email, who did you think it would be [turning up to the interview]?
> Miriam: Well, I saw your name – so you looked like what your name looked like. An Asian name. Why?
> Ali: Well there's a whole thing about whether people who are racialised differently can research people of different memberships.
> Miriam: Well, you know, we are a minority of brown people – we all have similar experiences really, even if we're from one continent or another. Because we're a minority here – obviously if I was in the Caribbean and you were in Asia we would have completely different experiences – but we have a British experience that's joint, that's common, people treat us the same in so many ways. I mean yeah, I mean, I haven't been followed around a gallery by security guards, but I have gone to markets, and yeah. Yeah, there's varying degrees of treatment but we all have similar experiences.

These insider moments show participants building some shared understanding of the way the world works with me. Such instances were emblematic of how the research experience itself can lead to a combined effort between the researcher and 'researched' to '[speak] back from the margins' to 'reveal how the power and the privileges of whiteness can be disrupted and an equitable landscape served'.[38] These moments thus showed me how my presence was often construed positively by my interviewees, where my research was praised for its anti-racist agenda. To help convey these positive intentions on my behalf, throughout my fieldwork I learned how to offer cues to participants that I was 'on their side' when it was appropriate. For instance, I would introduce topics of conversation by referring to my own experiences – such as being followed around art galleries by security guards – and asking if my participants had similar experiences.

I also experienced moments of outsider-ness and attempted to use this perspective of outsider-ness to avoid exaggerating tacit assumptions. These outsider moments were clearly visible in my ethnographic endeavours, where I would often be one of few non-Black people in certain spaces such as Black history walks, talks in the Black Cultural Archives, and Black professional networking events. For example, I turned up early to a Black history tour of the National Portrait Gallery and was greeted by Jacob, who I interviewed for my research a few weeks later. Jacob exclaimed 'Just the kind of demographic we need!' When he explained he meant young men, I said to him 'Oh, I thought you meant Asians!' which, after some laughter, led to a conversation on the breakdown of political Blackness and the greater acceptability that South Asians are afforded in middle-class spaces compared to Black folk. Thus, my pursuing this 'outsider moment' allowed me to engage someone in conversation with them fully knowing that I am coming from a different experiential background, but then using that different background and different experiences to highlight the intensity of racism in their own life.

Furthermore, my racialised identity was not the only 'category' which defined my insider-ness or outsider-ness. My membership at the University of Cambridge was often tantamount to my insider moments, especially when my interviewee had also attended this university. Three of my interviewees began by simply talking about their experiences of Cambridge without me asking them any question. Indeed, when I met Benjamin, an academic, in a North London café close to my home, before me 'getting a question in' he talked about Cambridge for long enough to fill two single-spaced typed pages of A4. Both Benjamin and Martin, who had both attended Cambridge, were often interested in whether Cambridge had changed that much from their own experiences several decades ago, where they were relatively isolated as the token 'Black person' in their college or degree course. In another interview with Keith, a chairman of a financial company, he immediately greeted me with a handshake and stated, 'I've always wondered what a Robinson [College] person looks like!', showing the insider-ness of the 'old boys' Oxbridge mentality.

Contrastingly, my age (being twenty-four years old for most of this research) was often a marker for outsider moments. For instance, Jacob, one of my oldest participants who is in his seventies, was recounting some of the cultural forms he grew up with as a child:

Let me give you the other side of that, I grew up with, erm, do you know who Billy Bunter is? [laughs] Do you know who Biggles is? [laughs] Dickson and Doppley? ... Ali I can see your eyes glazing up! [Laughs] So this is a pure generation thing, so like if my mates were here we'd all be here nodding [laughing] because that's what we like! [joking tone] But, for you ignorant young people!

Thus, throughout my interviews and ethnographic work, I was constantly aware of how I was shifting from moments of insider-ness and outsider-ness, and how dynamically moving between these two positions allowed for me to engage in my research simultaneously from (experientially) closer and farther distances. Naturally, some of this movement was outside my control, while sometimes I deliberately sought out positions of insider-ness or outsider-ness to collate deep narratives. This description of my individual reflexivity is intended to show my readers any possible interpretive bias in my research. Given that I am entering into a collaborative dialogue with a (hypothetical or 'real') community of critics, it also important to engage in two further forms of reflexivity which go beyond individual positioning, to discuss *sociology* and *scholasticism*.

Disciplinary reflexivity

Disciplinary reflexivity involves turning the eye back on to the discipline – in this case sociology – and questioning how this discipline itself can reproduce the status quo. This is especially pertinent in sociology, where classical and contemporary sociology have often worked to reproduce the dominant racial ideologies of their times – whether that be scientific racism, cultural racism, or colour-blindness.[39]

Within my work, disciplinary reflexivity thus guided my entire methodology as I sought to engage in a research project that contests, not reproduces, the racial status quo. My study unearths how racism is a continuing social problem which affects everyone in society (because all actors are placed in the racialised social system). I thus tailored my research question towards challenging the dominant racial order; I focus on a group who often claim to be invisible in public and political discourse, on a group who rarely appear in sociological texts and theories – the Black middle class – and I seek to ground understandings of racism through their excluded narratives.

At an epistemological level, my reflections on disciplinary reflexivity were a predominant reason that I came to adopt the aforementioned case-study logic. Such a case-study logic argues that every individual experience merits sociological attention, and that we can build sociological explanations from individualised, fragmented narratives. Such a case-study logic is thus pertinent for anti-racist research, as we can meaningfully pay attention to the multiple ways that different individuals experience, mediate, and are affected by the racialised social system without dismissing these individual experiences as disconnected from wider social processes. I thus *used* disciplinary reflexivity by pursuing this case-study epistemology, while this reflexivity also pushed me away from other means of data analysis. For instance, when I was working with the British Sociological Association (BSA) for a press release on my work in 2018, the BSA representative asked me,

> Can you say what proportion of the thirty-two said they felt uneasy at being stared at or confronted by security or other such discriminatory behaviour? ... If you're able to say roughly what proportion of your interviewees had attended some kind of cultural event and been made to feel uncomfortable ... roughly how many felt that way solely because they were the only Black people in the audience (and for no other reason), and how many because they were stared at or questioned, or overhead remarks, etc.?

While I can see a value in this approach of counting how many times participants had similar experiences, it is inconsistent with my epistemology. At an implicit level, this is an example of how certain methodologies can unintentionally reproduce the (racial) status quo through a 'White logic, White methods'[40] approach. Namely, the logic is that if *only* a minority of participants have an experience – such as being stared in an all-white space – then it does not merit sociological investigation. It reorients the 'burden of proof' on to those who suffer from social inequalities rather than aiming towards a critique of the people and structures *responsible* for this inequality.[41] Indeed, it becomes reminiscent of Toni Morrison's discussion of racism as distraction, whereby the racially subordinate have to constantly prove and refute racist tropes[42]:

> The function, the very serious function of racism is distraction. It keeps you from doing your work. It keeps you explaining, over and over again, your reason for being. Somebody says you have no language and you spend twenty years proving that you do. Somebody says your head isn't shaped properly so you have scientists working on the fact that it is. Somebody says you have no art, so you dredge that up. Somebody says you have no kingdoms, so you dredge that up. None of this is necessary. There will always be one more thing.

Expanding on Morrison's quote, racism often means that the racially subordinate have to constantly *prove* that racism exists, we have to constantly defend our experiences from structures and people who seek to downplay the continuing significance of race(ism).[43] My disciplinary reflexivity thus encouraged me to avoid pursuing forms of data analysis which are 'distracting' from my anti-racist research. I adopted a case-study epistemology which is less concerned with the burden of 'proving' that certain people have experienced racism, and more concerned with unearthing the ways that a similar social structure (the racial hierarchy) can shape different people's lives. Indeed, it is this focus on life in the 'real world' that is the focus of the final form of reflexivity.

Scholastic reflexivity

The final form of reflexivity aims to move away from 'the scholastic fallacy'.[44] The scholastic fallacy involves the researcher believing that the world they are studying is separate to the world they inhabit, consequently divorcing their understandings of the world from the lived experience of their participants.

My methodology moved me away from the scholastic idea that I was studying a 'separate world'. One of the reasons I used ethnographic methods was to distance myself from the view that my interview participants were all gatekeepers into a 'secret universe'. To find out that middle-class cultural spaces are dominated by white audiences, you do not need to meet a Black middle-class person to tell you this; you can simply go and see it for yourself. Indeed, on this very issue, many of the folk I talked to in my ethnographic work discussed 'white spaces', and how middle-class cultural spaces tend to be dominated by white audiences. This issue of white spaces is directly reminiscent of conversations I am constantly having with non-white friends at my institution at the University of Cambridge. It is therefore farcical to view my research as being in a separate universe to the one in which I live. Furthermore, as is highlighted in some autoethnographic reflections throughout my following chapters, especially in traditional middle-class spaces which were dominated by white audiences, I often fell victim to a racialised suspicion. This commonly involved security guards following me around art galleries, aggressively stopping me asking if I am lost, while I sometimes caused panic reaching into my backpack to retrieve my fieldwork journal. I have never been under such intense scrutiny as when I was waiting, on my own, by the National Gallery café to interview Jacob. Thus, the strength of racial ideologies meant I was incapable of endorsing the scholastic view that I am studying a separate world to the one in which I live, even if I wanted to.

Recognising myself as an 'enmeshed eye' rather than an 'objective I' in my research meant that I also avoided the scholastic fallacy of theorising only at a 'meta' level. Indeed, my very use of qualitative methods more broadly meant that my interpretations had to stem from the experience(s) of my study's participants. Bourdieu alludes to the efficacy of qualitative methods in avoiding scholasticism when he criticises survey methods.[45] Bourdieu's critique is that researchers often use surveys to ask participants about questions that these participants would *never* think about in their day-to-day lives, and thus are not prepared to answer.[46] In contrast to this, my own research was very firmly in an area that many of my participants had been thinking about outside of the interview setting. For instance, at the end of my interview with Ijeoma, a barrister, she mentioned how she had taught a lot of her white friends about issues faced by Black women. I thus asked her 'Out of interest do you tend to think about these issues [from the interview] quite a lot then?' She replied,

> I remember before, I went out with my ex-boyfriend – who was also white – his dad [starts laughing] we were sitting at dinner and he was like 'Ijeoma, why do you talk about race all the time?' And I remember just being like 'Because I'm thinking about it all the time!' It's such a stupid question. It's constant, it happens all the time. ... So yeah, I think about that stuff quite a lot, like all the time, you must do as well?

Ijeoma confirms that the issues discussed in the interview were not foreign to her, while her last comment 'you must do as well?' also confirms that *my position* in this research was not as an 'outsider to this universe', but rather someone who thinks about these issues both within and outside the academy. And of course, my thoughts about these issues – both within and outside the academy – are thus indebted to the many conversations I had with people throughout my fieldwork; their thoughts and experiences are the foundation of this book. Such is the nature of qualitative research – to demonstrate that research is collaborative between not only the research and other researchers, but between the researcher and the supposed 'researched'.[47]

The point of qualitative research

When conducting qualitative research, we meet a variety of people, and we get to know them. While conducting the research in this book, I helped with a participant's daughter's university coursework, I offered advice on another participant's PhD application, and I even stepped in at the last minute to help someone moderate a conference panel. The fact of the matter is that the sociologist is not the carrier of all sociological knowledge; the sociologist does not have a monopoly on the sociological. All people carry a practical knowledge of the world with them – it enables us all to act, and to comprehend our worlds. All people thus conduct their own 'folk ethnographies'[48] of the social spaces they inhabit and move through; qualitative research allows us to collate these folk ethnographies together and weave them into grander theories of processes and structures that shape the social world. Les Back summarises this simply when he remarks,[49]

> Perhaps the difference between a professor and a bus driver is that the professor can say stupid things with complete authority while the bus driver is not authorized to make brilliant insights.

Qualitative research is then, foundationally, about making sure the 'brilliant insights' into the social world get realised and recognised. Lamont and Swidler state, 'there are no good and bad techniques of data collection; there are only good and bad questions, and stronger and weaker ways of using each method'.[50] Within this chapter, I hope to have shown why my methodology was suitable for asking my research question on how racism and anti-racism affect Black middle-class cultural lives. Within this total book, I hope to have shown that this research question was worth asking in the first place.

Notes

1. Becker, 1992: 205.
2. See Du Bois, 1898; Earl Wright II, 2016.
3. For a discussion of disciplinary reflexivity, see Bourdieu, 2004; Emirbayer and Desmond, 2012; 2015; Moore, 2012.
4. Mellor, 2001.
5. Katz, 2015: 135.
6. Ragin, 1992a: 8–9.
7. Thomas, 2011.
8. Abbott, 1992; Thomas, 2011.
9. Ragin, 1992a: 6.
10. Small, 2009.
11. Small, 2009: 25.
12. Small, 2009.
13. Small, 2009: 22.
14. Peirce, 1935.
15. Thomas, 2010: 577.
16. Flyvbjerg, 2006: 228.
17. Becker, 2014: 5.

18 Becker, 2002: 80.
19 Becker, 2002.
20 As argued by Duneier, 2011; Hammersley, 2007; Katz, 2001; 2015.
21 Maxwell, 1992.
22 Maxwell, 1992.
23 Flyvbjerg, 2006: 238.
24 Ragin, 1992b: 224–225.
25 Maxwell, 1996.
26 Following the advice of Wolfinger, 2002.
27 Mills, 2014.
28 Anderson, 2011.
29 Bourdieu, 2004; Du Bois, 1898; Emirbayer and Desmond, 2012; Keith, 1992.
30 Bourdieu, 2004: 89 (italics in original).
31 Drawing on the division identified in Bourdieu, 2004; Emirbayer and Desmond, 2012; 2015.
32 Armstrong, 1979; Collins, 1986; 2000; Harding, 1987; 1991; 2004; Ladner, 1973.
33 Earle and Phillips, 2013; Meer, 2013.
34 Alexander, 2018; Andrews, 2016; Modood, 1994.
35 Du Bois, 1968: 198.
36 Nayak, 2006.
37 Nayak, 2006: 425.
38 Rollock, 2013: 492.
39 Bonilla-Silva, 2017b; Frazier, 1947; Solomos et al., 1982; Stanfield II, 2008; 2011a, b; Zuberi and Bonilla-Silva, 2008a, b.
40 Bonilla-Silva and Zuberi, 2008; Zuberi and Bonilla-Silva, 2008a.
41 Meghji, A. (Forthcoming), 'White Power, Racialized Regimes of Truth, and (In)Validity', *Sentio*, 1:1.
42 Morrison, 1975.
43 Morrison, 1975.
44 Wacquant, 2004a, b.
45 Bourdieu, 1998.
46 Bourdieu, 1998.
47 Sinha and Back, 2014.
48 Anderson, 2011: 11.
49 Back, 2007: 12.
50 Lamont and Swidler, 2014: 154.

References

Abbott, A. (1992), 'What do cases do? Some notes on activity in sociological analysis', in C. Ragin and H. S. Becker (eds), *What is a Case? Exploring the Foundations of Social Inquiry* (Cambridge: Cambridge University Press), pp. 53–82.
Achebe, C. (1996 [1959]), *Things Fall Apart* (Oxford: Heinemann).
Ahmed, S. (2007), 'A phenomenology of whiteness', *Feminist Theory*, 8:2, 149–168. 10.1177/1464700107078139.
Ahmed, S. (2012), *On Being Included: Racism and Diversity in Institutional Life* (Durham, NC: Duke University Press Books).
Ahmed, S. (2015), *The Cultural Politics of Emotion* (London: Routledge, 2nd edn).
Alexander, C. (1996), *The Art of Being Black: The Creation of Black British Youth Identities* (Oxford: Oxford University Press).
Alexander, C. (2018), 'Breaking black: the death of ethnic and racial studies in Britain', *Ethnic and Racial Studies*, 41:6, 1034–1054. 10.1080/01419870.2018.1409902.
Alexander, J. C. (2003), *The Meanings of Social Life* (Oxford: Oxford University Press).
Anderson, E. (2011), *The Cosmopolitan Canopy: Race and Civility in Everyday Life* (New York, NY: W. W. Norton & Company).
Anderson, E. (2015), '"The white space"', *Sociology of Race and Ethnicity*, 1:1, 10–21. 10.1177/2332649214561306.
Andrews, K. (2016), 'The problem of political blackness: lessons from the Black Supplementary School Movement', *Ethnic and Racial Studies*, 39:11, 2060–2078. 10.1080/01419870.2015.1131314.
Archer, L. (2011), 'Constructing minority ethnic middle-class identity: an exploratory study with parents, pupils and young professionals', *Sociology*, 45:1, 134–151. 10.1177/0038038510387187.
Armstrong, E. G. (1979), 'Black sociology and phenomenological sociology', *The Sociological Quarterly*, 20:3, 387–397.
Atkinson, R. (2000), 'Professionalization and displacement in Greater London', *Area*, 32:3, 287–295. 10.2307/20004081.
Atkinson, R. (2004), 'The evidence on the impact of gentrification: new lessons for the urban renaissance?', *International Journal of Housing Policy*, 4:1, 107–131. 10.1080/1461671042000215479.

References

Atkinson, W. (2017), *Class in the New Millennium: The Structure, Homologies and Experience of the British Social Space* (London: Routledge).

Austin, A. (2006), *Achieving Blackness: Race, Black Nationalism, and Afrocentrism in the Twentieth Century* (New York, NY: New York University Press).

Back, L. (2007), *The Art of Listening* (Oxford: Berg).

Bacqué, M-H., G. Bridge, M. Benson, T. Butler, E. Charmes, Y. Fijalkow, E. Jackson, L. Launay and S. Vermeersch (2015), *The Middle Classes and the City: A Study of Paris and London* (New York, NY: Macmillan).

Ball, S. J. (2003), *Class Strategies and the Educational Market: The Middle Classes and Social Advantage* (London: Routledge).

Ball, S. J., R. Bowe and S. Gewirtz (1996), 'School choice, social class and distinction: the realization of social advantage in education', *Journal of Education Policy*, 11:1, 89–112. 10.1080/0268093960110105.

Ball, S. J., N. Rollock, C. Vincent and D. Gillborn (2013), 'Social mix, schooling and intersectionality: identity and risk for black middle-class families', *Research Papers in Education*, 28:3, 265–288. 10.1080/02671522.2011.641998.

Banks, P. A. (2010a), 'Black cultural advancement: racial identity and participation in the arts among the black middle class', *Ethnic and Racial Studies*, 33:2, 272–289. 10.1080/01419870903121332.

Banks, P. A. (2010b), *Represent: Art and Identity Among the Black Upper-Middle Class* (New York, NY: Routledge).

Banks, P. A. (2012), 'Cultural socialization in black middle-class families', *Cultural Sociology*, 6:1, 61–73. 10.1177/1749975511427646.

Bassel, L. and A. Emejulu (2017), *Minority Women and Austerity: Survival and Resistance in France and Britain* (Bristol: Policy Press).

Becker, H. S. (1992), 'Cases, causes, conjunctures, stories, and imagery', in C. C. Ragin and H. S. Becker (eds), *What is a Case? Exploring the Foundations of Social Inquiry* (Cambridge: Cambridge University Press), pp. 205–216.

Becker, H. S. (1998), *Tricks of the Trade: How to Think About Your Research While You're Doing It* (Chicago, IL: University of Chicago Press).

Becker, H. S. (2002), 'The life history and the scientific mosaic', in D. Weinberg (ed.), *Qualitative Research Methods* (Malden, MA: Blackwell), 79–87.

Becker, H. S. (2014), *What about Mozart? What about Murder?* (Chicago, IL: Chicago University Press).

Bell, D. A. (1980), 'Brown v. Board of Education and the interest-convergence dilemma', *Harvard Law Review*, 93:3, 518–533.

Bennett, T., M. Savage, E. Silva, A. Warde, M. Gayo-Cal and D. Wright (2010), *Culture, Class, Distinction* (London: Routledge).

Benson, M. and E. Jackson (2013), 'Place-making and place maintenance: performativity, place and belonging among the middle classes', *Sociology*, 47:4, 793–809. 10.1177/0038038512454350.

Besbris, M. and S. Khan (2017), 'Less theory. More description', *Sociological Theory*, 35:2, 147–153. 10.1177/0735275117709776.

References

Bhambra, G. K. (2014), 'A sociological dilemma: race, segregation and US sociology', *Current Sociology*, 62:4, 472–492.

Bhambra, G. K. (2015), 'Black thought matters: Patricia Hill Collins and the long tradition of African American sociology', *Ethnic and Racial Studies*, 38:13, 2315–2321. 10.1080/01419870.2015.1058497.

Bhambra, G. K. (2017), 'Brexit, Trump, and "methodological whiteness": on the misrecognition of race and class', *British Journal of Sociology*, 68:1, 214–232. 10.1111/1468-4446.12317.

Bhatt, C. (2016), 'White sociology', *Ethnic and Racial Studies*, 39:3, 397–404. 10.1080/01419870.2016.1109684.

Bhopal, K. (2018), *White Privilege: The Myth of a Post-Racial Society* (Bristol: Policy Press).

Bobo, L. D. (2011), 'Somewhere between Jim Crow & post-racialism: reflections on the racial divide in America today', *Daedalus*, 140:2, 11–36. 10.1162/DAED_a_00091.

Bobo, L., J. R. Kluegel and R. A. Smith (1997), 'Laissez-faire racism: the crystallization of a kinder, gentler, antiblack ideology', *Racial Attitudes in the 1990s: Continuity and Change*, 15, 23–25.

Bonilla-Silva, E. (1997), 'Rethinking racism: toward a structural interpretation', *American Sociological Review*, 62:3, 465–480. 10.2307/2657316.

Bonilla-Silva, E. (1999), 'The essential social fact of race', *American Sociological Review*, 64:6, 899–906. 10.2307/2657410.

Bonilla-Silva, E. (2003), 'Racial attitudes or racial ideology? An alternative paradigm for examining actors' racial views', *Journal of Political Ideologies*, 8:1, 63–82. 10.1080/13569310306082.

Bonilla-Silva, E. (2010), *Racism Without Racists: Color-Blind Racism & Racial Inequality in Contemporary America* (Lanham, MD: Rowman & Littlefield, 3rd edn).

Bonilla-Silva, E. (2012), 'The invisible weight of whiteness: the racial grammar of everyday life in contemporary America', *Ethnic and Racial Studies*, 35:2, 173–194. 10.1080/01419870.2011.613997.

Bonilla-Silva, E. (2015), 'More than prejudice: restatement, reflections, and new directions in critical race theory', *Sociology of Race and Ethnicity*, 1:1, 73–87. 10.1177/2332649214557042.

Bonilla-Silva, E. (2016), 'Reply to Professor Fenelon and adding emotion to my Materialist RSS Theory', *Sociology of Race and Ethnicity*, 2:2, 243–247. 10.1177/2332649216628300.

Bonilla-Silva, E. (2017a), *Racism Without Racists: Color-Blind Racism and the Persistence of Racial Inequality in America* (Lanham, MD: Rowman & Littlefield, 5th edn).

Bonilla-Silva, E. (2017b), 'What we were, what we are, and what we should be: the racial problem of American sociology', *Social Problems*, 64:2, 179–187.

Bonilla-Silva, E. (2019), 'Feeling race: theorizing the racial economy of emotions', *American Sociological Review*, Online First. 10.1177/0003122418816958.

Bonilla-Silva, E., C. Goar and D. G. Embrick (2006), 'When whites flock together: the social psychology of white habitus', *Critical Sociology*, 32:2–3, 229–253. 10.1163/156916306777835268.

Bonilla-Silva, E. and T. Zuberi (2008), 'Towards a definition of White logic and White methods', in E. Bonilla-Silva and T. Zuberi (eds), *White Logic, White Methods* (Lanham, MD: Rowman & Littlefield), pp. 3–27.

References

Bourdieu, P. (1979), 'Les trois états du capital culturel', *Actes de la recherche en sciences sociales*, 30:1, 3–6. 10.3406/arss.1979.2654.

Bourdieu, P. (1986), 'Forms of capital', in Richardson, J. G. (ed.), *Handbook of Theory and Research for the Sociology of Education* (New York, NY: Greenwood Press), pp. 241–258.

Bourdieu, P. (1993), *The Field of Cultural Production* (Cambridge: Polity).

Bourdieu, P. (1998), *Practical Reason: On the Theory of Action* (Cambridge: Polity).

Bourdieu, P. (2004), *Science of Science and Reflexivity* (Cambridge: Polity).

Bourdieu, P. (2010), *Distinction: A Social Critique of the Judgement of Taste* (Abingdon: Routledge).

Bourdieu, P. (2013), 'Symbolic capital and social classes', *Journal of Classical Sociology*, 13:2, 292–302. 10.1177/1468795X12468736.

Bourdieu, P. and J. C. Passeron (1990), *Reproduction in Education, Society and Culture* (London: SAGE, 2nd edn).

Bourdieu, P. and L. Wacquant (1992), *An Invitation to Reflexive Sociology* (Cambridge: Polity).

Bridge, G., T. Butler and L. Lees (2012), *Mixed Communities: Gentrification by Stealth?* (Bristol: Policy Press).

Brown, C. (1984), *Black and White Britain: The Third PSI Survey* (London: Heineman Educational Books).

Brubaker, R. (2009), 'Ethnicity, race, and nationalism', *Annual Review of Sociology*, 35:1, 21–42. 10.1146/annurev-soc-070308-115916.

Brynin, M. and S. Longhi (2015), 'The effect of occupation on poverty among ethnic minority groups', *Joseph Rowntree Foundation*. Available at: http://www.jrf.org.uk/publications/effect-occupation-poverty-among-ethnic-minority-groups (Accessed: 28 May 2015).

Bull, A. (2016), 'El Sistema as a bourgeois social project: class, gender, and Victorian values', *Action, Criticism, and Theory for Music Education*, 15:1, 120–153.

Butler, T. (1997), *Gentrification and the Middle Classes* (Aldershot: Ashgate).

Butler, T. (2003), 'Living in the bubble: gentrification and its "others" in North London', *Urban Studies*, 40:12, 2469–2486. 10.1080/0042098032000136165.

Butler, T. (2007), 'Re-urbanizing London Docklands: gentrification, suburbanization or new urbanism?', *International Journal of Urban and Regional Research*, 31:4, 759–781. 10.1111/j.1468–2427.2007.00758.x.

Butler, T. and C. Hamnett (1994). 'Gentrification, class, and gender: some comments on Warden's "Gentrification as consumption"', *Environment and Planning D: Society and Space*, 12:4, 477–493. 10.1068/d120477.

Butler, T. and G. Robson (2001), 'Social capital, gentrification and neighbourhood change in London: a comparison of three South London neighbourhoods', *Urban Studies*, 38:12, 2145–2162. 10.1080/00420980120087090.

Butler, T. and G. Robson (2003a), 'Negotiating their way in: the middle classes, gentrification and the deployment of capital in a globalising metropolis', *Urban Studies*, 40:9, 1791–1809. 10.1080/0042098032000106609.

Butler, T. and G. Robson (2003b), 'Plotting the middle classes: gentrification and circuits of education in London', *Housing Studies*, 18:1, 5–28. 10.1080/0267303032000076812.

References

Campbell, P., D. O'Brien and M. Taylor (2018), 'Cultural engagement and the economic performance of the cultural and creative industries: an occupational critique', *Sociology*, Online First. 10.1177/0038038518772737.

Canham, H. and R. Williams (2017), 'Being black, middle class and the object of two gazes', *Ethnicities*, 17:1, 23–46. 10.1177/1468796816664752.

Carrigan, M. (2015), 'Life in the Accelerated Academy: anxiety thrives, demands intensify and metrics hold the tangled web together', *Impact of Social Sciences*. Available at: http://blogs.lse.ac.uk/impactofsocialsciences/2015/04/07/life-in-the-accelerated-academy-carrigan/ (Accessed: 5 April 2018).

Carter, P. L. (2003), '"Black" cultural capital, status positioning, and schooling conflicts for low-income African American youth', *Social Problems*, 50:1, 136–155. 10.1525/sp.2003.50.1.136.

CCCS (1982), *The Empire Strikes Back: Race and Racism in 70s Britain* (London: Hutchinson & Co).

Chambers, E. (2012), *Things Done Change: The Cultural Politics of Recent Black Artists in Britain* (Amsterdam: Rodopi).

Chan, T. W. and J. H. Goldthorpe (2005), 'The social stratification of theatre, dance and cinema attendance', *Cultural Trends*, 14:3, 193–212. 10.1080/09548960500436774.

Chan, T. W. and J. H. Goldthorpe (2007), 'The social stratification of cultural consumption: some policy implications of a research project', *Cultural Trends*, 16:4, 373–384. 10.1080/09548960701692787.

Clark, K. and S. Drinkwater (2007), 'Ethnic minorities in the labour market: dynamics and diversity', *Joseph Rowntree Foundation*. Available at: http://www.jrf.org.uk/publications/ethnic-minorities-labour-market-dynamics-and-diversity (Accessed: 1 September 2017).

Collins, P. H. (1986), 'Learning from the outsider within: the sociological significance of black feminist thought', *Social Problems*, 33:6, 14–32. 10.2307/800672.

Collins, P. H. (2000), *Black Feminist Thought: Knowledge, Consciousness, and the Politics of Empowerment* (New York, NY: Routledge).

Collins, P. H. (2004), *Black Sexual Politics: African Americans, Gender, and the New Racism* (New York, NY: Routledge).

Cosentino, D. J. (2000), 'Hip-hop assemblage: the Chris Ofili affair', *African Arts*, 33:1, 40–96. 10.2307/3337750.

Costa, A. E. D. (2016), 'Confounding anti-racism: mixture, racial democracy, and post-racial politics in Brazil', *Critical Sociology*, 42:4–5, 495–513. 10.1177/0896920513508663.

Crozier, G., D. Reay, D. James, F. Jamieson, P. Beedell, S. Hollingworth and K. Williams (2008), 'White middle-class parents, identities, educational choice and the urban comprehensive school: dilemmas, ambivalence and moral ambiguity', *British Journal of Sociology of Education*, 29:3, 261–272. 10.1080/01425690801966295.

Crozier, G., P. J. Burke and L. Archer (2016), 'Peer relations in higher education: raced, classed and gendered constructions and Othering', *Whiteness and Education*, 1:1, 39–53. 10.1080/23793406.2016.1164746.

Cunningham, N. and M. Savage (2015), 'The secret garden? Elite metropolitan geographies in the contemporary UK', *The Sociological Review*, 63:2, 321–348. 10.1111/1467-954X.12285.

References

Daye, S. J. (1994), *Middle-Class Blacks in Britain* (London: Macmillan Press).

De Noronha, L. (2018), 'The "Windrush generation" and "illegal immigrants" are both our kin', *Open Democracy*. Available at: https://www.opendemocracy.net/uk/luke-de-noronha/windrush-generation-and-illegal-immigrants-are-both-our-kin (Accessed: 31 May 2018).

Doane, A. 'Woody' (2017), 'Beyond color-blindness: (re) theorizing racial ideology', *Sociological Perspectives*, 60:5, 975–991. 10.1177/0731121417719697.

Du Bois, W. E. B. (1898), 'The study of the negro problems', *Annals of the American Academy of Political and Social Science*, 11, 1–23.

Du Bois, W. E. B. (1922a), 'An institute of negro literature and art', *The Crisis*, 24, 58–59.

Du Bois, W. E. B. (1922b), 'Negro art', *The Crisis*, 22, 107.

Du Bois, W. E. B. (1926), 'Criteria of negro art', *The Crisis*, 32, 290–297.

Du Bois, W. E. B. (1967 [1899]), *The Philadelphia Negro: A Social Study* (New York, NY: Schocken Books)

Du Bois, W. E. B. (1968), *The Autobiography of W. E. B. Du Bois: A Soliloquy on Viewing My Life from the Final Decade of its First Century*, ed. H. Aptheker (New York, NY: International).

Du Bois, W. E. B. (1990 [1944]), 'My evolving program for negro freedom', *Clinical Sociology Review*, 8:1, 27–57.

Du Bois, W. E. B. (2007 [1903]), *The Souls of Black Folk* (Oxford: Oxford University Press).

Du Bois, W. E. B. (2007 [1940]), *Dusk of Dawn: An Essay Toward an Autobiography of a Race Concept* (Oxford: Oxford University Press).

Du Bois, W. E. B. (2008 [1920]), 'The souls of white folk', in S. Appelrouth and L. D. Edles (eds), *Classical and Contemporary Sociological Theory: Text and Readings* (Los Angeles, CA: Pine Forge Press), pp. 305–309.

Duneier, M. (2011), 'How not to lie with ethnography', *Sociological Methodology*, 41:1, 1–11. 10.1111/j.1467–9531.2011.01249.x.

Earle, R. and C. Phillips (2013), '"Muslim is the new black": new ethnicities and new essentialisms in the prison', *Race and Justice*, 3:2, 114–129. 10.1177/2153368713483322.

Embrick, D. G., S. Domínguez and B. Karsak (2017), 'More than just insults: rethinking sociology's contribution to scholarship on racial microaggressions', *Sociological Inquiry*, 87:2, 193–206. 10.1111/soin.12184.

Emirbayer, M. and M. Desmond (2012), 'Race and reflexivity', *Ethnic and Racial Studies*, 35:4, 574–599. 10.1080/01419870.2011.606910.

Emirbayer, M. and M. Desmond (2015), *The Racial Order* (Chicago, IL: University of Chicago Press).

Equality and Human Rights Commission (2016), *Healing a Divided Britain – the Need for a Comprehensive Race Equality Strategy*. Available at: https://www.equalityhumanrights.com/sites/default/files/healing_a_divided_britain_-_the_need_for_a_comprehensive_race_equality_strategy_final.pdf (Accessed: 1 September 2017).

Evans, L. (2013), *Cabin Pressure: African American Pilots, Flight Attendants, and Emotional Labor* (Lanham, MD: Rowman & Littlefield).

Evans, L. and J. R. Feagin (2012), 'Middle-class African American pilots: the continuing significance of racism', *American Behavioral Scientist*, 56:5, 650–665. 10.1177/0002764211433804.

References

Evans, L. and J. R. Feagin (2015), 'The costs of policing violence: foregrounding cognitive and emotional labor', *Critical Sociology*, 41:6, 887–895. 10.1177/0896920515589727.

Evans, L. and W. L. Moore (2015), 'Impossible burdens: white institutions, emotional labor, and micro-resistance', *Social Problems*, 62:3, 439–454. 10.1093/socpro/spv009.

Fanon, F. (1986), *Black Skin, White Masks* (London: Pluto).

Feagin, J. R. (2006), *Systemic Racism: A Theory of Oppression* (New York, NY: Routledge).

Feagin, J. R. (2009), *The White Racial Frame: Centuries of Racial Framing and Counter-Framing* (New York, NY: Routledge).

Feagin, J. and S. Elias (2013), 'Rethinking racial formation theory: a systemic racism critique', *Ethnic and Racial Studies*, 36:6, 931–960. 10.1080/01419870.2012.669839.

Flyvbjerg, B. (2006), 'Five misunderstandings about case-study research', *Qualitative Inquiry*, 12:2, 219–245. 10.1177/1077800405284363.

Frankenberg, R. (1993), *White Women, Race Matters: The Social Construction of Whiteness* (London: Routledge).

Frazier, E. F. (1947), 'Sociological theory and race relations', *American Sociological Review*, 12:3, 265–271. 10.2307/2086515.

Frazier, E. F. (1957), *Black Bourgeoisie* (New York, NY: The Free Press).

Friedman, S. (2012), 'Cultural omnivores or culturally homeless? Exploring the shifting cultural identities of the upwardly mobile', *Poetics*, 40:5, 467–489.

Friedman, S. (2016), 'Habitus Clivé and the emotional imprint of social mobility', *The Sociological Review*, 64:1, 129–147. 10.1111/1467–954X.12280.

Friedman, S., M. Savage, L. Hanquinet and A. Miles (2015a), 'Cultural sociology and new forms of distinction', *Poetics*, 53, 1–8. 10.1016/j.poetic.2015.10.002.

Friedman, S., D. Laurison and A. Miles (2015b), 'Breaking the "class" ceiling? Social mobility into Britain's elite occupations', *The Sociological Review*, 63:2, 259–289. 10.1111/1467–954X.12283.

Fryer, P. (1984), *Staying Power: The History of Black People in Britain* (London: Pluto).

Fusco, C. (1999), 'Captain Shit and other allegories of black stardom: the work of Chris Ofili', *Nka: Journal of Contemporary African Art*, 10:1, 40–45.

Garfinkel, H. (1967), *Studies in Ethnomethodology* (Englewood Cliffs, NJ: Prentice Hall).

Gillborn, D. (2015), 'Intersectionality, critical race theory, and the primacy of racism: race, class, gender, and disability in education', *Qualitative Inquiry*, 21:3, 277–287. 10.1177/1077800414557827.

Gillborn, D., N. Rollock, C. Vincent and S. Ball (2012), '"You got a pass, so what more do you want?": race, class and gender intersections in the educational experiences of the Black middle class', *Race Ethnicity and Education*, 15:1, 121–139. 10.1080/13613324.2012.638869.

Gilroy, P. (1982), 'Steppin' out of Babylon – race, class and autonomy', in CCCS (ed.), *The Empire Strikes Back: Race and Racism in 70s Britain* (London: Hutchinson & Co.), pp. 276–314.

Gilroy, P. (1987), *There Ain't no Black in the Union Jack: The Cultural Politics of Race and Nation* (Chicago, IL: Chicago University Press).

Gilroy, P. (1990), 'The end of anti-racism', *Journal of Ethnic and Migration Studies*, 17:1, 71–83. 10.1080/1369183X.1990.9976222.

References

Gilroy, P. (1993a), *The Black Atlantic: Modernity and Double Consciousness* (Cambridge, MA: Harvard University Press).

Gilroy, P. (1993b), *Small Acts: Thoughts on the Politics of Black Cultures* (London: Serpent's Tail).

Gilroy, P. (1998), 'Race ends here', *Ethnic and Racial Studies*, 21:5, 838–847. 10.1080/014198798329676.

Gilroy, P. (2004), *After Empire: Melancholia or Convivial Culture?* (London: Routledge).

Gilroy, P. (2010), *Darker than Blue: The W. E. B. Du Bois Lectures* (Cambridge, MA: Harvard University Press).

Goddard, L. (2015), *Contemporary Black British Playwrights: Margins to Mainstream* (Basingstoke: Palgrave).

Goffman, E. (1983), 'The Interaction Order: American Sociological Association, 1982 Presidential Address', *American Sociological Review*, 48:1, 1–17. 10.2307/2095141.

Goldberg, D. T. (2009), *The Threat of Race: Reflections on Racial Neoliberalism* (Malden, MA: Wiley-Blackwell).

Grams, D. (2010), *Producing Local Color: Art Networks in Ethnic Chicago* (Chicago, IL: Chicago University Press).

Gunaratnam, Y. (2003), *Researching 'Race' and Ethnicity: Methods, Knowledge and Power* (London: SAGE).

Hall, S. (1980), 'Encoding/decoding', in S. Hall, D. Hobson and P. Willis (eds), *Culture, Media, Language Working Papers in Cultural Studies, 1972–79* (London: Routledge), pp. 117–127.

Hall, S. (1988), 'The toad in the garden: Thatcherism among the theorists', in C. Nelson and L. Grossberg (eds), *Marxism and the Interpretation of Culture* (Basingstoke: Macmillan), pp. 35–73.

Hall, S. (1993), 'What is this "black" in black popular culture?', *Social Justice*, 20:1–2, 104–114.

Hall, S. (1996), 'New ethnicities', in D. Morley and K-H. Chen (eds), *Stuart Hall: Critical Dialogues in Cultural Studies* (London: Routledge), pp. 442–451.

Hall, S. (2005), 'Assembling the 1980s: the deluge – and after', in D. A. Bailey, I. Baucom and S. Boyce (eds), *Shades of Black: Assembling Black Arts in 1980s Britain* (Durham, NC: Duke University Press), pp. 1–20.

Hall, S. (2016), *Cultural Studies 1983: A Theoretical History*, eds J. D. Slack and L. Grossberg (Durham, NC: Duke University Press).

Hall, S. (2017a), *Familiar Stranger: A Life Between Two Islands*, ed. B. Schwarz (Durham, NC: Duke University Press).

Hall, S. (2017b), *Selected Political Writings: The Great Moving Right Show and Other Essays*, eds S. Davison, D. Featherstone, M. Rustin and B. Schwarz (London: Lawrence & Wishart).

Hammersley, M. (2007), 'The issue of quality in qualitative research', *International Journal of Research & Method in Education*, 30:3, 287–305. 10.1080/17437270701614782.

Hamnett, C. (2003), 'Gentrification and the middle-class remaking of inner London, 1961–2001', *Urban Studies*, 40:12, 2401–2426. 10.1080/0042098032000136138.

Hannerz, U. (2004 [1969]), *Soulside: Inquiries into Ghetto Culture and Community* (Chicago, IL: University of Chicago Press).

References

Hanquinet, L. (2013), 'Visitors to modern and contemporary art museums: towards a new sociology of "cultural profiles"', *The Sociological Review*, 61:4, 790–813. 10.1111/1467-954X.12072.

Harding, S. (1991), *Whose Science? Whose Knowledge?: Thinking from Women's Lives* (Ithaca, NY: Cornell University Press).

Harding, S. G. (1987), *Feminism and Methodology: Social Science Issues* (Bloomington, IN: Indiana University Press).

Harding, S. G. (2004), *The Feminist Standpoint Theory Reader: Intellectual and Political Controversies* (London: Routledge).

Healy, K. (2017), 'Fuck nuance', *Sociological Theory*, 35:2, 118–127. 10.1177/0735275117709046.

Hey, A. P., A. Grimaldi-Christensen and M. Savage (2017), 'Elites in the UK: new approaches to contemporary class divisions', *Tempo Social*, 29:3, 161–179. 10.11606/0103–2070. ts.2017.125956.

Hill, J. (2018), *Learie Constantine and Race Relations in Britain and the Empire* (London: Bloomsbury).

Honneth, A. (2012), *The I in We: Studies in the Theory of Recognition* (Cambridge: Polity).

hooks, bell (2004), *The Will to Change: Men, Masculinity, and Love* (New York, NY: Simon and Schuster).

hooks, bell (2014), *Black Looks: Race and Representation* (New York, NY: Routledge).

Huber, L. P. and D. G. Solórzano (2015), 'Racial microaggressions as a tool for critical race research', *Race Ethnicity and Education*, 18:3, 297–320. 10.1080/13613324.2014.994173.

Hughey, M. W. (2010), 'The (dis)similarities of white racial identities: the conceptual framework of "hegemonic whiteness"', *Ethnic and Racial Studies*, 33:8, 1289–1309. 10.1080/01419870903125069

Hughey, M. W., D. G. Embrick and A. 'Woody' Doane (2015), 'Paving the way for future race research: exploring the racial mechanisms within a color-blind, racialized social system', *American Behavioral Scientist*, 59:11, 1347–1357. 10.1177/0002764215591033.

Hughey, M. W., J. Rees, D. R. Goss, M. L. Rosino and E. Lesser (2017), 'Making everyday microaggressions: an exploratory experimental vignette study on the presence and power of racial microaggressions', *Sociological Inquiry*, 87:2, 303–336. 10.1111/soin.12167.

Hunter, M. A. (2017), 'Racial physics or a theory for everything that happened', *Ethnic and Racial Studies*, 40:8, 1173–1183. 10.1080/01419870.2017.1285040.

Hyra, D. S. (2017), *Race, Class, and Politics in the Cappuccino City* (Chicago, IL: University of Chicago Press).

Imoagene, O. (2012), 'Being British vs being American: identification among second-generation adults of Nigerian descent in the US and UK', *Ethnic and Racial Studies*, 35:12, 2153–2173. 10.1080/01419870.2011.631556.

Imoagene, O. (2017), *Beyond Expectations: Second-Generation Nigerians in the United States and Britain* (Oakland, CA: University of California Press).

Jackson, E. (2019), 'Valuing the bowling alley: contestations over the preservation of spaces of everyday urban multiculture in London', *The Sociological Review*, 67:1, 79–94. 10.1177/0038026118772784.

References

Jackson, E. and T. Butler (2015), 'Revisiting "social tectonics": the middle classes and social mix in gentrifying neighbourhoods', *Urban Studies*, 52:13, 2349–2365. 10.1177/0042098014547370.

James, C. L. R. (1963), *Beyond A Boundary* (London: Stanley Paul & Co).

Jerolmack, C. and S. Khan (2014), 'Talk is cheap: ethnography and the attitudinal fallacy', *Sociological Methods & Research*, 43:2, 178–209.

Jones, C. (1949), 'We seek full equality for all women', *Daily Worker* (4 September 1949).

Jones, H., Y. Gunaratnam, G. Bhattacharyya, W. Davies, S. Dhaliwal, K. Forkert, R. Saltus and E. Jackson (2017), *Go Home?: The Politics of Immigration Controversies* (Manchester: Manchester University Press).

Joseph-Salisbury, R. (2018), '"Does anybody really care what a racist says?" Anti-racism in "post-racial" times', *The Sociological Review*, Online First. 10.1177/0038026118807672.

Kapoor, N. (2011), 'The advancement of racial neoliberalism in Britain', *Ethnic and Racial Studies*, 36:6, 1028–1046. 10.1080/01419870.2011.629002.

Katz, J. (2001), 'From how to why: on luminous description and causal inference in ethnography (Part I)', *Ethnography*, 2:4, 443–473. 10.1177/146613801002004001.

Katz, J. (2015), 'A theory of qualitative methodology: the social system of analytic fieldwork', *Méthod(e)s: African Review of Social Sciences Methodology*, 1:1–2, 131–146. 10.1080/23754745.2015.1017282.

Keith, M. (1992), 'Angry writing: (re)presenting the unethical world of the ethnographer', *Environment and Planning D: Society and Space*, 10:5, 551–568. 10.1068/d100551.

Khan, S. R. (2010), *Privilege: The Making of an Adolescent Elite at St. Paul's School* (Princeton, NJ: Princeton University Press).

Khattab, N. (2016), 'The ethno-religious wage gap within the British salariat class: how severe is the penalty?', *Sociology*, 50:4, 813–824. 10.1177/0038038515575865.

Lacy, K. R. (2006), 'Black spaces, black places: strategic assimilation and identity construction in middle-class suburbia', *Ethnic and Racial Studies*, 27:6, 908–930. 10.1080/0141987042000268521.

Lacy, K. R. (2007), *Blue-Chip Black: Race, Class, and Status in the New Black Middle Class* (Berkeley, CA: University of California Press).

Ladner, J. A. (1973), *The Death of White Sociology: Essays on Race and Culture* (Baltimore, MD: Black Classic Press).

Lamont, M. (1992), *Money, Morals, and Manners: The Culture of the French and the American Upper-Middle Class* (Chicago, IL: University of Chicago Press).

Lamont, M. (2000a), 'Meaning-making in cultural sociology: broadening our agenda', *Contemporary Sociology*, 29:4, 602–607. 10.2307/2654561.

Lamont, M. (2000b), *The Dignity of Working Men: Morality and the Boundaries of Race, Class, and Immigration* (New York, NY: Russell Sage Foundation).

Lamont, M. (2000c), 'The rhetorics of racism and anti-racism in France and the United States', in M. Lamont and L. Thévenot (eds), *Rethinking Comparative Cultural Sociology* (Cambridge: Cambridge University Press), pp. 25–55.

Lamont, M. (2004), 'A life of sad, but justified, choices: interviewing across (too) many divides', in M. Bulmer and J. Solomos (eds), *Researching Race and Racism* (London: Routledge), pp. 162–171.

References

Lamont, M. (2018), 'Addressing recognition gaps: destigmatization and the reduction of inequality', *American Sociological Review*, 83:3, 419–444. 10.1177/0003122418773775.

Lamont, M. and C. M. Fleming (2005), 'Everyday antiracism: competence and religion in the cultural repertoire of the African American elite', *Du Bois Review*, 2:1, 29–43.

Lamont, M. and A. Lareau (1988), 'Cultural capital: allusions, gaps and glissandos in recent theoretical developments', *Sociological Theory*, 6:2, 153–168.

Lamont, M. and V. Molnár (2001), 'How blacks use consumption to shape their collective identity: evidence from marketing specialists', *Journal of Consumer Culture*, 1:1, 31–45. 10.1177/146954050100100103.

Lamont, M. and V. Molnár (2002), 'The study of boundaries in the social sciences', *Annual Review of Sociology*, 28:1, 167–195. 10.1146/annurev.soc.28.110601.141107.

Lamont, M., G. M. Silva, J. S. Welburn, J. Guetzkow, N. Mizrachi, H. Herzog and E. Reis (2016), *Getting Respect: Responding to Stigma and Discrimination in the United States, Brazil, and Israel* (Princeton, NJ: Princeton University Press).

Lamont, M., G. M. Silva, J. S. Welburn, J. Guetzkow, N. Mizrachi, H. Herzog and E. Reis (2017), 'From the study of racism to destigmatization and the transformation of group boundaries', *Ethnic and Racial Studies*, 40:8, 1287–1297. 10.1080/01419870.2017.1303183.

Lamont, M. and A. Swidler (2014), 'Methodological pluralism and the possibilities and limits of interviewing', *Qualitative Sociology*, 37:2, 153–171.

Landry, B. (1987), *The New Black Middle Class* (Berkeley, CA: University of California Press).

Laurison, D. and S. Friedman (2016), 'The class pay gap in higher professional and managerial occupations', *American Sociological Review*, 81:4, 668–695. 10.1177/0003122416653602.

Lawler, S. (2012), 'White like them: whiteness and anachronistic space in representations of the English white working class', *Ethnicities*, 12:4, 409–426. 10.1177/1468796812448019.

Lefebvre, H. (2004), *Rhythmanalysis: Space, Time and Everyday Life* (London: Continuum).

Lessard-Phillips, L., V. Boliver, M. Pampaka and D. Swain (2018), 'Exploring ethnic differences in the post-university destinations of Russell Group graduates', *Ethnicities*, 1–22. 10.1177/1468796818777543.

Lewis, A. (2004), '"What group?" Studying whites and whiteness in the era of "color-blindness"', *Sociological Theory*, 22:4, 623–646. 10.1111/j.0735–2751.2004.00237.x.

Lewis, L. A. (2012), *Chocolate and Corn Flour: History, Race, and Place in the Making of 'Black' Mexico* (Durham, NC: Duke University Press).

Li, Y. (2015), 'Ethnic minority unemployment in hard times', *Runnymede Trust*, 35–37. Available at: https://www.research.manchester.ac.uk/portal/files/32380913/FULL_TEXT.PDF (Accessed: 6 April 2018).

Li, Y. and A. Heath (2008), 'Minority ethnic men in British labour market (1972-2005)', *International Journal of Sociology and Social Policy*, 28:5/6, 231–244. 10.1108/01443330810881277.

Li, Y., M. Savage and A. Warde (2008), 'Social mobility and social capital in contemporary Britain', *British Journal of Sociology*, 59:3, 391–411. 10.1111/j.1468–4446.2008.00200.x.

Lipsitz, G. (1998), *The Possessive Investment in Whiteness: How White People Profit from Identity Politics* (Philadelphia, PA: Temple University Press).

Lipsitz, G. (2007), 'The racialization of space and the spatialization of race theorizing the hidden architecture of landscape', *Landscape Journal*, 26:1, 10–23. 10.3368/lj.26.1.10.

References

Lorde, A. (1997 [1981]), 'The uses of anger', *Women's Studies Quarterly*, 25:1/2, 278–285.

Lorimer, D. (1978), *Colour, Class and the Victorians* (Leicester: Leicester University Press).

Lorimer, D. (2003), 'Reconstructing Victorian racial discourse: images of race, the language of race relations, and the context of black resistance', in G. H. Gerzina (ed.), *Black Victorians/Black Victoriana* (New Brunswick: Rutgers University Press), pp. 187–207.

Maxwell, J. A. (1992), 'Understanding and validity in qualitative research', *Harvard Educational Review*, 62:3, 279–300.

Maxwell, J. A. (1996), *Qualitative Research Design: An Interactive Approach* (Thousand Oaks, CA: SAGE).

McLennan, G. (2005), 'The "New American Cultural Sociology": an appraisal', *Theory, Culture & Society*, 22:6, 1–18. 10.1177/0263276405059411.

Meer, N. (2013), 'Racialization and religion: race, culture and difference in the study of antisemitism and Islamophobia', *Ethnic and Racial Studies*, 36:3, 385–398. 10.1080/01419870.2013.734392.

Meer, N. (2018), 'W. E. B. Du Bois, double consciousness and the "spirit" of recognition', *The Sociological Review*, Online First. 10.1177/0038026118765370.

Meghji, A. (2017a), 'Positionings of the Black middle classes: understanding identity construction beyond strategic assimilation', *Ethnic and Racial Studies*, 40:6, 1007–1025. 10.1080/01419870.2016.1201585.

Meghji, A. (2017b), 'Encoding and decoding Black and White cultural capitals: Black middle-class experiences', *Cultural Sociology*, Online First, 1–17. 10.1177/1749975517741999.

Meghji, A. (2017c), 'A relational study of the Black middle classes and globalised White hegemony: identities, interactions, and ideologies in the United States, United Kingdom, and South Africa', *Sociology Compass*, 11:9. 10.1111/soc4.12504.

Meghji, A. (2018), 'Activating controlling images in the racialized interaction order: Black middle-class interactions and the creativity of racist action', *Symbolic Interaction*, Online First. 10.1002/symb.398.

Meghji, A. (forthcoming), *Race and Class in 21st-Century Britain: Towards Racialised Class Formation* (London: Palgrave).

Meghji, A. and R. Saini (2018), 'Rationalising racial inequality: ideology, hegemony and post-racialism among the Black and South Asian middle classes', *Sociology*, 52:4, 671–687. 10.1177/0038038517726645.

Mellor, N. (2001), 'Messy method: the unfolding story', *Educational Action Research*, 9:3, 465–484. 10.1080/09650790100200166.

Mills, C. W. (1997), *The Racial Contract* (Ithaca, NY: Cornell University Press).

Mills, C. W. (1998), *Blackness Visible: Essays on Philosophy and Race* (Ithaca, NY: Cornell University Press).

Mills, C. W. (2014), 'White time: the chronic injustice of ideal theory', *Du Bois Review: Social Science Research on Race*, 11:1, 27–42. 10.1017/S1742058X14000022.

Mills, C. W. (2017), *Black Rights/White Wrongs: The Critique of Racial Liberalism* (New York, NY: Oxford University Press).

Modood, T. (1994), 'Political blackness and British Asians', *Sociology*, 28:4, 859–876. 10.1177/0038038594028004004.

References

Moore, K. S. (2008), 'Class formations: competing forms of black middle-class identity', *Ethnicities*, 8:4, 492–517. 10.1177/1468796808097075.

Moore, W. L. (2007), *Reproducing Racism: White Space, Elite Law Schools, and Racial Inequality* (Lanham, MD: Rowman & Littlefield).

Moore, W. L. (2012), 'Reflexivity, power, and systemic racism', *Ethnic and Racial Studies*, 35:4, 614–619. 10.1080/01419870.2011.630097.

Moreno Figueroa, M. G. (2010), 'Distributed intensities: whiteness, mestizaje and the logics of Mexican racism', *Ethnicities*, 10:3, 387–401. 10.1177/1468796810372305.

Morrison, T. (1975), 'A humanistic view', in *Public Dialogue on the American Dream Theme* (Portland, OR: Portland State University). Available at: https://soundcloud.com/portland-state-library/portland-state-black-studies-1 (Accessed: 6 June 2018).

Mueller, J. C. (2017), 'Producing colorblindness: everyday mechanisms of white ignorance', *Social Problems*, 64:2, 219–238. 10.1093/socpro/spw061.

Mueller, J. C. (2018), 'Advancing a sociology of ignorance in the study of racism and racial non-knowing', *Sociology Compass*, 12:8. 10.1111/soc4.12600.

Nayak, A. (2006), 'After race: ethnography, race and post-race theory', *Ethnic and Racial Studies*, 29:3, 411–430. 10.1080/01419870600597818.

Nayak, A. (2007), 'Critical whiteness studies', *Sociology Compass*, 1:2, 737–755. 10.1111/j.1751–9020.2007.00045.x.

Nayak, A. (2011), 'Geography, race and emotions: social and cultural intersections', *Social & Cultural Geography*, 12:6, 548–562. 10.1080/14649365.2011.601867.

Neal, S., K. Bennett, A. Cochrane and G. Mohan (2013), 'Living multiculture: understanding the new spatial and social relations of ethnicity and multiculture in England', *Environment and Planning C: Government and Policy*, 31:2, 308–323. 10.1068/c11263r.

O'Brien, D., D. Laurison, A. Miles and S. Friedman (2016), 'Are the creative industries meritocratic? An analysis of the 2014 British Labour Force Survey', *Cultural Trends*, 25:2, 116–131. 10.1080/09548963.2016.1170943.

Office for National Statistics; National Records of Scotland; Northern Ireland Statistics and Research Agency (2016): 2011 Census aggregate data. UK Data Service (June 2016 edn). Available at: http://dx.doi.org/10.5257/census/aggregate-2011-1 (Accessed: 1 January 2018).

Omi, M. and H. Winant (2015), *Racial Formation in the United States* (New York, NY: Routledge, 3rd edn).

Oría, A., A. Cardini, S. Ball, E. Stamou, M. Kolokitha, S. Vertigan and C. Flores-Moreno (2007), 'Urban education, the middle classes and their dilemmas of school choice', *Journal of Education Policy*, 22:1, 91–105. 10.1080/02680930601065791.

Pachucki, M. A., S. Pendergrass and M. Lamont (2007), 'Boundary processes: Recent theoretical developments and new contributions', *Poetics*, 35:6, 331–351. 10.1016/j.poetic.2007.10.001.

Parker, J. (2016), *A Report into the Ethnic Diversity of UK Boards*. Available at: https://www.gov.uk/government/publications/ethnic-diversity-of-uk-boards-the-parker-review (Accessed: 12 January 2017).

References

Parveen, N. and H. Sherwood (2016), 'Police log fivefold rise in race-hate complaints since Brexit result', *Guardian*. Available at: http://www.theguardian.com/world/2016/jun/30/police-report-fivefold-increase-race-hate-crimes-since-brexit-result (Accessed: 8 June 2018).

Pattillo, M. (2013), *Black Picket Fences: Privilege and Peril among the Black Middle Class* (Chicago, IL: University of Chicago Press, 2nd edn).

Peacock, D. K. (2015), 'The social and political context of black British theatre: the 2000s', in M. F. Brewer, L. Goddard and D. Osborne (eds), *Modern and Contemporary Black British Drama* (London: Palgrave), pp. 147–160.

Peirce, C. S. (1935), *Collected Papers of Charles Sanders Peirce, Volumes V and VI: Pragmatism and Pragmaticism and Scientific Metaphysics*, eds C. Hartshorne and P. Weiss (Cambridge, MA: Harvard University Press).

Pierce, J. L. (2003), '"Racing for innocence": whiteness, corporate culture, and the backlash against affirmative action', *Qualitative Sociology*, 26:1, 53–70. 10.1023/A:1021404020349.

Power, S., T. Edwards, G. Whitty and V. Wigfall (2003), *Education in the Middle Class* (Buckingham: Open University Press).

Prieur, A. and M. Savage (2013), 'Emerging forms of cultural capital', *European Societies*, 15:2, 246–267. 10.1080/14616696.2012.748930.

Putnam, R. D. (2001), *Bowling Alone: The Collapse and Revival of American Community* (New York, NY: Simon and Schuster).

Puwar, N. (2004), *Space Invaders: Race, Gender and Bodies Out of Place* (Oxford: Berg).

Ragin, C. C. (1992a), '"Casing" and the process of social inquiry', in C. C. Ragin and H. S. Becker (eds), *What is a Case? Exploring the Foundations of Social Inquiry* (Cambridge: Cambridge University Press), pp. 217–226.

Ragin, C. C. (1992b), 'Introduction: cases of "What is a case?"', in C. C. Ragin and H. S. Becker (eds), *What is a Case? Exploring the Foundations of Social Inquiry* (Cambridge: Cambridge University Press), pp. 1–18.

Ramdin, R. (2017), *The Making of the Black Working Class in Britain* (London: Verso Books).

Raveaud, M. and A. van Zanten (2007), 'Choosing the local school: middle-class parents' values and social and ethnic mix in London and Paris', *Journal of Education Policy*, 22:1, 107–124. 10.1080/02680930601065817.

Rawls, A. W. (2000), '"Race" as an interaction order phenomenon: W. E. B. Du Bois's "double consciousness" thesis revisited', *Sociological Theory*, 18:2, 241–274. 10.1111/0735-2751.00097.

Rawls, A. W. and W. Duck (2017), '"Fractured reflections" of high-status black male presentations of self: nonrecognition of identity as a "tacit" form of institutional racism', *Sociological Focus*, 50:1, 36–51. 10.1080/00380237.2016.1218215.

Ray, V. and L. Seamster (2016), 'Rethinking racial progress: a response to Wimmer', *Ethnic and Racial Studies*, 39:8, 1361–1369. 10.1080/01419870.2016.1151540.

Ray, V. E., A. Randolph, M. Underhill and D. Luke (2017), 'Critical race theory, Afro-pessimism, and racial progress narratives', *Sociology of Race and Ethnicity*, 3:2, 147–158. 10.1177/2332649217692557.

Reay, D. (1998), *Class Work: Mothers' Involvement in Their Children's Schooling* (London: University College Press).

References

Reay, D. (2007), '"Unruly places": inner-city comprehensives, middle-class imaginaries and working-class children', *Urban Studies*, 44:7, 1191–1201. 10.1080/00420980701302965.

Reay, D. (2008), 'Psychosocial aspects of white middle-class identities: desiring and defending against the class and ethnic "other" in urban multi-ethnic schooling', *Sociology*, 42:6, 1072–1088. 10.1177/0038038508096934.

Reay, P. D., D. G. Crozier and D. James (2011), *White Middle-Class Identities and Urban Schooling* (Basingstoke: Palgrave Macmillan).

Reay, D., G. Crozier, D. James, S. Hollingworth, K. Williams, F. Jamieson and P. Beedell (2008), 'Re-invigorating democracy?: White middle-class identities and comprehensive schooling', *The Sociological Review*, 56:2, 238–255. 10.1111/j.1467-954X.2008.00786.x.

Reay, D., S. Hollingworth, K. Williams, G. Crozier, F. Jamieson, D. James and P. Beedell (2007), '"A darker shade of pale?" Whiteness, the middle classes and multi-ethnic inner city schooling', *Sociology*, 41:6, 1041–1060. 10.1177/0038038507082314.

Reeves, A. and R. de Vries (2018), 'Can cultural consumption increase future earnings? Exploring the economic returns to cultural capital', *British Journal of Sociology*, Online First. 10.1111/1468-4446.12374.

Robinson, V. and R. Valeny (2005), 'Ethnic minorities, employment, self-employment, and social mobility in postwar Britain', in G. C. Loury, T. Modood and S. M. Teles (eds), *Ethnicity, Social Mobility, and Public Policy: Comparing the USA and UK* (Cambridge: Cambridge University Press), pp. 414–448.

Rollock, N. (2012a), 'The invisibility of race: intersectional reflections on the liminal space of alterity', *Race Ethnicity and Education*, 15:1, 65–84. 10.1080/13613324.2012.638864.

Rollock, N. (2012b), 'Unspoken rules of engagement: navigating racial microaggressions in the academic terrain', *International Journal of Qualitative Studies in Education*, 25:5, 517–532. 10.1080/09518398.2010.543433.

Rollock, N. (2013), 'A political investment: revisiting race and racism in the research process', *Discourse: Studies in the Cultural Politics of Education*, 34:4, 492–509. 10.1080/01596306.2013.822617.

Rollock, N. (2014), 'Race, class and "the harmony of dispositions"', *Sociology*, 48:3, 445–451. 10.1177/0038038514521716.

Rollock, N., D. Gillborn, C. Vincent and S. Ball (2011), 'The public identities of the black middle classes: managing race in public spaces', *Sociology*, 45:6, 1078–1093. 10.1177/0038038511416167.

Rollock, N., D. Gillborn, C. Vincent and S. Ball (2013), '"Middle class by profession": class status and identification amongst the Black middle classes', *Ethnicities*, 13:3, 253–275. 10.1177/1468796812467743.

Rollock, N., D. Gillborn, C. Vincent and S. Ball (2015), *The Colour of Class: The Educational Strategies of the Black Middle Classes* (London: Routledge).

Rose, T. (1994), *Black Noise: Rap Music and Black Culture in Contemporary America* (Hanover, NH: Wesleyan University Press).

Rosino, M. L. (2017), 'Dramaturgical domination: the genesis and evolution of the racialized interaction order', *Humanity & Society*, 41:2, 158–181. 10.1177/0160597615623042.

Saha, A. (2016), 'The rationalizing/racializing logic of capital in cultural production', *Media Industries Journal*, 3:1. http://dx..org/10.3998/mij.15031809.0003.101.

References

Saha, A. (2018), *Race and the Cultural Industries* (Cambridge: Polity).

Savage, M. (2015a), *Social Class in the 21st Century* (London: Pelican).

Savage, M. (2015b), 'Introduction to elites from the "problematic of the proletariat" to a class analysis of "wealth elites"', *The Sociological Review*, 63:2, 223–239. 10.1111/1467-954X.12281.

Savage, M., G. Bagnall and B. Longhurst (2001), 'Ordinary, ambivalent and defensive: class identities in the northwest of England', *Sociology*, 35:4, 875–892. 10.1177/0038038501035004005.

Savage, M., F. Devine, N. Cunningham, M. Taylor, Y. Li, J. Hjellbrekke, B. L. Roux, S. Friedman and A. Miles (2013), 'A new model of social class? Findings from the BBC's Great British Class Survey Experiment', *Sociology*, 47:2, 219–250. 10.1177/0038038513481128.

Silva, E. (2006), 'Distinction through visual art', *Cultural Trends*, 15:2–3, 141–158. 10.1080/09548960600712942.

Silva, E. (2008), 'Cultural capital and visual art in the contemporary UK', *Cultural Trends*, 17:4, 267–287. 10.1080/09548960802615414.

Silva, E. (2015), 'Class in contemporary Britain: comparing the Cultural Capital and Social Exclusion (CCSE) project and the Great British Class Survey (GBCS)', *The Sociological Review*, 63:2, 373–392. 10.1111/1467-954X.12286.

Sinha, S. and L. Back (2014), 'Making methods sociable: dialogue, ethics and authorship in qualitative research', *Qualitative Research*, 14:4, 473–487. 10.1177/1468794113490717.

Sivanandan, A. (1976), 'Race, class and the state: the black experience in Britain', *Race & Class*, 17:4, 347–368. 10.1177/030639687601700401.

Sivanandan, A. (1985), 'RAT and the degradation of black struggle', *Race & Class*, 26:4, 1–33. 10.1177/030639688502600401.

Skeggs, B. (1997), *Formations of Class and Gender* (London: SAGE).

Small, M. L. (2009), '"How many cases do I need?": On science and the logic of case selection in field-based research', *Ethnography*, 10:1, 5–38. 10.1177/1466138108099586.

Soja, E. W. (1980), 'The socio-spatial dialectic', *Annals of the Association of American Geographers*, 70:2, 207–225.

Soja, E. W. (1989), *Postmodern Geographies: The Reassertion of Space in Critical Social Theory* (London: Verso).

Solomos, J. (2003), *Race and Racism in Britain* (Basingstoke: Palgrave Macmillan, 3rd edn).

Solomos, J., B. Findlay, S. Jones and P. Gilroy (1982), 'The organic crisis of British capitalism and race: the experience of the seventies', in CCCS (ed.), *The Empire Strikes Back: Race and Racism in 70s Britain* (London: Hutchinson & Co), pp. 9–46.

Song, M. (2014), 'Challenging a culture of racial equivalence', *British Journal of Sociology*, 65:1, 107–129. 10.1111/1468-4446.12054.

de Sousa Santos, B. (2001), 'Nuestra America: reinventing a subaltern paradigm of recognition and redistribution', *Theory, Culture & Society*, 18:2–3, 185–217. 10.1177/02632760122051706.

Stanfield II, J. H. (2008), 'The gospel of feel-good sociology: race relations as pseudoscience and the decline in the relevance of American Academic Sociology in the twenty-first century', in T. Zuberi and E. Bonilla-Silva (eds), *White Logic, White Methods: Racism and Methodology* (Lanham, MD: Rowman & Littlefield), pp. 271–282.

References

Stanfield II, J. H. (2011a), *Black Reflective Sociology: Epistemology, Theory, and Methodology* (Walnut Creek, CA: Left Coast Press).

Stanfield II, J. H. (2011b), *Historical Foundations of Black Reflective Sociology* (Walnut Creek, CA: Left Coast Press).

St John, G. (2003), 'Post-rave technotribalism and the carnival of protest', in D. Muggleton and R. Weinzierl (eds), *The Post-Subcultures Reader* (Oxford: Berg), pp. 65–82.

Swidler, A. (1986), 'Culture in action: symbols and strategies', *American Sociological Review*, 51:2, 273–286.

Tate, S. (2013), 'The performativity of black beauty shame in Jamaica and its diaspora: problematising and transforming beauty iconicities', *Feminist Theory*, 14:2, 219–235. 10.1177/1464700113483250.

Telles, E. (2006), *Race in Another America: The Significance of Skin Color in Brazil* (Princeton, NJ: Princeton University Press).

Thomas, G. (2010), 'Doing case study: abduction not induction, phronesis not theory', *Qualitative Inquiry*, 16:7, 575–582. 10.1177/1077800410372601.

Thomas, G. (2011), 'A typology for the case study in social science following a review of definition, discourse, and structure', *Qualitative Inquiry*, 17:6, 511–521. 10.1177/1077800411409884.

Trades Union Congress (2016), 'Black workers with degrees earn a quarter less than white counterparts, finds TUC'. Available at: https://www.tuc.org.uk/equality-issues/black-workers/labour-market/black-workers-degrees-earn-quarter-less-white (Accessed: 6 April 2018).

Trades Union Congress (2017), 'Insecure work and ethnicity'. Available at: https://www.tuc.org.uk/research-analysis/reports/insecure-work-and-ethnicity (Accessed 1 September 2018).

Turner, B. (2009), 'Introduction: a new agenda for social theory?', in B. Turner (ed.), *The New Blackwell Companion To Social Theory* (Malden, MA: Wiley-Blackwell), pp. 1–16.

Veblen, T. (2005 [1899]), *The Theory of the Leisure Class: An Economic Study of Institutions* (Delhi: Aakar Books).

Vincent, C. and S. J. Ball (2007), '"Making up" the middle-class child: families, activities and class dispositions', *Sociology*, 41:6, 1061–1077. 10.1177/0038038507082315.

Vincent, C., S. Ball, N. Rollock and D. Gillborn (2013), 'Three generations of racism: black middle-class children and schooling', *British Journal of Sociology of Education*, 34:5–6, 929–946. 10.1080/01425692.2013.816032.

Vincent, C., N. Rollock, S. Ball and D. Gillborn (2011), *The Educational Strategies of the Black Middle Classes*, ESRC RES-062–23–1880sk (London: Institute of Education), pp. 1–21.

Vincent, C., N. Rollock, S. Ball and D. Gillborn (2012a), 'Being strategic, being watchful, being determined: black middle-class parents and schooling', *British Journal of Sociology of Education*, 33:3, 337–354. 10.1080/01425692.2012.668833.

Vincent, C., N. Rollock, S. Ball and D. Gillborn (2012b), 'Intersectional work and precarious positionings: black middle-class parents and their encounters with schools in England', *International Studies in Sociology of Education*, 22:3, 259–276. 10.1080/09620214.2012.744214.

Vincent, C., N. Rollock, S. Ball and D. Gillborn (2013), 'Raising middle-class black children: parenting priorities, actions and strategies', *Sociology*, 47:3, 427–442. 10.1177/0038038512454244.

Virdee, S. (2000), 'A Marxist critique of black radical theories of trade-union racism', *Sociology*, 34:3, 545–565.

Virdee, S. (2014a), *Racism, Class and the Racialized Outsider* (Basingstoke: Palgrave).

Virdee, S. (2014b), 'Challenging the empire', *Ethnic and Racial Studies*, 37:10, 1823–1829. 10.1080/01419870.2014.932408.

Virdee, S. (2017), 'The second sight of racialised outsiders in the imperialist core', *Third World Quarterly*, 38:11, 2396–2410. 10.1080/01436597.2017.1328274.

Wacquant, L. (1992), 'Making class: the middle class(es) in social theory and social structure', in R. F. Levine and S. G. McNall (eds), *Bringing Class Back In* (Boulder, CO: Westview Press), pp. 39–64.

Wacquant, L. (2004a), *Body & Soul: Notebooks of an Apprentice Boxer* (New York, NY: Oxford University Press).

Wacquant, L. (2004b), 'Following Pierre Bourdieu into the field', *Ethnography*, 5:4, 387–414. 10.1177/1466138104052259.

Wacquant, L. and A. Akçaoğlu (2017), 'Practice and symbolic power in Bourdieu: The view from Berkeley', *Journal of Classical Sociology*, 17:1, 55–69. 10.1177/1468795X16682145.

Wakeling, P. and M. Savage (2015), 'Entry to elite positions and the stratification of higher education in Britain', *The Sociological Review*, 63:2, 290–320. 10.1111/1467-954X.12284.

Wallace, D. (2015), 'Re-interpreting Bourdieu, belonging and black identities: exploring "black" cultural capital among black Caribbean youth in London', in J. Thatcher, N. Ingram, C. Burke and J. Abrahams (eds), *Bourdieu: The Next Generation: The Development of Bourdieu's Intellectual Heritage in Contemporary UK Sociology* (London: Routledge), pp. 37–54.

Wallace, D. (2017), 'Reading "race" in Bourdieu? Examining black cultural capital among black Caribbean youth in South London', *Sociology*, 51:5, 907–923. 10.1177/0038038516643478.

Wallace, D. (2018), 'Cultural capital as whiteness? Examining logics of ethno-racial representation and resistance', *British Journal of Sociology of Education*, 39:4, 466–482. 10.1080/01425692.2017.1355228.

Warde, A. (2011), 'Cultural hostility re-considered', *Cultural Sociology*, 5:3, 341–366. 10.1177/1749975510387755.

Warde, A. and T. Bennett (2008), 'A culture in common: the cultural consumption of the UK managerial elite', *The Sociological Review*, 56:1, 240–259. 10.1111/j.1467-954X.2008.00770.x.

Warde, A. and M. Gayo-Cal (2009), 'The anatomy of cultural omnivorousness: the case of the United Kingdom', *Poetics*, 37:2, 119–145. 10.1016/j.poetic.2008.12.001.

Warde, A., D. Wright and M. Gayo-Cal (2007), 'Understanding cultural omnivorousness: or, the myth of the cultural omnivore', *Cultural Sociology*, 1:2, 143–164. 10.1177/1749975507078185.

Warde, A., D. Wright and M. Gayo-Cal (2008), 'The omnivorous orientation in the UK', *Poetics*, 36:2, 148–165. 10.1016/j.poetic.2008.02.004.

References

Wiles, R., G. Crow and H. Pain (2011), 'Innovation in qualitative research methods: a narrative review', *Qualitative Research*, 11:5, 587–604. 10.1177/1468794111413227.

Williams, R. (1977), *Marxism and Literature* (Oxford: Oxford University Press).

Wingfield, A. H. (2007), 'The modern mammy and the angry black man: African American professionals' experiences with gendered racism in the workplace', *Race, Gender & Class*, 14:1/2, 196–212.

Wingfield, A. H. (2010), 'Are some emotions marked "whites only"? Racialized feeling rules in professional workplaces', *Social Problems*, 57:2, 251–268. 10.1525/sp.2010.57.2.251.

Wingfield, A. H. and J. Feagin (2012), 'The racial dialectic: President Barack Obama and the white racial frame', *Qualitative Sociology*, 35:2, 143–162. 10.1007/s11133-012-9223-7.

Wolfinger, N. H. (2002), 'On writing fieldnotes: collection strategies and background expectancies', *Qualitative Research*, 2:1, 85–93. 10.1177/1468794102002001640.

Wright, E. O. (1989), 'The comparative project on class structure and class consciousness: an overview', *Acta Sociologica*, 32:1, 3–22.

Wright II, E. (2016), *The First American School of Sociology: W. E. B. Du Bois and the Atlanta Sociological Laboratory* (Farnham: Ashgate).

Wright II, E. and T. C. Calhoun (2006), 'Jim Crow sociology: toward an understanding of the origin and principles of black sociology via the Atlanta Sociological Laboratory', *Sociological Focus*, 39:1, 1–18. 10.1080/00380237.2006.10571274.

Yosso, T. J. (2005), 'Whose culture has capital? A critical race theory discussion of community cultural wealth', *Race Ethnicity and Education*, 8:1, 69–91.

Zuberi, T. and E. Bonilla-Silva (2008a), 'Telling the real tale of the hunt: toward a race conscious sociology of racial stratification', in T. Zuberi and E. Bonilla-Silva (eds), *White Logic, White Methods: Racism and Methodology* (Lanham, MD: Rowman & Littlefield), pp. 329–341.

Zuberi, T. and E. Bonilla-Silva (eds) (2008b), *White Logic, White Methods: Racism and Methodology* (Lanham, MD: Rowman & Littlefield).

Index

acceptability 28, 151
Afro-centrism 13, 15, 16, 18, 30, 31, 41–46, 49, 65–66, 74, 87–89, 92, 95, 113–115, 122, 129, 147
anti-racism 3, 11–12, 15, 17, 19, 29, 31, 33, 36–38, 73–75, 85–87, 89–90, 95–97, 100–101, 108, 111, 113, 121–123, 132–134, 138, 144, 146–147, 150, 152, 154, 156
art galleries 59, 61–62, 65, 67, 78, 93, 150
authenticity 13, 78, 80–81, 88, 90, 92, 117–118, 122–123, 133

beauty 12, 39–40, 48, 81
Black history 27–28, 42–43, 57, 66, 78, 84, 99, 105–107, 109, 114–117, 151
Black spaces 78, 92, 95
boundaries 3, 10, 35, 49, 63–64, 82, 92, 98–99, 117–118, 136
Bourdieu, Pierre 9, 10, 20, 87, 125, 134, 148, 155
Brexit 100
browning 13, 16, 18, 22, 30, 31, 37–41, 43, 45–46, 95, 115–116, 122, 129, 147

classical music 54–56, 68–70, 73, 80, 131
class-minded 9, 12–14, 16–18, 23, 29–40, 43–50, 54, 56, 64, 67–70, 73–75, 87, 105, 108, 119–120, 123–124, 129, 135, 137, 147
code-switching 7–8, 12–13, 18, 26–29, 30–31, 32–33, 40–41, 49, 70–75, 90, 92–93, 95–96, 121–122, 125, 129, 135
colour-blindness 4–6, 54, 64, 127, 130
controlling images 16, 22, 79–81, 97, 133
critical race theory 2, 12, 89, 120, 125, 132–133
cultural capital
    Black cultural capital 78–87, 89, 91, 93, 95, 96, 97
    definition of 10–16, 20
    highbrow 6, 10, 18, 59, 113–114
    traditional middle-class 13–15, 18–19, 21–22, 29–30, 37, 46, 50, 53–55, 57, 59, 61, 63–67, 69–71, 73–75, 92, 94, 111, 113–115, 121–123, 125, 127, 129–131, 133, 146, 148, 154
    use of 10–11, 64, 70–71, 73, 75, 117–118
cultural equity 9, 12–15, 18, 28–29, 30–31, 70–75, 92, 113, 121–122, 125, 129
cultural membership 3–4, 7, 12, 24–26, 121, 124
cultural omnivore 6, 93, 96, 130–131
cultural repertoires 11–12, 30–31, 128–130

de-racialisation 13–14, 16, 18, 30–31, 37–39, 41, 43–44, 45–46, 67–68, 74, 123–124, 129
double consciousness
    as identity 102–106, 111–114
    as second sight 107, 111, 114–116
Du Bois, W.E.B. 9–10, 19, 81, 101–102, 107, 110

Index

elites 2, 10–11, 138–139
ethnoracial autonomous 2, 12–13, 15–16, 18–19, 22, 29–33, 35, 37, 39–42, 46–50, 54, 64–67, 73–74, 87–89, 91–92, 94–96, 111, 114–117, 120, 122–124, 128, 135, 137, 147
Eurocentric 12–13, 15–16, 18, 39–40, 46, 61–62, 65–66, 68, 123

gendered racism 40, 47–48, 58, 102–127, 149
Gilroy, Paul 41, 46, 100, 102, 104

Hall, Stuart 55, 62, 80, 100, 104

immigration 47, 100, 103
interactions 7, 26–27, 53, 55–57, 102–106, 109, 127–128

Jim Crow sociology 10

Lamont, Michèle 11, 49, 117, 156

methodological whiteness 4
microaggressions 53, 57–60, 63–65, 86, 95, 122, 127, 146
moral worth 11, 41, 57, 63, 123, 125

norms 7, 13, 26, 38–40, 44, 46, 120, 122–124, 147

opera 54, 58–59, 70, 80–81

phenomenology 57, 60, 130, 136
post-racialism 3, 12–13, 16–17, 30–31, 33–38, 45, 50, 57, 68–69, 73–74, 108–109, 123–124, 129, 134–135, 147

qualitative research methods 17, 48, 130, 138, 142–145, 148–149, 154–156
quantitative research methods 17, 126–127, 129–130, 137, 144–145

racial frame 88–90, 96–97
racial ideology 12, 24–25, 43, 75, 95, 121, 124, 132, 152

racialised emotional 24–26, 67, 76, 97, 121, 133, 138
racial salience 37–39, 43
recognition 2, 43, 63–64, 115
reflexivity
    disciplinary 143, 152–154
    individual 149–152,
    narcissistic 148
    scholastic 154–155
reggae 88–90, 113
resistance 8, 13, 16, 19, 39–41, 46, 48, 60, 79–81, 99, 100–101, 111, 114–116, 122, 132, 137–138, 144–147
respectability 7, 13, 28, 49, 72, 112, 113–114, 122, 124, 128
Rollock, Nicola 38, 51, 58, 102

social capital 2, 5–6, 28–29, 31, 125–126
social class
    ambivalence 7–8, 30, 32
    definition of 3–4
    need for qualitative analyses of 129–130, 132
stereotypes 5–6, 24–25, 35, 43, 59, 81, 83, 113, 124–125, 133
strategic assimilation 7–9, 12–16, 18–19, 22–33, 35, 37, 40–41, 47, 49–50, 54, 56, 65–67, 70–71, 73–75, 87, 89–93, 95–96, 111, 113, 115–117, 119–124, 129, 134, 137

triangle of identity 12–17, 30–31, 48–50, 56, 134–135

university 2, 10, 37, 39, 43, 115, 128, 151, 154–155

validity 145

Wallace, Derron 7–9, 20, 24, 78–79
white logic, white method 4, 153
white middle class 2, 4–9, 12–15, 18–19, 24–29, 32, 37–38, 44, 46, 54, 60,

64, 70, 72–75, 88, 92, 95–96, 99, 110, 120–123, 126–130, 132–133, 136

whiteness 4–7, 27, 29, 32, 38–39, 50, 54, 56, 58–63, 65–67, 69, 71, 73, 79, 90, 92, 100, 131, 135, 150

White sociology 4

white spaces
   physical 56–60
   political economy of 63–64
   symbolic 61–63

working-class 11, 28, 32, 47, 71, 114, 130, 133

EU authorised representative for GPSR:
Easy Access System Europe, Mustamäe tee 50,
10621 Tallinn, Estonia
gpsr.requests@easproject.com

www.ingramcontent.com/pod-product-compliance
Lightning Source LLC
Chambersburg PA
CBHW030121240426
43673CB00041B/1361